THE NONCONFORMITY
OF
RICHARD BAXTER

THE NONCONFORMITY
OF
RICHARD BAXTER

BY
IRVONWY MORGAN, M.A., Ph.D.

WIPF & STOCK · Eugene, Oregon

Wipf and Stock Publishers
199 W 8th Ave, Suite 3
Eugene, OR 97401

The Nonconformity of Richard Baxter
By Morgan, Irvonwy
Copyright©1946 Methodist Publishing - Epworth Press
ISBN 13: 978-1-5326-3054-5
Publication date 4/5/2017
Previously published by Epworth Press, 1946

Every effort has been made to trace the current copyright
owner of this publication but without success. If you have
any information or interest in the copyright, please contact the publishers.

PREFACE

A GROUP of men standing at a corner near my church in 1939 were debating fiercely the merits and demerits of the shelters that were being put in their tiny gardens by the Borough Council. Nearly all of them objected strongly to this upheaval of the only place where they could plant a few flowers, since the shelters took up the whole of the garden space. One man, however, was very pleased with the arrangement. He had concreted the floor of the shelter, fitted up an electric light and put in an armchair. 'I go there after tea', he said. 'It's the only place I can get a bit of peace in the house!'

Though we do not normally connect air-raid shelters with peace, I must confess that the fact that I had to live in an air-raid shelter during the 'blitz' of 1940 and 1941 gave me time and opportunity to do the reading necessary for this study in the life and importance of Richard Baxter. Some may consider that this work is merely another example of flogging a dead horse, but ideas which have rocked nations do not die as quickly as horses, and with the emergence of talk on Church reunion it is well that all parties should remind themselves of the origins and purpose of what is termed Nonconformity.

I would like to record my grateful thanks to those who have helped me; to the late Rev. Dr. H. Maldwyn Hughes, to whom this book is dedicated, whose kindness and consideration to me in College and after can never be repaid; to the Rev. Dr. R. Newton Flew, for encouragement when I started to put my thoughts on paper; to the Rev. Dr. E. S. Waterhouse, for allowing me to become a member of my father's old College at Richmond; to the Rev. Rupert Davies, M.A., B.D., for help and advice on Chapter Eleven, and especially to the Rev. Dr. S. G. Dimond, my Tutor, who so painstakingly advised me and patiently corrected what he was pleased to call my typing errors. I would also like to thank Mr. Stephen K. Jones, M.A., Librarian of Dr. Williams's Library, for the loan of precious books, and help in checking quotations, and Mr. Conan Nicholas, who compiled the Index and Bibliography.

The book itself has been approved as a thesis for the Degree of Doctor of Philosophy in the University of London.

I. MORGAN

POPLAR
1945

CONTENTS

	PREFACE	5
1	PURITAN PURPOSE	9
2	'C. OF E. AND A GOOD THING'	24
3	A REFORMED PASTOR	36
4	A PILLAR OF THE CHURCH	49
5	THE OUTCAST	62
6	THE BISHOP OF NONCONFORMITY	75
7	BAXTER'S DOCTRINE OF THE CHURCH	90
	(1) THE CHURCH UNIVERSAL	90
	(2) PARTICULAR CHURCHES	104
8	THE MINISTRY	117
	(1) ITS ORIGIN AND DEVELOPMENT	117
	(2) ITS AUTHORITY AND SUCCESSION	130
9	THE WORD OF GOD	144
10	THE SACRAMENTS	163
11	BAXTER AND THE HIERARCHICAL CONCEPTION	179
12	THINGS INDIFFERENT	196
13	A MERE NONCONFORMIST	210
14	SOME ASPECTS OF REUNION RECONSIDERED	224
	APPENDIX—PURITAN PROPAGANDA	244
	BIBLIOGRAPHY	256
	RICHARD BAXTER'S WRITINGS	258
	INDEX	259

Chapter I

PURITAN PURPOSE

PURITAN ORIGIN AND INFLUENCE

IF we can compare the Christian life of these islands to a broad river that throughout the years has fertilized the surrounding land, bringing forth in civil and religious life fruits that are worthy of esteem, then we can compare the Puritan contribution to one, and that not the least, of its tributaries; a tributary which owes its origin to many springs that have each added its contribution to the strength and purity of the parent flow. We now live in the broad stream of Christian life which bears many marks of the Puritan spirit, and though that spirit is no longer canalized in sect or party, we can still see the channel along which it once flowed, and the springs from which that flow was once fed.

For the springs that fed English Puritanism were many and various. Some can be traced back into the popular movements that disturbed the triumphant Medieval Church, others found their inspiration in the religious and intellectual stirrings of Reformation and Renaissance Europe, while others were fed by the study of the Scriptures, so belatedly made available in the vernacular. Dr. Scott Pearson sums them up in these words: 'The Revival of Learning, the consequent interest in the Greek New Testament, the various translations of the Scriptures into the vernacular, the lively heritage of Lollardism, particularly in the eastern counties and in such towns as London, Northampton, Leicester, and Norwich, and the direct influence of the Continental Reformation fostered the Puritan spirit. During Edward's reign such Reformers from abroad as Bucer, Fagius, Tremellius, Martyr, Alasco, and Knox from Scotland, by their learning and fervour favoured an advanced type of Protestantism. Such Bishops as Ridley and Hooper were advocates of a simple Reformed religion. Now the return of Roman Catholicism to England, by driving large contingents of Protestants overseas, helped to create the party, who constituted the immediate precursors of the Elizabethan Puritans.'[1]

But these influences inspired, in the reigns of Edward and of

[1] A. F. Scott Pearson, *Thomas Cartwright and Elizabethan Puritanism* (Cambridge University Press, 1925), p. 6.

Mary a spirit rather than a movement. A spirit at once anti-Popish and anti-superstitious. Many people objected to certain rites and vestments still retained in the Church, to the use of the ring in marriage, the use of the sign of the Cross in baptism and to kneeling at the Communion Table, because they were associated with Popery.[1] These were opinions which were to become closely identified with Puritanism, and were to cause dissension in the Puritan camp. It was a spirit that took a great delight in the singing of psalms, as Bishop Jewell wrote to Peter Martyr in 1560: 'You may see sometimes at Paul's Cross after the service six thousand persons . . . all singing together and praiseing God.'[2] The only thing that really united them was a special devotion to Holy Scripture. Dr. Hensley Henson in his book, *Puritanism in England*, quotes the words of Archbishop Cranmer, writing in 1552 with reference to Puritan objections against the second Prayer-book: 'They say that kneeling is not commanded in Scripture: and what is not commanded in Scripture is unlawful. *There is the root of the errors of the sects!*'[3] It was their devotion to Holy Scripture which was the spiritual meeting-point of the reforming aspirations of all those who formed the precursors of the Elizabethan Puritans.

To canalize this spirit so that it became a movement there were needed two things, a definite stimulus and a definite leadership. The stimulus came from Elizabeth's desire for uniformity in the Church, and the leadership from the genius and character of Thomas Cartwright, Lady Margaret Professor of Divinity in the University of Cambridge. The water from the springs began then to converge into a stream which flowed with varying fortunes through the reigns of Elizabeth, James I, and Charles I, through the Commonwealth into the reign of Charles II. This period saw the rise of the movement with definite aims and definite leadership, the triumph of one phase of the movement in the Commonwealth period, and the final repudiation of the movement by the Anglican Church in the days of Charles II.

PURITAN ROOTS IN THE MODERN WORLD

The results of the struggle in our national and religious life are very different from that which was aimed at by either protagonist. Indeed some of the results, which we have learned to appreciate,

[1] H. Hensley Henson, *Puritanism in England* (Hodder & Stoughton, 1912), p. 10.
[2] ibid., p. 18.
[3] ibid., p. 17.

would have been heartily condemned by both the leaders of the Puritans and of the Episcopal party. The persistence of both sides in their ideas, and the failure of either side to crush or convert the other, has resulted in the general acceptance by the nation of the principle of Liberty of Conscience, and its consequence, the spirit of Toleration. The establishment of Protestant Dissenting churches with definite rights has necessitated the corollary of freedom of worship and propaganda for Roman Catholic Dissenters. Meanwhile, the futility of the cruelties practised by both sides has strengthened the traditional British dislike of persecution.

In other ways too the Puritan movement has permanently affected our national life. The freedom of the Press is almost the direct outcome of the Puritan pamphleteers' struggle to preach their gospel to the people, despite High Commission and Star Chamber. Their idealization of romantic love within marriage, particularly in the poetry of Spenser and Milton, has affected our conception of marriage, resulting in the gradual death of those *mariages des covenances*, arranged by families rather than by the persons concerned, which, even to-day, are common in countries with a strong Roman Catholic tradition. This too has affected our attitude to divorce. The Puritans were the first people, in any numbers in England, to advocate the institution of divorce.[1] This was not because they were anti-social, or because they viewed marriage as merely a contract, but because they looked on marriage as a spiritual as well as a physical union.[2] Anything which destroyed the spiritual union, such as unfaithfulness, naturally destroyed the physical union as well. It is due to the Puritan conception[3] of idealized, romantic love within the marriage bond that, until recently, adultery was the main reason for allowing divorce in this country. To the Puritan Milton, adultery was not only a form of thievery, or the breaking of faith, as Chaucer said it was, it was a pollution of the body and soul, a worse form of fornication, which, letting 'in defilement in the inward parts, the soul grows clotted by contagion'. It is this idealized, romantic view of sexual love which dominates our modern attitude to courtship and marriage.

In the world of business and commerce, too, the Puritan

[1] cf. M. M. Knappen, *Tudor Puritanism* (University of Chicago Press, 1939), pp. 456–61.
[2] cf. William Haller, *Rise of Puritanism* (Columbia University Press, 1938), p. 121.
[3] ibid., p. 122.

movement has left its mark. The Puritan view that all worthy occupations were vocations brought dignity to labour, and their inward spiritual discipline was reflected in their devotion to their own particular work,[1] and contributed to their success in business. The London merchants were strong supporters of the movement, and in Baxter's day the great towns of Manchester and Sheffield, newly grown and not incorporated, came to be called 'Cities of Refuge' by the Nonconformist victims of the Five-Mile Act who were able to take refuge there.[2]

Lastly, the Puritans have suffered much from the erroneous view that their creed was so other-worldly that they looked with disgust upon the natural pleasures of this world, and that their main purpose was to dragoon the people by an all-embracing code of prohibitions. Macaulay's remark that 'the Puritans hated bear-baiting, not because it gave pain to the bear, but because it gave pleasure to the spectators', sums up the popular view of Puritanism. Yet if this view is true it is impossible to explain the wide support given to the movement by such full-blooded Elizabethan courtiers as Burghley, Walsingham, Leicester, Warwick, Howard, Hatton, Shrewsbury, and Croft, who were all members of the Privy Council. J. B. Marsden, in his *History of the Early Puritans*, says: 'Amongst the Puritans were found, together with a crowd of our greatest divines, and a multitude of learned men, many of our most profound lawyers, some of our most able statesmen, of our most renowned soldiers, and (strangely out of place as they may seem) not a few of our greatest orators and poets.'[3] Bacon supported them, and Essex, when he came to die, sought consolation from them. The Royal Navy and the Merchant Navy had strong Puritan tendencies, which in the Civil War helped to bring them into the conflict on the side of the Puritans and Parliament. In fact, Puritanism was much more than 'a table of prohibitions. It was the programme of an active, not a monastic or contemplative, life.'[4] It was only in the time of the Civil War, when the more fanatical section of them—namely, the Separatists—came into power, that an attempt was made to regiment the people by dictatorial methods.

[1] William Haller, *Rise of Puritanism* (Columbia University Press, 1938), p. 121.
[2] George Eayrs, *Richard Baxter* (National Council of Evangelical Free Churches, 1912), p. 97.
[3] J. B. Marsden, *History of the Early Puritans* (1852), p. 4.
[4] William Haller, *Rise of Puritanism* (1938), p. 123.

The main solid body of the Puritans were kindly, respectable, hardworking folk, what the French would call *sérieuse*. Baxter, for instance, tells how in his day the vulgar rabble gave the odious name of 'Puritan' to those simple respectable folk, who, having no preaching at home, went to hear the few constant, competent preachers who lived near him,[1] and for no other reason apparently than that they went to hear the preaching. The attitude of the majority of Puritans to this world is well expressed by Sibbes, one of the leaders of the Society for the extension of Puritan preaching, in his *Saint's Cordials*, quoted by William Haller: 'Worldly things are good in themselves, and given to sweeten our passage to Heaven. . . . This world and the things thereof are all good, and were all made of God, for the benefit of his creature.'[2]

THE EMERGENCE OF THE PURITAN PARTY

But to return to the Puritans of Elizabeth's day. Elizabeth, like nearly all the Tudors, was a great ruler. She knew what she wanted, and used every art to obtain her will. And what she wanted was to reign as Queen of England and live.[3] Nor in the turmoil of English sixteenth century society were these negligible ambitions. Only a great person could have succeeded. She found herself when she came to the throne, the nominal ruler of a divided nation. The majority of her subjects were Protestants of a sort, especially about London, but a large, and partly hostile minority were Roman Catholic. The only unifying force of those days—namely, the Church—had lost, in the turbulence of the three previous reigns, a great deal of its prestige and its moral authority. Anything might have happened. The Church was still, however, a 'going concern', but where it went to depended to a large extent on who controlled it, and with it went England. Elizabeth determined that she was going to control it. To quote Haller: 'Her father may be said to have seized the Church: Her brother and sister before her had in contrary ways and with unhappy results tried to reform it. She perceived she must govern it or be ruined.'[4] So she

---

[1] *Autobiography of Richard Baxter* (Everyman Edition, Dent, 1931), p. 4.

[2] William Haller, *Rise of Puritanism* (1938), p. 123; cf. W. Usher, *Reconstruction of the English Church* (D. Appleton, New York, 1910), vol. I, p. 245.

[3] M. M. Knappen, *Tudor Puritanism* (1939), p. 167.

[4] William Haller, *Rise of Puritanism* (1938), p. 6.

appointed bishops she could rely on, and saw to it that they asserted their authority and her own.

Yet in her persecution of the Puritans, which she conducted through her bishops to bring the Puritans to conformity, she was careful that the odium should be attached to the bishops and not to her. The Privy Council, which we have seen had a number of men in it with strong Puritan leanings,[1] used their moderating influence on several occasions in favour of the Puritans. These actions were known to the Queen, and were approved because they brought her the credit of being merciful, while the world could reflect on the cruelty of the bishops.[2] In fact, the bishops frequently complained of being hampered by the Councillors in doing their duty. 'For their literal devotion to duty they received neither thanks nor support.'[3]

The attitude of the Queen to the Puritans was in fact determined by political considerations. She persecuted them because she saw a threat to her royal supremacy implied in their doctrines, she was lenient to them when it would redound to her credit, or when the Spanish and Roman Catholic danger necessitated the support of such strong Protestant supporters. After the defeat of the Armada, she allowed the bishops to silence them.[4]

The immediate reason for the emergence of a Puritan party was the effort of the bishops, on Elizabeth's orders, to secure uniformity in the rites and ceremonies of the Church.[5] A book of articles was drawn up by Archbishop Parker in 1564–5, known as *Parker's Advertisements*, in which such uniformity was enjoined. There were immediate protests from the universities of Oxford and Cambridge, and from many of the clergy. Some of the clergy, particularly in London, who refused obedience were suspended. The result was the consolidation of dissent, and a party emerged to which the name 'Puritan' was applied.[6] Beside consolidating Puritan feeling into a party, there also emerged side by side as it were, but very much smaller in numbers, people who, though Genevan in principle as the rest of the Puritans were, broke away from the Established Church to worship separately. These were called 'Separatists', and are the ancestors of the modern Congregational and Baptist denomi-

[1] Henry Soames, *Elizabethan Religious History* (1839), p. 366.
[2] cf. A. F. Scott Pearson, *Thomas Cartwright and Elizabethan Puritanism* (1925), p. 125.
[3] ibid., p. 235.   [4] cf. ibid., p. 236.
[5] J. B. Marsden, *History of the Early Puritans* (1852), p. 40.
[6] cf. A. F. Scott Pearson, *Thomas Cartwright and Elizabethan Puritanism* (1925), p. 18.

nations. They were, too, the forerunners of the 'Sectaries' who came to power in the Commonwealth, and produced Cromwell and Milton. It was partly their excesses in regimentation and narrowness in outlook when they did achieve power that earned for the name 'Puritan' the odium which now attaches to it.

So far the Puritan party may be called a negative party. A party of objection without a positive programme, embodying among its adherents all those who considered that the Reformation in England had, in the Elizabethan settlement of the Church, compromised with Roman Catholicism. But it was soon to find a positive programme, and a leader of ability in Thomas Cartwright. In 1569 Cartwright was appointed Lady Margaret Professor of Divinity at Cambridge, and opened his lectures with a study of the first two chapters of the Acts of the Apostles. In these lectures he dealt with the question of Church government, and came to the conclusion that the form of Church government revealed in the New Testament was not Episcopacy, but Presbyterianism. His lectures caused a sensation in the university, so much so that he was finally deprived of his professorship. Before this, however, Cartwright submitted to the Vice-Chancellor the marrow of his teaching in the following six articles:

(1) The names and offices of archbishops and bishops should be abolished, in their stead the offices of bishops and deacons, as described in the New Testament, should be established;

(2) The bishop should have a purely spiritual function, and the deacon should care for the poor;

(3) The government of the Church should not be entrusted to chancellors or bishops, or officials of archdeacons, etc., but to the minister and the Presbytery of the Church;

(4) Each minister should be attached to a definite congregation;

(5) No one should, like a candidate, seek the office of a minister, and none should be created ministers by the authority of bishops, but should be elected by a Church;

(6) All should promote this reformation according to their several vocations, i.e. the magistrate by his authority, the minister by preaching, and all by their prayers.[1] The importance of these articles for our study of Baxter is that, as we shall see, they form, with certain modifications, the substance of his own view of Church government. It is also easy to see that the result of such

[1] ibid., p. 28, and J. B Marsden, *History of the Early Puritans* (1852), p. 77.

a reformation would have been the total abolition of diocesan episcopacy, and the establishment of Presbyterianism after the model of the Scottish Church. No wonder there was a stir in college, deanery, and court! But there was a stir in Puritan circles also, for Cartwright had propounded a policy that was to turn Puritanism into new channels,[1] and both parties were conscious of the change.

TWIN DANGERS TO THE STATE

We have seen how the Queen's desire for uniformity in the Church had led to the 'Vestment Controversy', and brought to a head the half-formed antipathy to anything that savoured of Popish religion. It was not any purely religious motive that dictated her policy, but the necessity of controlling the main instrument of propaganda in the country—namely, the Church. The Queen also saw that there were two religious movements which might imperil her authority: one being the strong Roman Catholic minority, and the other the Puritan movement, with its political implications. The first danger was complicated by the Spanish intention of invading and conquering England, and bringing the land which had been known in earlier times as 'Mary's Dowry' back to the Roman Catholic obedience. The Roman Catholics in England were a possible source of sympathy for the Spanish cause, and a potentially dangerous Fifth Column.

The Spanish danger grew and came to a head in the years 1569–87. The Northern rebellion occurred in 1569, and the Papal Bull of Excommunication in 1570. After the Pope had attempted to destroy Elizabeth by maintaining his right to free her subjects from her allegiance, the danger to the throne from inside the country became more evident. The Jesuit missionary campaigns, the Roman Catholic supporters, both English and foreign, who came from the Continent to overthrow Elizabeth, the invasion of Ireland by Spain and Rome, the various plots connected with the Queen of Scots, the attempted invasion of England by the Spanish Armada, all showed that the danger was real and immediate, and indeed was only dissipated with the defeat of the Armada. Until 1570 Roman Catholics had been lightly treated, 'Beyond fines for non-attendance at church, irregularly levied, she [Elizabeth] had not persecuted the

[1] A. F. Scott Pearson, *Thomas Cartwright and Elizabethan Puritanism* (1925), p. 33, and M. M. Knappen, *Tudor Puritanism* (1939), p. 227.

Catholic laity for their opinions'.[1] But after the Papal Bull of Excommunication their treatment was different, and the missionary agents of the Pope-King were harried to death. The Queen's first leniency was inspired by political considerations, for she did not wish to alienate the moderate Roman Catholics,[2] who, though they might have fought for Mary against her, would certainly support her against Philip of Spain.

With the Puritans the case was different. Whatever their difficulties with the Throne and the bishops, they would have undoubtedly supported the Throne against any threat from a Roman Catholic source, consequently there was not so much need to be light-handed. At first, although the main movement was left alone, proceedings were taken against the leaders. In 1573, for instance, an inquisition was made in all English dioceses to report to the Queen's Council the names of all nonconforming ministers. Stroud, the Puritan printer, Dering, and many others were silenced; Cartwright went into hiding in London and a warrant was issued for his arrest, at which, to avoid prison or exile, he fled to Germany.[3]

With the silencing of their leaders, the Puritan movement remained at a very low ebb, although they were not inactive in a quiet manner. While the vigilance of the authorities was probably a contributing cause of this silence, Dr. Scott Pearson thinks that the main cause was the use the Puritans were making of the 'Prophesyings', or 'Exercises', 'By means of which they were able to associate, to nourish, and propagate their ambitions, and prepare for future triumph.'[4] These meetings were calculated to deepen the knowledge of the Scriptures among the clergy, and improve the quality and numbers of the preachers. They were approved by several of the bishops, and professed to be based upon the prophesyings of the Early Church. However, these 'Exercises' did not win the approval of the Queen, and she decided that they must be suppressed. She asked Archbishop Grindal to carry out her commands, but he wrote to her in 1576 declining to join in their suppression. He explained to her the nature and value of the meetings, and declared his willingness to become a Nonconformist for their sake. He was sequestered and suffered the Queen's displeasure.[5]

[1] G. M. Trevelyan, *History of England* (Longmans, 1927), p. 353.
[2] M. M. Knappen, *Tudor Puritanism* (1939), p. 168.
[3] A. F. Scott Pearson, *Thomas Cartwright and Elizabethan Puritanism* (1925), p. 121.
[4] ibid., p. 155. [5] ibid., p. 156.

But despite the opposition of the Queen and the bishops, the atmosphere was favourable to the Puritans. The Council and Parliament had strong Puritan leanings, which became more pronounced as the Roman Catholic and Spanish danger increased. To suppress such strong Protestants would under the circumstances have been foolish, because it would have caused dissension in Church and State, and weakened the national front against the Roman Catholic menace. The Puritans took advantage of this state of affairs by resuscitating the 'Exercises'. Fuller, in his *Church History of Britain*, states that 'The year [1582] proved very active, especially in the practises of Presbyterians, who now found so much favour, as almost amounted to a connivance at their discipline. For, whilst the severity of the State was at this time intended to the height against Jesuits, some lenity, of course, by the very rules of opposition, fell to the share of the Nonconformists, even on the score of their notorious enmity to the Jesuitical party.'[1] But in 1583 Whitgift, now Archbishop of Canterbury, acted again against the Puritans by publishing a set of articles to which the clergy were required to subscribe. There was widespread opposition in the Puritan ranks, which led to many suspensions. A great number of prominent people tried to intercede on behalf of the suspended clergy. Sir Francis Knollys besought Whitgift, because of the Popish danger, to stop his crusade against them. Robert Beale, Clerk of the Council, worked hard to procure them favour. Burghley himself severely criticized Whitgift, and many members of the Council joined with him to try to stay the hands of the Archbishop. But this was of no avail, and only succeeded in drawing the Puritan forces more closely together.

They decided finally to present another Bill to Parliament, which was in the form of a petition desiring the conversion of the Church of England into a Presbyterian organization. Parliament had a strong Puritan flavour, and the attempt was in keeping with the accepted Puritan strategy of striving for the conversion of the Church from inside it, and by the authority of 'the magistrate', a strategy condemned by the Separatists, and particularly by Robert Browne, and called by them, reformation by 'tarrying for the magistrate'.[2] Some time was wasted in argument, and

---

[1] cf. quotation by A. F. Scott Pearson, *Thomas Cartwright and Elizabethan Puritanism* (1925), p. 238, note 5.
[2] cf. Robert Browne's *A Treatise of Reformation without Tarying for Anie*.

the Bill never came to a reading. Elizabeth, taking advantage of this, sent for the papers and suppressed them. The reformation by tarrying for the magistrate had signally failed. The result was that many of the Puritans came to the conclusion that their efforts at reform were useless as long as the bishops held to their intransigent attitude.

The radical section of the Puritans had flared up in the antiepiscopal Marprelate tracts, but by the end of 1589 they too were silenced. The press which printed them was found and the printers fined. Bancroft, afterwards Bishop of London, unearthed masses of incriminating evidence relating to the Conferences and to *The Book of Discipline*, a book associated with the name of another great Puritan leader, Walter Travers, and written that the aims of the party might be definitely known, and that through its guidance there might be unity in the party's demands. Finally, Cartwright and others were arraigned before the Star Chamber and imprisoned, the Conferences were stopped, the movement lost some of its most powerful supporters, such as Leicester and Walsingham, by death, and the Queen effectively muzzled any move in Parliament to redress Puritan grievances.[1] The hard measures passed against Protestant and Roman dissent in 1593 made any such dissent impossible. Banishment or conformity were the only alternatives. Large numbers of Separatists fled to Holland to worship there according to their consciences, but the Puritans proper remained at home giving their 'wonted allegiance to the Establishment, but waiting for a better day in which to renew their effort in favour of Presbyterianism'.[2]

By this time too the Anglicans had developed better literary opponents to the Puritans in Sutcliffe, Bancroft, and, above all, Richard Hooker, while the Puritans remained practically silent. Hooker's work, *The Laws of Ecclesiastical Polity*, is the classic defence of the Church of England against the Puritanism of Cartwright. But, as has been pointed out, its arguments are not inherently Anglican, for they can be cited to support Papacy or even Presbyterianism. If, as Hooker maintained, there is no unalterable Church polity laid down in Holy Scripture, then there need be no limits to the evolution of Church orders. If monarchical episcopacy grew out of the degrees of ministry existing in the Apostolic Church, then there seems no logical

---

[1] A. F. Scott Pearson, *Thomas Cartwright and Elizabethan Puritanism* (1925), p. 359.
[2] ibid.

reason why monarchical papacy should not grow out of them. The Puritans, in view of this, would not go beyond Holy Scripture for either Faith or Order,[1] neither by adding doctrines to the Faith once delivered to the saints, nor by superimposing extra degrees or orders to the deposits of Apostolic practice. Thus they focused attention on the paramount place of the Scriptures in the Church.

POLITICAL IMPLICATIONS OF PURITANISM

We have seen that Puritanism, which commanded the allegiance of a very large minority of the clergy, was yet persecuted and silenced by the Throne, despite the support of many influential men among the Lords, Commons, and the merchant classes. Why, therefore, we may ask ourselves, did the Queen persist in her attitude of antagonism to the movement? Was it solely because of her preference for episcopal forms and ceremonies, or was it that she detected another issue behind the controversy? The answer is to be found in a letter which she wrote to King James of Scotland in 1590. The General Assembly of the Church in Scotland, in sympathy for their persecuted Presbyterian brethren in England, had recommended that prayers be said for them. When Elizabeth heard of this she was furious, and wrote to James asking him to put a stop to this action. In this letter she gives her real reason for her hatred of Presbyterianism. For, she says, 'Ther is risen, bothe in your realme and myne, a secte of perilous consequence, suche as wold have no kings but a presbitrye, and take our place while the inioy our privilege with a shade of Godes word, whiche non is juged to folow right without by ther censure the be so demed. Yea looke we wel unto them. Whan the have made in our peoples hartz a doubt of our religion, and that we erre if the say so, what perilous issue this may make I rather thinke than mynde to write. *Sapienti pauca.* I pray you stap the mouthes, or make shortar the toungz, of suche ministars as dare presume to make oraison in ther pulpitz for the persecuted in Ingland for the gospel. . . . I hope . . . you wil not suffar a strange king receave that indignitie at suche caterpilars hand.'[2]

As we see from this letter, what Elizabeth feared was the

[1] cf. J. B. Marsden, *History of the Early Puritans* (1852), p. 88.
[2] A. F. Scott Pearson, *Thomas Cartwright and Elizabethan Puritanism* (1925), p. 343, and 'Letters of Queen Elizabeth and King James', *Camden Society*, XLVI (1849), p. 63.

political implications which lay behind the Puritan concern for the government of the Church. On the accession of Elizabeth the Church was settled on anti-papal lines. But the chief moulder of the Church of England was the Queen herself, and she was lawful governor of the Church, believing firmly in her supremacy both in civil and ecclesiastical affairs.[1] What she saw was that the view that the Church was the State in its spiritual aspect, governed by the monarch, who is really priest and king, was incompatible with the Presbyterian-Puritan view. For the Presbyterian theory of the relationship between the Church and State sees them as two separate, organic bodies, 'bound together by a principle of reciprocity. As the Church needs the State so the State needs the Church, and each has duties to the other.'[2] This distinction 'is expounded by Cartwright when he deals with the two questions:

(1) the magistrate's authority in ecclesiastical causes; and
(2) the performance of civil offices by ecclesiastical persons. His conclusions are, "that as wel in the decision of the doctrine, as in the chois of the variable ceremonies of the church, the principal autority belongeth unto the ministery", and "that it is unlawful in an established estate of the church that a minister of the church should bear civil office".'[3] He proclaims the Sovereignty of God and the duty of earthly monarchs to obey his commands as given in Scripture, and accordingly to yield allegiance to the Church prescribed by God in His Word. This means for Cartwright the submission of civil magistrates to the Presbyterian Church.[4] For besides being an earthly ruler, the Godly magistrate is a member of the Church, and as such is subject to the ordinary ecclesiastical discipline. ' "That princes", says Cartwright, "should be excepted from ecclesiastical discipline and namely excommunication I utterly mislike." '[5] Travers too maintains the same position that civil magistrates, even kings, as spiritual beings, are under the charge of the ecclesiastical magistrates. Thus the Puritans emphasized the divine right of Presbyterianism as the form of government of the Church, and denied the divine right of kings in the secular sphere. Although Cartwright protested that he did not dislike the present form of civil government, when pressed he has to admit that a monarchical government is not an absolute necessity for the wellbeing

[1] cf. A. F. Scott Pearson, *Church and State* (Cambridge University Press, 1928), p. 6.
[2] ibid., p. 20.   [3] ibid., p. 9 (and notes).   [4] ibid., p. 27.   [5] ibid., p. 27.

of society. Thus the logical implications of Presbyterianism might, in the hands of some, give them a reasonable ground for doing away with the monarchy, the least that could happen would be the curtailing of the monarchy's authority, if only because the monarch would be subject to the Church in spiritual matters.

It was Whitgift who first pointed out these implications in Puritan doctrine, and drew the Queen's attention to them.[1] He classed Puritans and Papists together in their advocacy of similar principles, and appealed against the claims of clericalism. The Queen was quick to see these implications, and it is this that lies behind her antipathy to the movement. Dr. Scott Pearson, in his masterly study of the political aspects of sixteenth-century Puritanism, states: 'Elizabeth, Whitgift, Bancroft, and other protagonists of the *status quo* were, therefore, from their point of view, justified in regarding Puritanism as a political danger and the suppression of it as an urgent duty. To foster it was to prepare a rod for their own backs.'[2] But while all this is true, the Puritan leaders repudiated any thought of disloyalty to the monarch. Cartwright took the Oath of Supremacy several times, and protested that he was willing to take it again. In 1591 he and other Puritan leaders, in their imprisonment, wrote to Burghley defining the Puritan attitude to the oath, and saying that they had all been sworn to Her Majesty's supremacy, and were willing to swear it again.'[3] The Privy Council in 1592 were satisfied with Cartwright's protestation of loyalty and even glad that the charges of sedition, which had been preferred against him, had failed, but they still considered Presbyterianism politically dangerous. It was the political implications of Presbyterianism which the Queen saw were incompatible with the settled constitution of Church and State in her day. Therefore she muzzled any possibility of the Puritans gaining control of the Church by legal means. It was not until the next century when Puritan strategy in Elizabeth's day had failed, and the form of Puritanism called Separatism in the sixteenth century had become more powerful, that the political implications came to the surface in the Civil War.

Even so, it is wrong to assume that the Elizabethan Puritan leaders were mainly politicians masquerading as religious reformers. This was the criticism levelled at them by the bishops,

---

[1] A. F. Scott Pearson, *Church and State* (Cambridge University Press, 1928), p. 127.
[2] ibid., p. 130.   [3] ibid., p. 57.

and it was the root of Elizabeth's antipathy. But Cartwright and the other leaders objected strongly to the accusation that they were 'shooting at' (to use Whitgift's words) the head of the State, and complained that they had been misrepresented to the Queen. It would seem that the crux of the conflict lay in the fact that the Puritans were reformers, not merely in the realm of morals, but their reforms were aimed at the organization of the Church. Doctrinally they were, at least at first, in agreement with the Episcopal party, for both were Calvinists, it was in their conception of Church order that they differed. And here it was that political consequences were implied. To the Episcopal party any change in Church order, implying a transference of authority to ministers and congregations, cut at the root of the authority, not merely of the bishops, but of the monarch, the sole governor of the Church. (King James's assertion, 'No Bishop, no King', was to be the rallying cry in the next century of those who opposed reform.) The Puritans, on the other hand, genuinely failed to see why any altering of Church order need necessarily affect the State. It was a conflict between two different conceptions of the interdependence of Church and State which were mutually incompatible, and it was only resolved long after the Puritan movement had apparently failed, by the development of the principle of toleration, whereby separate expressions of Church order could exist and live in the same State side by side.

Chapter II

'C. OF E. AND A GOOD THING'

ELIZABETH AND THE NATIONAL CHURCH

IN the month of March, in the year 1603, the great Queen lay dying. The gaunt face no longer wore its mask of powder and paint, and the cadaverous body no longer wore clothes so outrageous in their impropriety that the Spanish Ambassador had almost blushed for shame. Outside the Palace rumours and panic had laid hold of the people. Rich merchants were burying their treasures. The Privy Council, afraid of meeting in London, were meeting in Richmond. Catholic lords were mustering their tenantry, and Protestant nobles feverishly sought to organize for the anticipated conflict. The trained bands were out night and day to try to prevent civil war. For it was no ordinary monarch who was dying; it was the mother and mistress of England. Already she had become a legend. The panic displayed was the measure of how much she had penetrated into the sense of stability of Englishmen. Her policy had always been to be firm in the saddle, but light on the reins. Like a great general, she knew when to retreat, and like a great woman, she knew how to retreat. Despite her autocratic Tudor nature, she had never despised the affection of her people. Even two years before her death, when, it might be thought, she could have neglected public opinion with impunity, she withdrew the unpopular trade monopolies, thus regaining her popularity in Parliament at a stroke. 'Though God hath raised me high', she said, 'yet this I count the glory of my crown, that I have reigned with your loves.'

Yet while she lay dying, and the mass of the people mourned, the leaders of the Episcopal, Catholic, and Puritan parties were turning to the future. As Bancroft knelt by her bed, he saw slipping away from him, not the soul of a woman, albeit a queen, but the soul of that opposition against which he had so often struggled in vain.

The Puritans and Catholics waited eagerly the coming of James VI of Scotland, with whom they had each had conferences and received vague promises. None guessed that what was dying was not merely the Queen, but the English national Church.

During her reign Puritans, Episcopalians, and moderate Catholics had all been embraced in one Church. True, the excommunication of Elizabeth had clarified the position of those Catholics who were more loyal to Rome than to the Queen; true, the separatist Puritans had also small organizations of their own outside the national Church. But what Elizabeth had done was to make it easy for moderates of either faction to remain in the Church. She did this by refusing to have defined who was or who was not a member of the Church, and by refusing to give the bishops sufficient authority to enforce their views. The Church was there to support the monarchy, and the only real test was the test of the Oath of Supremacy. If she had to rely on the bishops mostly for her unifying policy, she saw to it that they got all the kicks and none of the halfpence.

It was Elizabeth's personality that had kept this uneasy state of affairs in hand. It was her good fortune, on ascending the throne, not to be faced with a united band of returning reformers, covered in the glow of successfully evaded martyrdom. The reformers faced her individually, with no united policy, and got individual bargains. The brilliant scheme of the Geneva group of reformers, backed by John Knox, to present Elizabeth with a united front for reform, had foundered for lack of agreement among the reformers themselves. And as time wore on, and no agreed policy matured, one by one they slipped their cables and sailed for home and preferment. They were met at Westminster by one of the most astute of England's rulers, well able to use for her own ends the mixed motives and ambitions of the returned exiles. Consequently, there was scarcely any hard and fast rule as to who might minister, and who might communicate in the Church. All was determined by expediency. Anyone might serve in a benefice if he would take the Oath of Supremacy and could read the Book of Common Prayer. There was no agreement as to the nature of the Episcopate; all that could be said was that Elizabeth had settled the Church to be ruled by bishops, and these were considered to be more officers of the Crown than *Pastores pastorum*. For the bishops had little or no authority over the candidates for benefices. Five-sixths of the livings were in the hands of the laity or the Crown, and the bishops had to accept and induct whoever was presented by the patron. Nor had the bishops sufficient authority to impose Canon Law in their own dioceses, even if there had been any

Canon Law to impose. Indeed, it was not at all settled that Episcopacy would remain in the Church. The early reformers had not bothered much about Episcopacy as an institution. Cranmer and Jewel, to name two such, had expressly said that there was no special grace in the Episcopal office. It was a convenient institution, and had the merit of being a tangible link with the pre-Reformation Church. But, as we have seen, many thought that another form of Church government might better suit the Church, and be more free from the taint of Popery. Elizabeth's aim was to maintain this vagueness, that the monarchy and the Protestant succession might survive free from the tyranny of clericalism, whether Catholic or Puritan.

But during her lifetime the balance of ecclesiastical party power had changed. The Roman Catholic community had emerged, and were served on the accession of James by some two hundred priests. The Episcopal party in the national Church had gained greater authority, an authority soon to be confirmed by the King. For the national Church, on the accession of James, differed from the Church at the accession of Elizabeth in three important respects.

1. There was a more definite Episcopal party, with a firmer belief in the desirability of government by bishops. The representatives of this party held many of the more important offices in the Church.

2. The High Commission was using its authority to supplement the power of the bishops.

3. The codification of Canon Law was near completion.

The Puritans for the most part were still in the Church. They, in common with the other Church parties, were quietly negotiating with James, and storing up until a convenient time their aim to set up a national Presbyterian Church. But the opposition they faced was, by this time, stronger and more united.

This gradual change had come about through a variety of causes. The defeat of the Armada had made England more nationalist and patriotic. As a result, the sort of Church which the Queen apparently favoured shared in this fervour. Then again the telling use which Bancroft was able to make of the fortunes of the Church in Scotland, governed as the Puritans wanted the Church to be governed, shed a more kindly light on Episcopacy. But beyond all this was the devotion, brains, and hard work of Whitgift, Bancroft, and Hooker.

THE HARDENING OF EPISCOPAL CLAIMS

The success of these three in moulding the opposition to Puritanism is illustrated by the hardening, as it were, of Episcopal claims, as the years moved on. Whitgift taking up the cudgels against Cartwright's attack on Episcopacy, pleaded for Episcopacy on the ground of expediency and tradition. Both he and Cartwright believed in the sufficiency of Scripture for salvation, but he differed from his great Puritan antagonist in that he did not believe that Scripture specified the offices of the Church. In some points it was left to the liberty of the Church to rule herself according to the state of times, places, and persons. Episcopacy was permissible by all the traditions of the Church. He could not believe that for fifteen hundred years the true government of the Church had been neglected. Because this was so, there could not be only one Church government divinely ordained by Christ. Episcopacy, therefore, not being repugnant to Scripture, was permissible. Bancroft and Hooker did not alter his main argument, but strengthened it. Bancroft was able to plead, not only that Episcopacy was permissible, but that it was desirable. Presbyterianism had been tried near home, and in Bancroft's view it was certainly not better than Episcopacy—in fact, in many ways it was much inferior.

Hooker, following on, gave a philosophical justification for the form of Church government of the national Church. The difficulty under which Whitgift and Bancroft laboured was that they could not give an answer to the Puritans who asked why the form of Church government should be determined by expediency. After all, doctrine was not left to expediency, it was laid down in Scripture, and as they firmly believed that the Church was necessary to salvation (for, following Calvin, they held that the Church was the saved community), it seemed extraordinary to them, therefore, that anyone could believe that God should specify the doctrine, but not the discipline. Again, the Scriptures talked of bishop and presbyter as the same kind of person, and seemed to support the Presbyterians. Hooker, however, did succeed in giving them an answer. He said that the universe itself was governed by natural laws which were God's laws, and to them everything must conform. Being God's laws, they supplied the key to the opening of the Scriptures. These laws were determined by man's reason, aided by all the sources of light and truth which surrounded him. Therefore, if man's reason said that Episcopacy was a good thing, and if it seemed to be the best solution, taking into consideration all the weight of history, tradition, and suitability, then it should be upheld. It was plainly not contrary to Scripture, and was well established in the Church of England. In fact, to use the immortal words of that excellent history book, *1066 and All That*, it was 'C. of E. and a good thing'. The same argument might be applied to the Church of Rome in Italy, or the Presbyterian Church in Scotland, and with equal success. But it served its purpose in justifying the Episcopate in the English national Church.

BANCROFT AND THE HIGH COMMISSION

Coupled with this development was the use Bancroft made of the High Commission in supplementing the bishop's authority. The main problem of the Elizabethan settlement was an administrative one. In 1558 Thomas Sampson, returning from exile on the Continent, wrote to his friend Peter Martyr that he felt he ought not to accept a bishopric, 'Because through want of Church discipline, the Bishop or Pastor is unable to discharge his office'. This was the crux of the administrative problem, the lack of coercive authority in the Episcopal office. The Puritans produced one solution, which they outlined in the *Book of Discipline*. But the Episcopal party at first had no real solution. The bishops had little or no control over presenting a man to a benefice. Nor could they fine or imprison. The visitations, arranged by the archdeacons, were chiefly a method of inquiry, and hardly aided the bishops at all, save to give them some information which they found difficult to act on. A clergyman could indeed be deprived of his living, but only after a long legal process, and after being proved guilty. The old hierarchic system of the Medieval Church, in which the priest was responsible to his bishop, the bishop to his metropolitan, and the metropolitan to the Pope, had collapsed in England, with the alienation of livings to the laity, and the shifting of ecclesiastical control to the Crown. The coercive power which the bishops might have been given to restore something of the old authority was denied them by the Queen. Elizabeth did not want to see either the moderate Catholics or the moderate Puritans driven out of the Church. The government of the Church by the

Crown meant that the Privy Council did most of the work, and the section of the Council that did the work was the High Commission. It was virtually the ecclesiastical arm of the Privy Council, existing to enforce the Oath of Supremacy, the Thirty-nine Articles, and to punish Puritan and Catholic offences. It was Bancroft who first saw that the coercive power the bishops needed could be obtained through the High Commission. He realized that what could be used for enforcing a test of political loyalty could be used to enforce ecclesiastical conformity. The High Commission had the additional advantage that its jurisdiction was the whole of England. It could fine or imprison a man, whereas the bishops could only censure, excommunicate, and finally deprive. The High Commission, properly used, could find out what was hidden from the bishop, and supplement his authority in his own diocese. The bishops were not long in realizing that here was a weapon that did not break in their hands. Soon the knowledge that the bishop had the High Commission behind him was sufficient to produce obedience to an order, which earlier would have been laughed at.

THE CODIFICATION OF CANON LAW

The third difference between the Church at the accession of James and the Church at the accession of Elizabeth was that by the time of the Stuarts there was in hand a code of Canon Law. This had been prepared by Bancroft and it defined the nature and usage of the Church as Bancroft wanted it to be defined. He had come to believe that the national Church would not function properly if the Puritans were to remain in it. 'They were in the Church, but not of it',[1] he had said. In this he differed from Hooker, who wrote his great book on ecclesiastical polity, not only to justify Episcopacy, but as an irenicon to include the Puritans. This lack of a Canon Law was partly the reason for the difficulty in administering the Church in Elizabeth's day. There had been, in 1585 and 1587, certain canons enacted, but nowhere was there to be found any clear definition as to who should or who should not be considered a member of the Church. Nor was there any definition as to how the laity might communicate, nor any statement, for instance, on the vexed question of the position of the Communion table. A certain judicious liberty was allowed, to

[1] W. Usher, *Reconstruction of the English Church* (1910), vol. I, p. 76, note 2.

embrace all who would remain in moderate quietness. Nor is it easy to see how, or why, there could be any such definitions, if the Church was to embrace all, or even a majority of the nation. The bishops had striven for years to gain some small control over the ministry by issuing 'Injunctions', 'Advertisements', and forms of subscription, but the cry of Whitgift, 'Let us know, not what we may do on sufferance, but what we may do of right', was left unanswered by the astute Queen. Bancroft set himself to remedy this, and prepared his codification of Canon Law. This was finished in 1604 and hurried through Convocation. These canons made definite the Episcopal nature of the Church, as Bancroft and his friends understood it. They set the seal on the ultimate necessity of excluding the non-conforming Puritans. In effect, they were the beginning of a movement to turn the national Church into what seemed an Episcopal sect, although an established one.

THE HAMPTON COURT CONFERENCE

The culminating point in this process of 'sectarianizing' the national Church came when James coupled the monarchy with Episcopacy. It was the triumph of the policy of Whitgift and Bancroft. Realizing the impossibility of remedying the administrative difficulties of the Church, they both saw the Crown as the one power that could help them. Now James had justified their policy. He would have bishops. Not merely because he thought that they were the best form of government for the Church, but because he thought that without bishops there could be no king. Elizabeth had been careful not to identify the continuation of monarchy with the existence of episcopacy. The bishops were officers of the Crown, her servants, but not necessary to her throne.[1] James made the error of casting in his lot with what was, after all, only a sect, and a sect which could never command a majority in Parliament.

It is appropriate to our theme to inquire why he did so, for he was not committed to any ecclesiastical party on his accession, and had had dealings with all. He had received the Millenary Petition quite graciously, and his statement that he wished the universities to follow his example in handing over their impropriations to the improvement of Church livings, which frightened Bancroft and the universities, was exactly the Puritan

[1] cf. R. L. Ottley, *Lancelot Andrewes* (Methuen, 1894), p. 42.

policy. But after Bancroft had entertained the King and Queen at Fulham on their way to London, the Puritans found the going a little more difficult. Still, the King had conferred a certain dignity on them by agreeing to a conference between them and the Episcopal party. It was during this conference at Hampton Court that the Puritans were really discomfited. It was here that the King finally plumped for Episcopacy of the Bancroft kind, for which he received the gratifying assurance from the bishops that he 'spoke with the special assistance of God's Spirit'.

A readable account of the Conference will be found in the *Reconstruction of the English Church*, Vol. I, by Dr. Usher; but the whole of the work is slightly biased in two ways. Firstly, Dr. Usher is at pains to make out at every turn the numerically small numbers of Puritans in the country. Secondly, he assumes that the national Church was in fact what Bancroft wanted it to be in law, and that the Puritans had never had any right to be in it. But the facts seem to indicate otherwise. The Puritans were strong enough to command nearly always a majority in Parliament.[1] So they must have commanded a large following, if not of out-and-out Puritans, at least of people who favoured their views of reformation. Then again, the national Church had been framed to include all who would behave, whatever their personal views of Church government. The Puritan ministers, whether deprived or not, certainly considered themselves legally entitled to exercise their ministry in it. The process of 'sectarianizing' the national Church was a long one, and was valiantly opposed by the Puritans in their attempt to reform and control the Church.

In his account of the Conference, Dr. Usher follows Barlow's account, written at the Royal command, and undertaken at the express direction of Bancroft. He also prints five other accounts in the Appendix to the second volume of the work mentioned above. One is favourable to the bishops, and four are favourable to the Puritans. It would seem that the Puritan delegates first of all asked for very moderate reforms, as they had been instructed to do by their brethren. But the more radical section, headed by Hildersham, Egerton, and Fleetwood, drew up ten demands more suited to their views, and handed them to the delegates. It is probable that this was the paper

[1] cf. M. M. Knappen, *Tudor Puritanism* (1939), p. 333, note 24.

Dr. Raignolds produced when he asked for the establishment of 'Classes'. Although the various accounts vary considerably from one another, being biased on one side or another, it would appear that James tried to be fair to both sides. He did not hesitate to reprimand the bishops when necessary, and showed himself to be a Calvinist against any Episcopal tendency to Arminianism. But on one point he stood firm, and unequivocally proclaimed his position. This was when there was any question of changing the government of the Church into the Presbyterian form. He was as adamant as Elizabeth in his opposition to it. The question first arose over confirmation. The Puritans wished the parish ministers to have the right of examining the faith of their people, and judging themselves whether they were fit to proceed to the Supper of the Lord. But James was quick to see where this would lead. He 'smelt whereunto that tended to make every one in his cure to be Bishop which he liked not of'. He therefore confirmed the customary method of examination and approval by the diocesan bishop. The same stumbling-block occurred when Dr. Raignolds asked for the appointment of Classes in the Church. The King saw that it meant the establishment of Presbyterianism, and this he refused to sanction. He had sufficiently tasted the mischiefs of 'presbytry' in Scotland, and when he wished to live again under such a system he would go back to Scotland. His root objection was the same as Elizabeth's: a fear that Presbyterianism would diminish his prerogative of supreme governor of the Church. The upshot of the conference was that the Puritans were foiled again. The bishops won a resounding victory, and the King had identified the monarchy with the continuance of Episcopacy.

It now remained to be seen whether James could carry out his policy of harrying the Nonconformists into conformity or out of the Church. There was a certain reluctance on the part of many bishops to carry out his orders. Whether this was due to charitableness on the part of the bishops, as Usher thinks, or to the fear of provoking a good number of able clergy and laymen, or to weakness in the Church's administrative machine, it is impossible to determine accurately. Probably all three reasons combined to make the bishops reluctant. But James had his way, and certain clergy were deprived of their livings. In the Parliamentary debates of 1606, Yelverton asserted that three hundred ministers were deprived; but Bancroft insisted that only sixty were so punished. It is probable that three hundred were admonished, and some sixty deprived. Many Puritans conformed, and some who were deprived of their livings were straightway restored. It seems safe to say too that much Nonconformity was winked at.[1]

THE CHANGE IN PURITAN POLICY

In fact, the Puritans, though disorganized, were not demoralized. They still continued as an active force in the Church. Outside the Church, the Puritan Separatist sects were on the increase. While in Parliament, and the growing mercantile class, were many who, in their opposition to the authoritarianism of the Crown and of the bishops, made common cause with the Puritans. Because of this, the venue of the Puritan struggle moved closer and closer to the Parliamentary arena, where they could always command a hearing and good support. Parliament in the succeeding years was faced with two issues in the religious realm which affected it in what it conceived to be its own authority. One was the legality of the canons of 1604, which had not been passed by Parliament, and the other was the wider question whether Parliament had the right to decide ecclesiastical issues, or whether that right resided only in the Crown. In these issues the Parliamentary attack was given a *casus belli* by the Puritan complaints. Coupled with these was the question of the augmentation of ecclesiastical incomes. It was certainly necessary that the monetary value of Church livings should be increased if better men were to be attracted into the Church. There seemed only two sources from which such an increase could come. One was the deprivation of Episcopal incomes, and the other was the return to the Church of the impropriations of tithes and Church lands. This latter alternative would mean that many of the men in Parliament would have to return to the Church the sources of their new wealth. It seemed better to them that the bishops should suffer. They tended therefore to support the Puritans against the bishops, although the return of Church lands was a Puritan ideal also, but the danger from the bishops was more immediate. The situation, even so early in James's reign, was clarifying into a struggle between Parliament, supported by the Puritans, and the Crown supported by the bishops.

[1] M. M. Knappen, *Tudor Puritanism*, p. 328.

The ensuing years were filled with the attempts by the Puritans to reinstate the deprived ministers, through the authority of Parliament. The clergy in Convocation, meanwhile, were busy preparing the canons of 1606. These canons were concerned to provide a historical and logical basis for the Royal supremacy, with particular reference to Holy Scripture. Usher draws attention to the fact that 'Nowhere do we find the words "Divine Right" applied to either kings or bishops'.[1] In fact, it is pointed out that though the present form of Church and State has God's approval, they are not the only forms that He might approve. Although Bancroft strengthened both the hold of the bishops on the national Church, and the arguments for their government, he always held that a man could be saved in any of the Reformed Churches. To him Episcopacy was not a *sine qua non* of salvation.

The Commons meanwhile were still restive, and at the 1606–7 session challenged the legality of the 1604 canons, as they had not been confirmed by Parliament. The usual Puritan petition of grievances was produced. The Speaker, however, informed the House that the King had told him that he knew what was in the petition, and had done his best to redress the grievances; therefore there was no need to present them. The House was in favour of going on with them, but the Speaker pointed out that there were plenty of precedents for similar orders from the Crown on religious subjects in past days. The House doubted his word, and a committee was appointed to look into the matter. They confirmed the Speaker's ruling, and the House allowed the Bill to 'sleep'. But at one time there seemed to be a majority of the House in favour of going on with the petition, orders or no orders.

That Parliament should even contemplate disregarding the express orders of the Monarch showed a change in the attitude of the Puritans. In Elizabeth's day they were firmly convinced of the wisdom of passive resistance and obedience to the Monarch. But now their temper was changing. In 1605, when James goaded the bishops on to deal with the Puritans, Sir Edward Montagu and the Knightleys presented him with a petition from the gentry of Northamptonshire. The significant thing about the petition was not what it contained, but the words which accompanied it. James was told that, if he did not grant it, several thousands of his subjects would be seriously offended

[1] W. Usher, *Reconstruction of the English Church* (1910), vol. II, p. 128.

at him. It was almost a threat. James had noticed a change in the attitude of some of the Puritans before this. At the Hampton Court Conference he told them how the Presbyterians in Scotland began to question his authority, holding him to be no competent judge over them. 'Even according as some heare in England already have begun to deal with me. ffor at first theye prayed for me as supreme gouernor ouer all causes and persons, but after they began to abate their tearmes of my superiority.'[1] It was obvious that the Puritans, acting mainly through Parliament, were becoming more aggressive in tone. The attack on the High Commission centring around the Puritan lawyer, Nicholas Fuller, witnessed to the same thing. It was this same spirit which was behind the quarrel of the Common Lawyers with the High Commission. The incidence of the quarrel was the issuing of prohibitions by the Common Pleas to restrain the High Commission's suits against its various victims. But behind this procedure was the growing intransigence of the Puritans, and it was directed against the growing power of the bishops. Bancroft's work in strengthening Episcopal authority was gaining enemies, who were coming more and more into the open. His death in 1610 robbed the Episcopal party of its main driving force. The new Archbishop, Abbott, was content to leave things as they were during his long tenure of office. He was more interested in theological than in administrative problems, but when Laud succeeded to the Archbishopric, the Episcopal party gained a leader in the highest office of the Church more vigorous than even Bancroft. His work paved the way for what Bishop Henson calls 'The emphasis both sinister and unprecedented' that was placed on Episcopacy after the failure of the Savoy Conference in 1661. 'The Church of England had always been Episcopal, it now became Episcopalian, that is, what had been a matter of practical policy became the requirement of religious principle.'[2] While it is true that the 'emphasis' was unprecedented, the ground had been prepared by Bancroft and Laud. From being expedient, Episcopacy became desirable, and from being desirable it became necessary. And not only had it become necessary, but a particular kind of Episcopacy became necessary, that which was called in Baxter's day by the name of Prelacy.

[1] Harleian MSS., No. 828.
[2] H. Hensley Henson, *Church of England* (Cambridge University Press, 1939), p. 123.

Chapter III

A REFORMED PASTOR

BAXTER'S EARLY LIFE AND THE GROWTH OF PRELACY

ON Sunday morning, 12th November 1615, at the time of divine worship, a son was born to Richard and Beatrice Baxter at Rowton in the County of Shropshire. The following Sunday the boy was christened Richard, the name held by his father and grandfather. The year after he was born William Shakespeare died, and twelve years before his birth Thomas Cartwright, the great Puritan leader of Elizabeth's reign, had died; so near was his birth to the splendid Elizabethan age, and to the origin of the Puritan movement. Some of the early Puritan leaders, such as Travers, were still alive. Arthur Hildersham and John Dod were to live far into the seventeenth century, Hildersham to die in 1632 and John Dod, settled at Fawsley by Richard Knightly, was to hold that pulpit until his death in 1645 at ninety years of age. Renowned for his racy speech, his generous hospitality, and his sage counsel, John Dod was, to quote Cartwright, 'the fittest man in the land for a Pastoral function'. Sibbes, the great preacher and writer, was alive, and Chaderton, 'nuzzled in Popery', seventy years or so before Baxter's birth, shuffled off this mortal coil in 1640, nearly a hundred years old!

Baxter's early years were spent at a time when Puritanism seemed a lost cause. It had apparently received its quietus at the Hampton Court Conference. The great Elizabethan Puritan courtiers had long since passed away, and the prevailing tendency at Court was to support the Episcopal party, of which Andrewes and Laud were dissimilar but eager supporters. Throughout James's reign this party had been gaining ground. It was the party of men who regretted the Reformation, and looked with nostalgia to the powerful pre-Reformation Church. They sought in tradition and the early Fathers a more 'Catholic' faith than that of the Puritan steeped in his Bible. But their main purpose was to restore the power of the bishops, and also to resurrect the ancient influence of the Church by securing its economic independence. This group of men were in direct succession to Whitgift, Bancroft, and Hooker. Each of these had in some measure emphasized the principles for which the Episcopal party stood. Each had laid some little of the foundation for the development of Prelacy. Whitgift had chosen to redeem rather than alienate his Church lands, Hooker had preached an Apostolic English Church in direct and uninterrupted succession from the Apostles, while Bancroft had repudiated the Parliamentary control of the Church. This group were known as Arminians by their more orthodox Calvinist opponents, because of their predilection for the more gentle theology of Arminius. In time they came to hold high positions in the Church. In fact, when one of them was asked, in the days of Charles I, what the Arminians held, he replied that they held the best bishoprics and deaneries in England![1]

But in the days of James I only one of this party held high office in the Church. This was the saintly Bishop Andrewes, whose title to holiness was partly due to the fact that, much to everyone's surprise, he had obtained preferment in the Church without simony. He was a 'safe' man and would take no part in politics, although he was a Privy Councillor.[2] But it was also a surprise when James elevated the Calvinist Abbot rather than Andrewes to the vacant see of Canterbury, although it was in keeping with James's policy of trying to preserve a balance between the two rival parties. So that while Andrewes preached the divine right of bishops in the Apostolic English Church, without seriously attempting to apply his theories, Abbott continued to give his official support to the Puritans, and to let ecclesiastical politics take their course without too much pressure from the throne of Augustine.

But while Andrewes was content to formulate his ideals without applying them, in the odour of sanctity which escaped occasionally from his study, his disciples were not so content. The most brilliant, restless, and energetic of them, William Laud, gathered the reins of the Episcopal party into his own hands, and proceeded as a good son of Israel to harry the hosts of Midian, which, as the hymn says, prowled and prowled around. The hosts of Midian were, of course, the Puritans, the Parliament, the lay-holders of tithe, the lazy clergy—in fact, anyone who in Laud's view defaced the Bride of Christ, soon to be guided from Canterbury by 'little Laud' himself. Baxter's boyhood and youth

---

[1] H. R. Trevor-Roper, *Archbishop Laud* (Macmillan, 1940), p. 29.
[2] R. L. Ottley, *Lancelot Andrewes* (1894), p. 50.

were passed while Laud was gaining control of his party and consolidating his power.

How much there was needed to be done to make the Bride of Christ spotless is told us in the account which Baxter gives of his own village. 'We lived in the country', he says, 'that had but little preaching at all. In the village where I was born, there were four readers successively in six years' time, ignorant men and two of them immoral in their lives, who were all my schoolmasters. In the village where my father lived, there was a reader of about eighty years of age that never preached and had two churches about twenty miles distant.'[1] He tells of another cleric whose orders were forged, and of another who was a drunkard. Within a few miles of his home were a dozen ministers who were nearly eighty years old apiece and never preached, most of them being also of scandalous lives. There were only three or four constant, competent preachers, all conformable save one, who were the common marks of the people's reproach.

BAXTER'S CONVERSION AND HIS ENTRANCE INTO THE MINISTRY

But despite all this, it pleased God to convert his father by the bare reading of Scripture. His changed way of life got him the odious name of Puritan from the villagers who spent the Sabbath dancing round the maypole not far from his door. Often the boy had a mind to be with them, but when he heard them call his father a Puritan, it did much to cure him and alienate him from them. For he considered his father's method of spending the Sabbath much better than their games. At fifteen he was converted. The two books which most influenced him were written by two authors almost poles apart, at least in their own estimation. One was *Bunny's Resolution*, written by Parsons the Jesuit and corrected by Edmund Bunny, while the other was *The Bruised Reed*, written by Dr. Sibbes, the Puritan preacher. In his account of his conversion, Baxter gives us an interesting glimpse of the way literature was disseminated in the seventeenth century. He tells us that *Bunny's Resolution* was an old torn book lent to his father by a poor day labourer, who used to read in church for the old parson, while *The Bruised Reed* was bought at the door from a poor pedlar who came selling 'ballads and some good books'. It gives us an indication of the difficulty which Laud's censorship of literature had in trying to suppress

[1] *Autobiography* (Everyman, 1931), p. 3.

opposition pamphlets and books. The pedlars were still, as in the Middle Ages, almost the sole means of communication between village and village, and if books could be printed at all they would be assured of a market through the all-pervasive bagman.

About his seventeenth year Baxter had a taste of the world, and decided that he preferred the Gospel! On one occasion God cured his inclination to gambling by the curious method of letting him win when all seemed lost, in a game of chance at Ludlow Castle. According to all human calculation, he should have lost the game, but he refused to give up until all his tablemen were lost. At the last set-to the dice turned up his number so often that he won. His conclusion was that the Devil had the ruling of the dice, and allowed him to win to entice him deeper into the mire. He returned the stake to the loser. The other taste of the world which he had was when he was persuaded to set aside his thoughts of the ministry and go to Court as being 'the only rising way'. He was only there a month, staying with Sir Henry Herbert, the Master of the Revels. He saw a stageplay on Sunday instead of hearing a sermon, and the little preaching that was there was mostly against the Puritans. He was glad to return home, which he was able to do the easier as his mother had fallen ill and desired his return.

He was troubled continually with illness, and doubted as to the working of the Spirit in his heart. But he studied hard, plunging into the works of Aquinas, Duns Scotus, Durandus, and Ockham; a course which gave him an excellent facility in splitting hairs, and strengthened his natural bent to casuistry. But as he says, he counted it a mercy of God that he was never overwhelmed with real melancholy, while by exercise, temperance in eating, and beer, as hot as his throat would drink it, to make him sweat, he managed to evade an untimely death. All this while he was satisfied in the matter of conformity. But when he was about twenty he met some godly Nonconformists whose stories of persecution by the bishops gave rise to a prejudice in his heart that those who silenced and troubled such men could not be genuine followers of the Lord of Love. But he had no real scruple about subscribing, and he was ordained by the Bishop of Worcester, and had a licence to teach. He settled at Dudley and decided to study seriously the question of conformity. He found he could agree to most things in the Church, except to subscribing *ex animo* that there was nothing in the Book of Ordinances, the Homilies, and the Common Prayer contrary to the Word of God, nor could he agree to the use of the sign of the Cross in baptism, nor to the promiscuous giving of the Lord's Supper to immoral persons that were not excommunicated by the bishop or Chancellor. But he kept most of these things to himself and daily disputed against the Nonconformists. True to his nature, he found their tendency to separatism a great evil.

After nearly a year at Dudley, he moved to Bridgenorth as assistant to Mr. Madstard, the pastor there. The place was privileged from episcopal jurisdiction, the Archbishop visiting it once in three years. There were six parishes with this privilege, having an ordinary of their own who kept an ecclesiastical court. Mr. Madstard himself was the ordinary. Here Baxter had a full Church to preach to, who often applauded his sermons, but stubbornly refused to reform! Here he had freedom from those things at which he scrupled. He often read the Common Prayer, but did not celebrate, nor baptize with the sign of the Cross, nor wear a surplice. It was while he was here that Convocation passed the *Et cetera* Oath, which caused such a furore in the country, and impelled Baxter to study more closely the nature of Episcopacy. The canons in which this oath was included were passed by the Convocation called at the same time as the Short Parliament. They were part of the policy of the Laudian party to make high-churchmanship not merely a policy within the Church, but a principle of the Church.[1] These canons were the culminating point of that course, begun by Whitgift and Bancroft, and continued by Andrewes and Laud, to make the Church of England Episcopalian. They aroused widespread opposition, and the *Et cetera* Oath was tacitly dropped until a more convenient time. Not that the Laudian party had repented, but the opposition was now so strong that only civil war could resolve the impasse.

BAXTER AND THE CIVIL WAR

Soon Baxter moved to Kidderminster, which was to be the scene of his greatest and happiest labours. The people of Kidderminster had got up a petition against their Vicar and his two curates, whom they considered unfit to minister to them.

[1] H. R. Trevor-Roper, *Archbishop Laud* (1940), p. 391; and cf. H. Hensley Henson, *English Religion in the Seventeenth Century* (Murray, 1903), pp. 147–8.

But before the petition was presented, the Vicar compromised by promising to pay for a lecturer, to be appointed by the people to take the place of his town curate. Baxter was eventually chosen unanimously for the post. The beginnings of his ministry were not without incident. At one time some of the people were raging mad at him for preaching the doctrine of original sin, which they interpreted as meaning that God hated and loathed infants! Another time one of the drunken beggars of the town accused him of 'being under a tree with a woman'—that is, a woman of ill repute. However, he got the slanderers bound over to good behaviour, and the one who spread the story confessed that he had made a mistake. At that Baxter asked the magistrate to release them.

When the Civil War broke out, he was much put about as to what to believe about the conflict, as his instincts were Royalist, but his sympathies were Parliamentarian. He points out that both sides claimed to be for the King, but that the Parliament men said, of course, that they were for 'King and Parliament'. He finally came to the conclusion that the real traitors, whoever they were, were those who divided the King and Parliament. The Puritans as a whole sided with Parliament, even those who, like Baxter, preferred a monarchy, partly because Parliament was opposed to the bishops, and partly because the Parliament soldiers were more devout men. This was admitted by many who Baxter knew were personally for the King. The common people saw the Royalist soldiers living in debauchery, heard them curse and abuse the name of God, while their opponents flocked to sermons, prayers, and psalm-singing. Baxter's sympathies with Parliament inflamed the Royalists of the town against him. The mob on one occasion sought his life, for which he dealt with them plainly the next Lord's Day and offered to leave Kidderminster. But it turned out that, despite their fury, the people were loath to part with him. On several occasions he deemed it wise to leave Kidderminster for a time, because of the dangers, and from 1643–5 he lived at Coventry.

In 1645 he went to visit friends in the Parliamentary army at Naseby. Here he found that things had changed since the beginning of the war. The New Model Army under Cromwell's control had become revolutionary. No longer was there talk of defending King, Parliament, and the liberties of the people, but there were hints which intimated their intention to subvert both

Church and State. The Anabaptists in the army were increasing, and the sectaries, under Cromwell's encouragement, were gaining complete control. They took the King for a tyrant, and thought they might justly kill or conquer him. There was also great talk of liberty of conscience, which greatly disturbed Baxter. In fact, the change in the sentiments and purpose of the army since the rise of Cromwell not only astonished him, but worried him. Things were obviously getting out of control. He blamed the ministers for this, because they had remained at home and not joined the army as chaplains, and so kept the sectaries under control. He blamed himself more, because he had refused Cromwell's invitation to become chaplain to his own troop, which he had considered turning into a 'gathered Church'. For, despite his antipathy to 'gathered Churches', Baxter now felt that had he accepted the invitation things would have been different, especially as many of the original troop now held high offices in the New Model Army. So in order to try to stem the rising tide of sectarianism in the army, Baxter accepted the invitation of Captain Evanson to come to his regiment as chaplain. This extraordinary step illustrates not only his courage and his tender conscience, but also his faith in the power of reason to bring men to a better frame of mind, a faith which never left him all his life, despite the failure of many of his most cherished schemes. He pursued his work in the army with diligence, disputing with all those who seemed to him to be corrupted theologically, and following the army in its train of successes. He was sneered at by Cromwell's secretary, and ignored by men such as Captain Berry, who had once been his friends. But his career in the army was cut short by illness, just when he thought there might have been some success to it. And after a period of convalescence at the home of Sir Thomas and Lady Rous, he returned to Kidderminster.

BAXTER'S ATTEMPT TO CREATE A UNITED CHURCH

Baxter commenced the second period of his ministry at Kidderminster in very different circumstances. A few years of Laud's government had made the hierarchy extremely unpopular. Even Lord Digby, who spoke in defence of Episcopacy in Parliament, had to confess: 'I do not think that any people hath been ever more provoked than the generality of England of late years by the insolencies and exorbitances of the prelates.'[1] His speech gives a picture of persistent harrying by the bishops of all sorts and conditions of men. But he still believed in Episcopacy as a system. Indeed, when the Long Parliament first met, there was not much opinion hostile to Episcopacy as such, but only to the prelatical methods of Laud and his party. But the Civil Wars had made a great change. The original purpose of the Long Parliament was merely to reform Episcopacy, but the early defeats of their army forced them to rely more upon the Scots, who insisted on them taking the Solemn League and Covenant as a price of their help. Parliament wriggled as hard as it could, but the Scots had them in their grip. So Parliament had to give up its idea of merely reforming the Episcopal system, and accept, with certain modifications, the Presbyterian system which was implied in the Covenant.

It is one thing to legislate a new form of Church government, but quite another thing to make it work. For the Presbyterian system, as we have seen in the earlier chapters, necessitated the co-operation of the laity, particularly in electing Church elders, and, with the exception of London and Lancashire, where the new system was adopted, the laity refused to co-operate. The system also presupposed the friendly co-operation of the civil power, the godly magistrate of Cartwright's thesis, but after the triumph of the army this co-operation was refused. Without the co-operation of the civil power, there was no means of making the parishioners elect lay elders, and without lay elders there was no means of 'fencing the tables'—that is, of producing a system of examination of the whole parish so as to allow only fit parishioners to communicate. And without 'fencing the tables' the Presbyterian scheme of discipline broke down. In their disappointment at the failure of their system, the Presbyterian clergy, almost in a body, made up their minds not to administer the Sacrament at all where they could not do so in the way they wished.

Such was the position in the earlier years of Baxter's second period at Kidderminster. He was greatly exercised by the question of administering the Sacraments to the Church. He could see the impasse into which the Church was driven. On the one hand, the old method of exercising discipline by the bishop's court was destroyed with the destruction of the Episcopal

[1] H. Hensley Henson, *English Religion in the Seventeenth Century* (1903), p. 80.

system, in any case he could not support that method as it had been practised. On the other hand, the Presbyterian system had broken down; the people as a whole did not like it, as it was too inquisitorial. Baxter also could not persuade himself that the system of elected lay elders was of necessity Scriptural. The result was that the people would not accept any Church discipline at all because their pastors were not agreed about the right method. The problem was how to get as much discipline as might reduce the Churches to order, satisfy the ministers in administering the Sacraments, and stop the more religious people from separating because there was no discipline. The formation of the Worcestershire Association was his attempt to solve this problem.

Fundamentally, the problem was one of Church unity, and his great desire for the Church was its visible unity. But the sectarian mind was rampant, not only in the sects, but just as much in the large Church parties. Baxter realized this, and consequently applied himself to those in all parties, and of no party, who did not confuse their own opinion with the Catholic Church. He set forth his views to the leaders of the various Church parties, the Erastian, the Episcopal, the Presbyterian, and the Independents. Their attitude for the most part was discouraging. So he decided to make a practical beginning at home in Worcestershire. There was already a group of ministers meeting at his house every month, and in the spring of 1652 he approached them with his idea, and found that it was immediately welcomed. He was commissioned to draw up a scheme of Church order and discipline, which he did. After several meetings, about half the ministers in the county subscribed to it. It consisted of a scheme which embodied as much of Church order and discipline as the Episcopal, Presbyterian, and Independent were agreed in, as belonging to the pastors of each particular church. However, no Presbyterian or Independents joined in, and only four or five men who had definite views in favour of Episcopacy. For some years the Association prospered, and other associations were formed in Cambridgeshire, Cheshire, Cornwall, Devon, Norfolk, Nottingham, Shropshire, possibly in Herefordshire, and in North Wales. The Prelatical party, led by Dr. Hammond, would have nothing to do with it. Nor for the most part would the Presbyterians. They disliked it because it looked like Presbyterianism in practice, but was definitely not in principle.

Baxter pleaded with them to help him. It was wrong, he said, to forbear all administration of the Lord's Supper, and all exercise of discipline in the Church, as some ministers had done, simply because they had been unable, so far, to get full classical Presbyterianism in the country. But it was of no avail. However, the work that was done was good and necessary, and even some of the leading Baptists began to take him seriously.

Unfortunately, the death of Cromwell and the return of Charles put an end to Baxter's hopes of unity in the Church. The Prelatical faction gained control of the Church, due, so Baxter thought, to the lack of unity in those who were opposed to them, and his whole scheme collapsed. Had Cromwell lived, then Baxter's scheme might have served as a basis for a real Church of England, for whatever Cromwell's personal views were, there would have been toleration for the country to work out gradually an amicable settlement. Baxter disliked Cromwell, even calling him 'the Usurper', but he had to confess that he had a liberty under the Protector which was denied him under a monarch, and that under Cromwell's protectorate the quality of the clergy was greatly improved. 'For all the faults that are now among us', he says, 'I do not believe that ever England had so able and faithful a ministry since it was a nation, as it hath at this day.'[1]

THE WORCESTERSHIRE ASSOCIATION

The articles of association which formed the basis of the scheme of discipline in Worcester may be found in Baxter's book, *Christian Concord*, dated 1653, or conveniently set out in the first Appendix of J. T. Wilkinson's *Reformed Pastor*. They are in two parts: firstly, the propositions agreed to by the associated ministers of the county, and, secondly, a profession of faith taken by the ministers and to be taken by Church members. The purpose of the articles is to give a moral, persuasive authority to the pastoral work of each minister, and to provide some means of consultation between the ministers in cases of discipline. The Association was also to receive complaints by members of the Churches against any ministers in cases of scandal, false doctrine, or maladministration. But it is not indicated what should happen to the offending brother if

---

[1] *The Reformed Pastor by Richard Baxter*, edited by J. T. Wilkinson (Epworth Press, 1939), p. 94, note 1.

the case against him was proved. Presumably, he would be cast out. Provision was also made for the setting up of elders in the Churches who would assist the ministers, and be ordained for their particular tasks. The Association had to agree that these elders were properly ordained Church officers, but whether they should administer the Sacraments was to be left alone. The ministers might agree in practice, but each man's principles in such a knotty problem should be left to his own judgement. This clause would satisfy Presbyterians, but leave men like Baxter, who did not agree that lay elders were necessarily authorized in Scripture, to do what was convenient. In the county of Worcestershire there were to be five associations, and they were to meet once a month at five centres, viz. Worcester, Upton, Evesham, Kidderminster, and Bromsgrove, where they should keep up a public lecture. At these meetings the names of all those who had been put out of communion in any particular Church should be made known, so that other Churches should not receive them into their communion. Similarly, no one should receive as a Church member a person living in another parish, unless there was sufficient reason given. The sufficiency of the reason would be decided by the Association and not by the individual minister. The Association was more than a consultative assembly, it also had definite disciplinary powers, and was meant to supply the place of the old ecclesiastical courts, but with purely spiritual penalties. This was in keeping, as we shall see later on, with Baxter's desire for the reform of the bishops' courts to deal with purely spiritual issues, and with purely spiritual penalties.

One thing seems to stand out when reading the articles of Association—namely, that the framer of them and those who accepted them conceived of the Church as a voluntary association, in which people were asked to accept a moral discipline, as well as a definite profession of faith. The assumption behind the articles seems to be that the Church is not co-extensive with the nation, and that the Elizabethan ideal had broken down, with the result that the parish system was not working properly, and the 'godly' of the parish tended to leave the parish churches and join the Independents. The Association can be viewed as an attempt to save these people, who were very often the only morally earnest people of the parish, for the Church of England, and at the same time frame a form of Church government which would bring into co-operation the Independents, Presbyterians, and moderate Episcopalians. Baxter did, however, conceive the Church to be co-extensive with the nation, and it is only when we read the articles out of their historical context that they seem to presuppose a voluntary Church in the Independent sense. The fact is that the Association was an experiment in Church union, which Baxter hoped would have led to a national English Church. In this Church the magistrate would have exercised whatever compulsory authority was necessary. Baxter again and again repudiated the use of force by the clergy; consequently he and those concerned with discipline in the Church had to know who would accept the discipline voluntarily, since the Cromwellian government (the chief magistrate) refused to compel people to attend church worship.

The method to be adopted was to draw up a profession of faith, based on the Apostles' Creed, to which the people were asked to profess assent, and also to draw up a form of oath in which the people would, by signing their names, consent to be members of a particular Church, and to submit to the pastoral oversight of a particular pastor. This would give a basis for the exercise of discipline in the parish. There would then be three types of people in the parish; first of all, those who consented, who would be reckoned as members certain; then those who denied their consent, who would not be reckoned as members of that Church; lastly, the people who were uncertain for some reason or other. Only those who consented to the discipline were to be admitted to Communion, and others who were uncertain were to be considered as *catecumeni*, to be preached to and instructed. An interesting forerunner of the Methodist Societies of the next century is to be found in Article XIX, Rule 11, which reads: 'If there be not enough in one Parish that will consent (after our sufficient waiting) we shall joyn them to the next Parish by consent; yet continuing still our meetings for preaching to the rest that consent not, and not medling with alterations of the Ministers maintenance.' The ministers were still parish ministers, but the parishioners who accepted the discipline could either meet for fellowship in their own parish, if there were enough of them, or with the 'godly' of an adjoining parish. Similarly, the early Methodists met with those of any parish who were of like mind, and attended their own parish for Communion and public worship.

Baxter organized his parish at Kidderminster according to this system, and of 1,600 persons old enough to be admitted to Communion only 600 were deemed fit to do so. Commenting on this, Dr. Henson says that the 'unreconciled majority, nearly two-thirds of the people, were chafing against the humiliations imposed on them and the restraints imposed on their liberty by Puritanical magistrates'.[1] A statement for which he has no authority—at least, no authority that he mentions. No doubt the 'unreconciled majority' did not want Baxter's form of discipline, and were satisfied with something less than the 600 communicants, but from Baxter's own statement, which is all we have to go on, it is most unlikely that they were 'chafing against the humiliations imposed on them'. The majority of the people must have been at public worship each Sunday, for although the Church was capacious, five extra galleries had to be built after his going to Kidderminster. His own judgement was that before he went there, there was about one family in each street who worshipped God, but when he went away he left a people who were, for the most part, practising Christians and a town where there were some streets where not a single family could be found who did not worship God publicly. It was a truly astonishing achievement, and almost unrivalled in the history of the Christian Church. It demonstrated to the Church how 'a reformed pastor' should work, and how it was possible to preserve the unity of the Church despite the sectarian minds who strove continually to destroy it. One thing was necessary for success, before all else, and that was liberty to preach the gospel. His work at Kidderminster, looked at against the background of his later persecution, convinced Baxter that despite all that he had 'written against licentiousness in religion, and for the magistrates' power in it', he would count 'that land happy that hath but bare liberty to be as good as they are willing to be', and for this reason he would 'not hereafter much fear such toleration nor despair that truth will bear down adversaries'.[2]

---

[1] H. Hensley Henson, *English Religion in the Seventeenth Century* (1903), pp. 118–19.
[2] *Autobiography* (Everyman, 1931), p. 80.

Chapter IV

A PILLAR OF THE CHURCH

THE success of the Worcestershire Association in bringing a certain measure of discipline and unity into the Church marked Baxter out as one of the most important leaders in the Church. Although the movement failed, as it was bound to fail, with the return of Charles and the sectarian-minded Episcopalian party, it showed that Baxter was a force to be reckoned with in any settlement of the Church.

BAXTER AND CROMWELL

Cromwell had long before recognized his worth when he had invited him to be the chaplain to his troop of horse. His ready pen and eagerness to defend the Faith as he knew it had increased his influence in the land. It is no surprise, therefore, to find him giving his views on the essentials or fundamentals of religion at the time when Cromwell appointed a committee of divines to devise a religious test to be operative for the toleration Cromwell desired. Baxter was for presenting for the consideration of Parliament, the Creed, the Lord's Prayer, and the Decalogue alone, as containing all that was necessary for salvation. And that all those who would consent to these fundamentals should have freedom of worship. The others, however, would not agree to his scheme, and so Baxter set himself, as he says, to hinder them from doing harm.[1]

His brush with Dr. Owen shows us just where he differed from the Independents, who wanted a test based purely and simply on the Scriptures. Dr. Owen, in extolling the Scriptures, said that no man could know God to salvation by any other means. Baxter replied that this was not a truth nor a fundamental, for if anyone, even a Papist, should believe through the teaching of another, without ever knowing that there were any Scriptures, he should be saved, because it was promised that whoever believed should be saved. Dr. Owen was silent awhile, and then said that there could be no other way of presenting the saving revelation of Jesus Christ. Baxter then pointed out

[1] ibid., p. 139.

that Christ was savingly revealed by preaching many years before the New Testament was written. One cannot help feeling that Baxter had, not only the freer and more elastic mind of the two, but also a surer grasp of the fundamental continuity of the historic faith.

Cromwell thought sufficiently well of him to ask him to preach before him. Baxter grasped the opportunity of provoking the Protector to do his duty, by preaching on the text, 1 Corinthians i. 10: 'Now I beseech you, brethren, through the name of our Lord Jesus Christ, that ye all speak the same thing, and that there be no divisions among you.' In the sermon he showed what a mischievous thing it was for politicians to maintain divisions in the Church for their own ends, and to keep the Church in a state of weakness, lest it grow too powerful and so able to offend them. He was convinced that this was Cromwell's policy, and had no hesitation in saying so. Cromwell was not pleased with the sermon. He sent for Baxter later on and tried to justify his government as being under God's providential care, enumerating what great things had been done abroad. Baxter then told him bluntly what must have been his chief objection to Cromwell's régime: 'We took', he said, 'our ancient monarchy to be a blessing, and not an evil to the land.' Cromwell, not unnaturally, flew into a passion. Another time Cromwell sent for him to know his judgement on toleration, and wearied Baxter by haranguing him at length. Baxter offered him a manuscript to read, in which he had set forth his opinions, but did not think that Cromwell ever bothered to read it.[1]

Baxter's attitude to Cromwell was governed by an extraordinary dislike. Knowing his saintly character, we cannot suppose that it arose from Cromwell's treatment of him when he was with the Army. More probably it arose, at first, because Cromwell encouraged the sectaries, and was brought to a head by the killing of the King. This attitude of opposition was not lessened by Cromwell's purging of Parliament and his repudiation of the Solemn League and Covenant. Baxter had no particular love for the Covenant—indeed, he had prevented Kidderminster and Worcester from subscribing to it—but he felt that those who had subscribed should at least keep it. Consequently, he preached against the new engagement enacted by the Rump Parliament, in which was the promise to be faithful to the Commonwealth

[1] *Autobiography*, pp. 140-1.

as established without King or House of Lords. But even these reasons do not seem sufficient to explain his opposition. There was at bottom a psychological reason: Baxter's dislike of autocracy, whether in Protector or prelate. This was aggravated by the fact that Baxter distrusted mystics. Mystics are by nature autocratic, their visions justify their actions irrespective of law or custom, and Cromwell's autocracy was in its fundamental energy mystical. Dr. Powicke points out that when George Fox met Cromwell they were drawn together at once. There was a sympathy between them which was outside Baxter's understanding. Baxter was intensely honest—painfully so, in fact—and he saw in Cromwell's appeals to God's guidance, which so often cut across what Baxter conceived to be justice, only hypocrisy.[1] The peculiar thing is that both were working to the same end—namely, unity in the Church—but by different means. Cromwell's avowed religious policy of allowing liberty of worship to all who worshipped God through Jesus Christ, coupled with Baxter's scheme before described, would have formed a real national Church with the breadth and tolerance of the Elizabethan settlement.

THE FAILURE OF THE PURITAN EXPERIMENT

We have emphasized in the preceding chapters the fundamental aim of Puritanism—namely, the organization of the nation in the form of a Church governed by Presbyterian principles. This was the persistent aim of the Elizabethan Puritans, and that aim was not forgotten, despite the rebuffs administered by James I at the Hampton Court Conference and the growth of Prelacy under Laud.

But unfortunately for the Presbyterian Puritans the section of Puritanism which triumphed in the wars was the Independent section under the leadership of Cromwell, with the Army as their instrument. By 1649 the Independents had cleared everything away that stood opposed to them, and they were ready for the millennium. The people of God had been led out of bondage into liberty, and they set out 'to combine a religious settlement which must be enforced on an unwilling nation, with a political theory which derived the authority of the Commons from the sovereignty of a free people'.[2]

[1] F. J. Powicke, *A Life of the Reverend Richard Baxter, 1615–19* (Cape, 1924), p. 126.
[2] I. Deane Jones, *The English Revolution* (Heinemann, 1931), p. 89.

The task they had to perform was quite impossible, and Cromwell, in order to preserve his religious settlement of toleration of worship, had to dispense with Parliament and rule as a dictator. Once more the Presbyterian Puritans were foiled, and had to accept a religious settlement as odious to them as to the Prelatical party.

But the tendency to separatism, which Baxter disliked in the Independents, was to be their downfall. There had already been a split in the Puritan ranks between 1644-9 on the question of toleration. The Presbyterian Puritans gave up their attempt to coerce Charles, and joined with the moderate Episcopalians in opposition to Independency. This was the first split. Soon the Independents began to quarrel among themselves, composed as they were of the most argumentative of the Puritans, Republicans, Levellers, and Fifth Monarchy men. When the Army returned from its battles in 1651, they found that the Parliament had done nothing to revive a 'Godly' ministry, and soon they were at loggerheads with each other over the scheme of John Owen, Cromwell's chaplain, for a voluntary national Church. Parliament had little interest in the scheme, and wished to shelve it. It was here that the Rump Parliament made the same mistake as the King and the Presbyterians had done: they defied the wishes of the all-powerful Army. In 1653 the Army crushed the Rump Parliament, and once more Independency was weakened. From 1653 to 1658 Cromwell had perforce to rule alone, striving all the while to find some instrument which would give unity and representative government to the nation, but without success. This history of faction and fighting seems to witness to a decline in moral force and the consequent rise of selfish parties in the ranks of the Saints. In fact, Sir Charles Firth in his *Oliver Cromwell* attributes the fall of the Protectorate to these two things. Oliver himself was able to offset this moral decline by controlling and using these selfish factions, but Richard Cromwell found them too much for him and had to retire.

The nation was tired of experiment and reform, and cried in Cromwell's own words for 'settlement that we may know where we are'.[1] Cromwell's answer to them was the Humble Petition and Advice, which was also his confession of failure. But more than that, it was the beginning of the Restoration, for it set up

[1] Speech to the Committee of Parliament, 11th April 1657.

a sham monarchy and House of Lords in which all but two peers refused to sit. It also brought to a head the differences between the Protector and the Army. In the end Cromwell had to surrender to the Army, who refused to serve him as King. He was still strong enough to purge the Army of malcontents, but the Protectorate he envisaged was seen to be a broken reed when the Protector was a civilian, even though he was Cromwell's own son. But the idea of a fresh experiment in kingship had been mooted abroad, and when 'the Protectorate fell before that alliance between the Republicans and the malcontents in the army which Cromwell had always been strong enough to prevent',[1] the way was left open, through a year of intrigue, desperation, and treachery, for the return of Charles Stuart to the throne.

THE RETURN OF CHARLES

The main reason for the Restoration was that the rank and file of the Army deserted its officers. Its creator having died, no other man could inspire the Independents with ideals worth fighting for. There then began a scramble for material gain. Lambert's men slipped away to Monk, who seemed liberally supplied with money from Scotland; the officers who had received grants of land began to buy up the promissory notes given to the soldiers at heavy discounts to themselves; there arose a greedy set of land speculators, and the rank and file saw themselves getting poorer and poorer, while the officers got richer and richer. These speculators had everything to lose from the Restoration, but they could get no support from the soldiers, who had Charles's promise that he would pay them. So when Monk had purged the Army, all that was left was a highly professional force of mercenaries 7,000 strong, and he who controlled this force was master of England. Throughout the Army there arose a defeatist spirit with regard to the ideals of the Revolution, which had long ago made itself felt in the other sections of Puritanism, and all that was left of the Puritan glory was the Declaration of Breda, and a few weeks' pay. The mighty indeed were fallen and the weapons of war perished. It was fitting that the man who was to rule a defeatist and corrupt nation was the man whose conduct was governed by

[1] Charles Firth, *Oliver Cromwell* (Putnam, 1923) p. 446.

no higher motive than the determination 'never to go on his travels again'.

If Monk was the military agent of the Restoration, the Presbyterian party, under his guidance, carried it through. This party, with whose policy Baxter had most in common, had always been constitutional. The Solemn League and Covenant might have been their ultimate aim, but its establishment must come about through Parliament. The great Puritan lords, such as Hollis, Manchester, and Fairfax, had always given the party a monarchist lead, and were very chary of any harm coming to the King's person. The Scots had always been suspicious of them, saying that they intended nothing but 'a lame Erastian Presbytery'. The party, too, was strong in London among the merchants, and as it was a London petition which had sowed the seeds of civil war, so it was London which led the reaction against military rule. The temporary alliance between Presbyterian and Cavalier, started in the second Civil War, was vitalized by Monk's declaration for a 'free Parliament'. But what transpired from the deliberations of this Parliament was that the Royal line was restored, but not the Royal power. Charles was wise enough to enjoy his comforts and his mistresses, with only spasmodic attempts to assert himself, and so keep his throne and his head, leaving it to James to try to restore the royal power at the expense of Parliament and be exiled from the country. Though the Presbyterians carried through the Restoration, they did it at the expense of their own existence, for the Cavaliers, who returned to power in the wake of the King, soon turned against their one-time allies and gradually destroyed them.

BAXTER AND THE RESTORATION

The complete disappearance of the great Presbyterian party from English politics is one of the most astonishing features of the seventeenth century, and Baxter's career is the most illuminating commentary on it. Although not actually a Presbyterian, he was allied to them in his views of Church government, and political sympathies. His aim was a single, comprehensive, national Church, combining what he thought were the best features of Episcopacy and Presbyterianism, and he fell between these two stools. After the Act of Uniformity he was never completely at home either in Anglicanism or in Dissent, though he still attended Anglican services.

His contact with Sir Ralph Clare, one of his parishioners, had kept him posted on the moves to restore Charles, for Sir Ralph was a leading spirit in the Royalist cause. Otherwise, he and Baxter had little in common, and had already had a dispute over the Sacrament. Sir Ralph desired Baxter to give him the Sacrament kneeling on a specific day, and not with those who took it sitting. Baxter refused to give it to him, although he points out in the letter he wrote to Sir Ralph that if any in his pastoral charge considered it a sin to take the Sacrament sitting, then he would condescend to their weakness and give it to them kneeling. They would, however, have to make a public confession 'that they take not the Bread for the Substantial Body of Christ nor worship the Bread'. But he refused Sir Ralph for the same reason as he refused others of his parish, because they would not live under discipline. 'I will be Pastor to none', he says, 'that will not be under Discipline.' But Sir Ralph knew that, though he and Baxter might differ in religious views, they were both favourable to a re-establishment of the monarchy. So he gave Baxter all the news he received of the progress of the schemes for the return of the King: news he received from Dr. Hammond, leader of the Prelatical party, who received his news in turn from Dr. Morley, who was with the King.

But Baxter was worried, for he saw that the opinions of Dr. Hammond's party had grown so high as to deny the 'very being of the Reformed Churches and Ministry'. This party was the successor to the Laudian party of a previous generation, and earned its name of Prelatical because of these opinions. 'Prelacy' was a word bandied about a great deal in the seventeenth century, but it is a word difficult to define accurately, particularly as used by Baxter. Baxter certainly did not object to bishops as such, not even to bishops who were given some of the magistrates' power of the sword and had great lands and titles. As we shall see in the chapter on Particular Churches, he would say nothing against them, provided it was recognized that the pastors of churches had the full pastoral authority and the power of the keys, and that it was also recognized that the office of bishop was not to be reckoned different in kind from that of a pastor, but only in degree. What he seems to have meant by prelacy was that body of opinion in the Church which considered the Episcopal office different in kind from that of the ordinary pastor, and insisted that such an office was a *sine qua non* of the being of a true Church. Baxter recognized that such opinions must deny the name 'Church' to all non-episcopal Churches, and deny any validity to non-episcopal ministries.

And this was why Baxter was worried, for he knew that Dr. Hammond's party, once they got into power, would restore as much as they could of the Laudian Church, and woe betide those ministers ordained non-episcopally! Sir Ralph Clare tried to reassure him that such a policy was not intended. 'Any Episcopacy how low soever would serve the turn and be accepted,' he said. Still Baxter was not satisfied, for he saw that the last word would not be with the King, who seemed very amenable to Presbyterian suggestions, but with Dr. Hammond's party. He therefore set himself to win over Dr. Hammond, and drew up fourteen proposals for a common basis of Church government among Christian folk, and presented them to the Doctor, asking for his support. Dr. Hammond, however, threw the onus of decision upon King and Parliament, and did not answer Baxter's request that he should do his best to support it. In fact, the Doctor had decided to let the parties fight it out. It was not a happy augury for the future. It is obvious, when reading Baxter's autobiography, that although Sir Ralph Clare and others in high places pretended friendship for him, the Prelatical party were determined not to allow Baxter any chance of effecting a compromise. They even kept him out of the living of Kidderminster on the ground that the parishioners did not want him, despite the fact that the King, Chancellor Hyde, and 1,600 of the 1,800 parishioners wished him to return to them.

BAXTER'S EFFORTS FOR CHURCH UNITY

In 1660 Baxter went to London for an interview with the Earl of Lauderdale. The Earl, who was in close contact with the King, regarded the winning of the Presbyterians as of prime importance to the success of his scheme of restoring Charles to the throne. Indeed, he knew that without the Presbyterians the thing was impossible. So he set himself to persuade Baxter of the legality of the Restoration, knowing that if he won him he would have gone a long way in winning the others. Baxter suddenly found himself a person of great importance, and the

Earl was very attentive to him. His arguments persuaded Baxter, who did not need much persuading, and he and his friends, Mr. Calamy, Dr. Manton, and Dr. Reynolds, became warm supporters of the King's return.

But still Baxter was very troubled, knowing something of the secret negotiations that were going on among the Prelatical divines. He set himself, therefore, to promote unity in the Church by his own private efforts, and was delighted to find some 'moderate Episcopal' men who were advocating, not merely reconciliation and union with the Presbyterians, but a reward to them also for bringing in the King. The Presbyterians had some friends at Court, and the Lord Chamberlain, the Earl of Manchester, was their agent near the King. It was also considered a good sign that some dozen leading Presbyterian divines, of whom Baxter was one, were nominated to be the King's chaplains. He attended several conferences with a view to agreement, and at the one held in the Lord Chamberlain's lodgings the King promised to bring about the desired union. The King also desired the ministers to set down their proposals for agreement, and undertook to get from the bishops the uttermost they would give way to for concord.

The Presbyterians then held a series of lively conferences at Sion College, and drew up 'The First Address and Proposals of the Ministers'. This, with Dr. Usher's *'Reduction of Episcopacy unto the Form of Synodical Government received in the Ancient Church'*, was submitted to the King with high hopes. The King referred the document to the bishops, who returned an unqualified rejection. The ministers then prepared a defence, which ended with the despairing words: 'We perceive your counsels against peace are not likely to be frustrated. Your desires concerning us are like to be accomplished. You are like to be gratified with our silence and ejection, and the excommunication and consequent sufferings of dissenters.'[1] The ministers saw what was in store for them with uncanny accuracy, and desired to give up any attempt to come to terms with the intransigent bishops. But Baxter was not so easily deterred. With that tenacity which we have seen exemplified in the game of chance at Ludlow Castle, he stuck to his cause and persisted in suing for peace. His hopes were raised when he was commanded to preach before the King, and though Charles and his

[1] F. J. Powicke, *A Life of the Reverend Richard Baxter, 1615–91* (1924), p. 193.

dissolute Court could hardly have heard such a sermon before, he ordered it to be printed. Whether this was because it touched his heart or as a smack to the bishops for their stubbornness will never be known. At any rate, Baxter never had that honour again.

The King then took the matter into his own hands, and drew up a 'Declaration' concerning ecclesiastical affairs, and a meeting was held at Worcester House to hear the Declaration read. At first sight, the ministers found it disappointing, and sent a petition to the King with their comments on it. At the meeting each party was to speak to what they disliked, but there was to be no discussion. The Baptists and the Independents were not represented, but sent a petition themselves asking, according to their tradition, for freedom of worship. The King added a clause to this document, permitting others freedom of worship provided they did not disturb the peace. When the Chancellor read this out, all could see that it would permit Papists and Socinians a toleration which was at that time denied them. Baxter desired to speak against it, though his friends tried to persuade him to let the bishops speak first. However, he felt he had to explain publicly his own opposition, and refused to be a party to toleration for these two sects. This speech of his, brave as it was, cooled the King's ardour for a fair settlement, and played right into the bishops' hands. Incidentally, it also alienated the Independents still more, as Baxter was now reckoned an opponent of theirs. The conference then broke up, Baxter going home in despair.

But some days after he bought a paper from a newsboy giving the King's Declaration. On reading it, he found such alterations as any 'sober, honest minister may submit to'. He hurried immediately to the Chancellor to say that he would do his best to procure the full consent of others to this. He was again offered a bishopric, but refused it, asking only for the living of Kidderminster, if another place as a prebendary could be found for the Vicar. If this was impossible, then he was quite content to act as the Rev. Mr. Dance's curate. It is important to notice that at this time, and under the new order of the King's Declaration, Baxter was willing to serve as a minister in the national Church. The reason was that in the amended Declaration Presbyters were associated with the bishops, and each pastor was given a due measure of authority in his own parish.

It was just such a solution as Baxter was longing for, and he was certain that the other ministers would be willing to accept it also.

With this apparently favourable background it remained for Baxter to make one more effort for unity. He was incessant in begging Chancellor Hyde to bring the two sides together. If, together with the alterations stated in the King's Declaration, an alternative liturgy could be drawn up for the use of those who scrupled at the old liturgy, and if this could be settled by law, then, said Baxter, their divisions were at an end. Accordingly, a Royal Commission was set up to consider the reform of the liturgy, and Baxter was nominated as one of the Presbyterians. He begged to be left out because he felt that he was unacceptable to his superiors, but his friends refused to release him. The conference was called at the Savoy Palace, and the bishops soon showed their temper by stoutly defending the liturgy as it was, and refusing any consultation for its amendment until it had been proved defective, the onus of which was put on the ministers. They carefully avoided the fact that the Commission had been especially called to consider this. Like the Bourbons, they showed that they had learned nothing and forgotten nothing since the Hampton Court Conference. They had nothing to say until their opponents had brought their forms and alterations in writing. The ministers agreed to this, and Baxter was given the task of drawing up the 'additions' to the liturgy, while the other ministers would draw up the exceptions. Baxter worked night and day for a fortnight, and at the end of that time produced, to everyone's amazement, a complete liturgy, which a century afterwards drew from Dr. Johnson the praise 'That it was one of the first compositions of the ritual kind he had ever seen'.[1] This liturgy was drawn up in Scriptural phrases, and was not intended to supplant the old liturgy, but to act as an alternative for tender consciences.

It is interesting to note Baxter's opinion of the old liturgy as he explained it to the ministers. He did not take it to contain false doctrine or false worship, nor was it idolatrous. Its chief faults to him were disorder and defectiveness, and yet a Christian might join in its order of worship, failing anything better, without sin.[2] Thus in 1661 he expounded the position he took up

---

[1] George Eayrs, *Richard Baxter* (1912), p. 68.
[2] *Autobiography* (Everyman, 1931), pp. 163-5.

after 1662, when he became a Nonconformist. He also pointed out that old Simeon Ash, one of the oldest Puritan ministers in the land, had told him that this was the judgement of the old Nonconformists before the Revolution.

But as the debates wore on, Baxter could see that the bishops were getting more and more annoyed at what he calls 'our frequent crossing of their expectations', particularly Bishop Morley of Worcester, who overrode the whole Conference. It seemed to Baxter that the bishops disliked being spoken to on terms of equality as regards the subject of their discussions. The Restoration had returned to them such a façade of power that the greatest lords were glad of their favour, and they expected the ministers to be overawed by their formidable display of ecclesiastical authority. Even if they had had a hundred more ceremonies, and could afford to do away with some, he doubted whether they would abate one of them to keep the dissenters from being cast out. Their spirit, he thought, was more like that of the Papists than even their formal discipline and worship was.

When the last day of the Conference was come, nothing had been agreed. So it was decided that both sides should give their views in writing to the King, with a general statement that, while all were agreed on the ends, the Church's welfare, unity, and peace, and also the King's happiness and welfare, they could not agree as to the means of attaining these desirable objectives.

The ministers met once more to draw up their statement, and once more the willing horse obliged. Baxter drew up the statement to lay before the King, with a petition for his promised help. The Chancellor, who glanced through the statement before it went to the King, found some passages too pungent for his Majesty's ear, so also did the Lord Chamberlain, the Puritan Earl of Manchester, and Baxter had perforce to withdraw these passages. He was made to feel by these noble lords that he was the man responsible for the failure of the Conference, and that he was 'severe and strict, like a Melancholy Man and made those things sin which others did not'. It is true that Baxter spoiled the Conference from the bishops' point of view, as without his stiffening the Presbyterians might have given way. The result of all his efforts as far as he was concerned was that he had succeeded in unwittingly offending the King, Chancellor Hyde, the Puritan Manchester, and the bishops.

Yet it is doubtful, even if Baxter had trimmed his conscience, a thing he was incapable of doing, that there would have been any lasting reconciliation between the Episcopal party and the Puritans. For the real power in the land was not the King nor the bishops, nor the great lords, but the Cavalier Parliament, who were determined to punish those who had conquered and humiliated them in the Civil Wars.

Chapter V

THE OUTCAST

ECCLESIASTICAL AND POLITICAL SETTLEMENT

BAXTER's judgement of the Savoy Conference, that the bishops had no intention of abating one iota of their position to gain the Dissenters, is confirmed by Bishop Burnet in his *History of His Own Times*. He points out that the King, by Clarendon's design, desired an accommodation with the Presbyterians, but that the bishops determined to exclude them from the Church. The Presbyterians held most of the greatest benefices in the Church, particularly in the City and the two Universities. They were men of great influence, particularly in the election of Members to Parliament, and it was Burnet's opinion that the bishops set out deliberately to deprive them of their livings, and to preclude them from any claim of merit, or power of doing ill.[1]

In Convocation too, which was called a fortnight after the opening of the Savoy Conference, the bishops had their way. In London, where the Presbyterians predominated, the ministers elected Baxter and Calamy to Convocation, but Dr. Sheldon, the Bishop of London, exercised his right of choosing two out of four, or four out of six men elected by the ministers, and left out Baxter and Calamy in favour of less formidable candidates. Throughout the country the elections went in favour of the Episcopal party. In many cases this was due to the fact that some ministers had been deprived of their livings at the return of the King, and the old pre-Cromwellian clergy reinstated. This Convocation revised the Book of Common Prayer and, in indecent haste, made some alterations in the liturgy. This they sent to the King, who sent it in his turn to Parliament. Upon this the Act of Uniformity was prepared, but it had a considerable opposition and was passed with no great majority. It is significant of the feeling in the country that even the Cavalier Parliament found difficulty in passing the Act.

For the Cavalier Parliament was a packed Parliament. No influence necessary to achieve the object of the Court—namely,

[1] Bishop Burnet, *History of His Own Times* (Everyman Edition, Dent, 1906), p. 41.

a Parliament favourable to the Episcopal party and purged as much as possible of Presbyterians—was withheld from conscientious scruples. Stoughton, in his *Church and State Two Hundred Years Ago*, gives an instance where letters were intercepted at the Post Office, and seized by the Government. They were letters from Londoners telling their friends in the country how that in the Parliamentary elections in the Guildhall, four Presbyterians had been elected. Some letters deplored the event, but most of them expressed the hope that the country would do the same. But all letters, whether for or against the Presbyterians, which conveyed the unwelcome news were held back. One can only assume that they were seized to stop the London result from influencing the elections in the country. Government influence was sought in some places to bring in members favourable to the Court, while other members were bribed, as was subsequently shown. In addition, several corporations, who returned Members to Parliament, were purged by Royal order of men likely to be inimical to the Government. The result was a Parliament made up of men favourable to the Royalist side in the Civil Wars and opposed to Presbyterianism. The Presbyterian-Royalist alliance was broken, and the way was open for the Cavaliers to crush their original enemy.

Never again did Presbyterianism rise to be a political power in the country. Some of them gravitated back to Episcopacy, which, though High Church, was definitely Protestant. Others joined the sects they had originally despised, but as an organized party their power was destroyed. I. Deane Jones attributes their fall to three causes.[1] Firstly, they rose and fell as a political power with their Scottish connexion. Thus when Charles, on the advice of Lauderdale, abandoned the old Stuart policy of trying to unite the two countries, for the policy of fostering the differences between them, both Presbyterian parties were left in hopeless isolation. Secondly, the English party were left leaderless by the bribing of the Presbyterian lords, who looked after themselves and left their followers to their fate. This left them exposed to the revenge of the Episcopal party, whom they had treated badly during the Protectorate and previously. Lastly, the Cavalier gentry in the Lower House ignored the Lords, the King, and Clarendon, and set themselves to expel the poison of rebellion out of the nation. What made them so formidable

[1] I. Deane Jones, *The English Revolution* (1931).

was that they not only made the laws, but enforced them as the local Justices of the Peace. 'Organized Puritanism fell, as Stuart despotism had fallen, before the invincible combination of the Commons and the Commissions of the Peace.'[1]

The House of Commons was the only institution fully restored to power and repute at the Restoration. The Lords tacitly accepted their secondary place, and the younger lords found an outlet for their energies, not in Parliament, but in the Court, with its endless intrigues. The Commons extended its authority over the clergy too. The right of making grants to the King was taken away from them, but they were given a vote instead! Any ideas which the Episcopal party may have had of resurrecting Laud's scheme of an independent state of the clergy were crushed at the source. They too were to be brought under the thumb of the victorious Commons. The restored King found himself more completely controlled by Parliament than ever his father was; he was tied hand and foot to the Commons, who, while they gave him tunnage and poundage for life and a hereditary Excise, fixed the rates by statute, so that he always had to come to them for money.

The Church approached the Commons in the completeness of its restoration, but only approached it. All the trappings of Laudian ecclesiastical policy were restored by the Episcopalian clergy. But the essence of Laud's policy, an independent estate of the Church, was carefully guarded against by Parliament. The bishops were great lords, with a million and a half of income between them, but the Church had little voice in ruling the country, except when the bishops' policy coincided with that of the Commons, as in their common enmity towards the Presbyterians. But whereas Parliament did contain within itself the possibility of representing the opinions of the nation, just because it was an elective assembly, the Church, not being an elective assembly, had to face its problems in a different way. In the State, the two sides, Episcopal and Presbyterian, crystallized out into Tory and Whig during the next century, but the only solution the Church could find was to become the province of the most powerful 'sect' and exclude all Dissenters from its life. Sheldon determined to get purity of doctrine, as he understood it, by exclusion, and Clarendon was forced away from his first ideal of a comprehensive Church, supporting the Crown, to the

[1] I. Deane Jones, *The English Revolution* (1939).

exclusive legislation of the Clarendon Code. The name 'English' was replaced by the name 'Anglican', and never again would the Church embrace the whole or even a majority of the nation. This policy was a complete reversal of the traditions of the Reformation, as understood by Tudor and early Stuart statesmen. It was implemented by the abolishing of the Royal prerogative of ruling the Church (the centre of Henry VIII's and Elizabeth's settlement) when the Commons overrode the Declaration of Indulgence of December, 1662, and passed the Act of Uniformity. The Church became the monopoly of the Tory Party, and the logical consequence of its confession of failure (for such its policy was) was the Toleration Act of 1689.

THE HARROWING OF DISSENT

The all-powerful Commons, with the assistance of the bishops, who in the Savoy Conference of 1661 had confirmed the decision of the Hampton Court Conference to make no concessions even to moderate Presbyterians, set itself out to crush the Dissenters. The instrument which they shaped to carry out their design was five enactments, framed in the years 1661–7, and called the Clarendon Code, although Clarendon was out of office before the last Act was passed. Dr. Sheldon had the chief hand in framing these Acts, and the Commons forced their acceptance, despite certain opposition, at least at the beginning of the reign, by the King and Clarendon. The five Acts struck at Presbyterianism in its vital points. First of all, as the Presbyterians had refused the Prayer Book, so Parliament ordered the Solemn League and Covenant to be burnt by the common hangman, and made the use of the Prayer Book obligatory on all incumbents. Secondly, as the Presbyterians had deserted the Elizabethan ideal of a comprehensive Church, so Parliament took a leaf out of the Presbyterian book, deserted that ideal themselves, and by the Act of Uniformity in 1662 threw their opponents into the limbo of Dissent. Thirdly, as the Presbyterians had aimed to organize society into the form of a Presbyterian Church—in other words, to define citizenship by churchmanship—so the Corporation Act of 1661 and the Five-mile Act of 1665 made municipal franchise (and so Parliamentary franchise) dependent on loyalty to the new Anglican Church. Lastly, as one of the cardinal points of Presbyterianism had been its intolerance of other forms of Church government and worship, so the Conventicle Acts of 1664 and 1670 denied such tolerance to them.

The final result was that the civic and parliamentary influence of the Presbyterians, which had been very great in the towns, was almost completely destroyed. Nearly 2,000 ministers gave up their livings on St. Bartholomew's Day, 1662, and they and their families were left to the mercy of the charitably minded. None but Episcopal ordination was recognized—a rule unknown before in England—and the Anglican Church was separated from the communion of the Lutheran and other Continental Churches. Service in the Church was made conditional upon taking a political oath. In addition, the dissenting clergy were persecuted by the bishops' informers; they were fined and imprisoned until the jails were full of them.

THE PERSECUTION OF BAXTER

Baxter's life after 1661 is typical of those clerics and laymen who were unable, for conscience' sake, to comply with the full demands of the Clarendon Code. Having refused a bishopric, and having been denied the living of Kidderminster, he was soon forbidden to preach in the Diocese of Worcester by Dr. Morley, the Bishop. This was a great blow to him, as it meant that he could not preach to his beloved flock at Kidderminster. But soon a greater trial befell him by the passing of the Act of Uniformity. Some months before St. Bartholomew's Day, he preached his last sermon for thirteen years in the Anglican Church at Blackfriars. He did not wait until the day the Act came into force to announce his nonconformity, for two reasons: first, he wished others to know that he could not conform, and, secondly, because some lawyers interpreted a doubtful clause in the Act to mean that the liberty of lecturers (his only remaining link with the Anglican Church since his silencing by the Bishop of Worcester) was ended at once. His thoughts at this time were very painful, and there is a hint in his account of what was to him an unexpected and painful treachery on the part of the Episcopal party. But he resolved to do nothing that would finally bolt the door of the Church to him. Although he was not allowed to minister in the Church, he was, by virtue of his baptism, a member, and, wherever he was, Sunday saw him worshipping in the parish church.

In 1662 he was living in Dr. Micklethwaite's house in Little

Britain, and on 10th September of the same year he was married in St. Benet Fink Church to Margaret Charlton, who, with her mother, had followed him from Kidderminster. He took a house at Moorfields, and it was while he was at Moorfields that he had his first taste of the application of the Act of Uniformity. Already in January his old friend Dr. Calamy had been committed to Newgate for preaching the funeral sermon of the Rev. Simeon Ash in his old pulpit in Aldermanbury. The imprisonment did not entail great hardship, but it was the beginning of the great revenge. Baxter and Dr. Bates had agreed to meet at the house of a Mr. Beal to pray for his wife, who was sick. But it turned out that for some reason they could not be there. However, the authorities, not knowing this, sent two justices of the peace with the Parliament Sergeant-at-Arms to arrest them, who, when they failed to find them there, entered the room where Mrs. Beal lay dying, took the names of all those who were there and returned disappointed. Baxter now felt that he ought to get out of London, so he took a house at Acton, where he lived for six years, and gained the friendship of Sir Matthew Hale, afterwards Lord Chief Justice of the King's Bench. Baxter sat next to him in church, but did not speak to him, as he was afraid of compromising him. But when the ice was broken, Sir Matthew made his friendship with Baxter as obvious as possible.

AT ACTON

At Acton, on the whole, his routine of intense study went on without much trouble from the outside world. But there were two incidents which reminded him that the Conventicle Act, passed in 1664, was still in force. The first one occurred when he was preaching in his own home on Sunday 25th March 1665. A bullet came through the window and narrowly missed his sister-in-law, the wife of Canon Upton. Baxter does not say much about it, but he obviously thought it was a demonstration against his preaching service. The other incident was a visit from a lady who came with her family to hear him preach. Fortunately, they failed to open the door when she first knocked, and when she returned the service was finished. Baxter appointed her another time to come to hear him, but found out when she was gone that she only came to accuse him of keeping a conventicle. No doubt he would have been troubled with the

Conventicle Act sooner had it not been for the fact that the authorities were more concerned with the plague which broke out in 1665, and the Great Fire which broke out in Pudding Lane in the September of the next year.

The plague spread to Acton, and Baxter moved to the house of Richard Hampden, the son of the famous John Hampden, in Buckinghamshire. This has been used against him as a sign of selfishness and cowardice, but the naïve simplicity of the account he gives tells us that he himself, usually so quick to accuse himself, saw nothing wrong in his conduct. In fact, we can see the hand of Mrs. Baxter in this move. No doubt she did not want the responsibility of a sick man on her hands in the midst of a plague. She, of course, stayed behind to look after the maids. About 100,000 people died in London alone, and that mostly among the poor, for, as Baxter records, the rich and those who could afford it moved out of the city. Most of the Anglican clergy moved away, and many of the churches were left without services, the dead without Christian burial, and the sick with no comfort for soul or body. It was at this time that the nonconforming clergy earned an undying name for themselves. Many who had been ministering secretly to a few resolved that no law of man should forbid them ministering to the souls and bodies of the panic-stricken people. They stayed with the people and occupied the forsaken pulpits. Crowds flocked to hear them preach, and, as Baxter says, 'religion took that hold on people's hearts, as could never afterwards be loosed'. This devotion of the nonconforming ministers so enhanced their reputation in people's eyes that it was impossible even by guards of soldiers or imprisonment to keep people from hearing them, and this courage contributed as much as anything to the toleration which was eventually given to them.

We can only attribute to meanness and cruelty what was meanwhile done at Oxford. There the King and his Court had fled, and there Parliament met on 9th October. The question of the plague hardly bothered Parliament at all, for they did little about it. What did occupy their time was the continuation of their policy of revenge against the dissenting churchmen. With great swiftness, they passed the Five-mile Act, which forced Nonconformists to live at least five miles distant from any incorporated town or city, or any place where they had preached since the Act of Oblivion. The King, whose consent to the Bill was necessary, was sweetened by a subsidy of £125,000, and the Duke of York by another of £129,002 15*s*. 8*d*. With the Act was included an oath known as the Oxford Oath, which required all to swear that it was not lawful under any pretext whatsoever to take up arms against the King, or to endeavour any alteration in the government of Church or State. Failure to take the Oath was to be punished with banishment, and those who remained in forbidden areas were to be fined £40. The Earl of Southampton, who was the Lord Treasurer, in opposing the Oath, said that no honest man could take it. The Act came into force on 24th March, and during the next few months Baxter tells us that the number of ministers imprisoned increased so much that he could not count them. Very soon the Act was forgotten in the menace of the Great Fire, and again these ministers who were still at liberty preached in the vicinity of the burned churches whose clergy had gone. The Independents were as active as the Presbyterians, and Baxter does not fail to tell us that some of the Anglican clergy did their part also in comforting the people. These clergy were for the most part the more moderate sort, and people heard conformable and nonconformable ministers alike, making no distinction between them. The result of these calamities was to bring to the notice of the nation the worth of the nonconforming ministers, and foster a great deal more discussion on toleration. Indeed, on Clarendon's fall, the new favourite Buckingham came out for whole-hearted toleration for all parties.

This attitude of Buckingham's induced Lord Keeper Bridgman and one or two others to seek an accommodation with the Presbyterians, and toleration for all sound Christians. They got into communication with Baxter, who agreed to meet their representatives from the Anglican clergy. However, it came to nothing, partly because of the attitude of the bishops, who were said to be favourable at first, and partly because Baxter and his friends would not agree to any toleration which included Papists. In any case, Parliament was thoroughly opposed to any move to meet the Presbyterians. The first thing that it did on meeting was to veto any proposals for an accommodation or toleration, and to clinch this policy they passed the Second Conventicle Act. There was some delay in passing the Act, due to repeated adjournments of Parliament, but it was during this period that Baxter was imprisoned for the first time. The first Conventicle

Act expired in October 1668, and until the second one was made law it would seem that there could be no objection to Nonconformists holding their services. At any rate, that was the view that Baxter took of it, and so he threw his service, which he held at home, open to all. His next-door neighbour, Colonel Phillips, a courtier of the Bedchamber, reported it to the King, who took no notice of it, apart from telling a few Nonconformist ministers that they should be a little more circumspect, and instancing Baxter's conduct. But soon the King, at the request of the Rector of Acton, ordered Baxter's meeting to be suppressed, and he was arrested. He was tendered the Oxford Oath, but refused to take it, and so he was put in Clerkenwell Jail for six months. The Oxford Oath was similar to the *Et cetera* Oath, which Baxter had refused before the Civil Wars, and he refused the new Oath for the same reasons—namely, that to take the Oath would mean that he considered that the government of the Church by diocesan bishops was divinely ordained, a view he could not justify from Holy Scripture. He was not long in Clerkenwell. On the advice of friends, he sued for a writ of Habeas Corpus, and was freed because there were faults in the Mittimus. The judge warned him that he had been freed on a purely technical ground, and not because he was a good man, nor because there was no case against conventicles. Baxter soon found this out when he heard that a new Mittimus was being executed to commit him, this time with the thieves and murderers of Newgate Jail.

AT TOTTERIDGE

It was urgent, therefore, that he should leave Acton, and after some trouble he found a house at Totteridge, where he lived from 1670–3, devoting his time to study. He and his wife were happy in the companionship of the Rev. and Mrs. Corbet, the ejected minister of Bramshot in Hampshire, who came to live with them. It was while he was at Totteridge that a rumour originated that he was about to conform, which brought him the offer of a bishopric, or any position he preferred, in the Scottish Church. This offer was made to him by the Earl of Lauderdale. When Baxter refused it, he asked only that the Earl should use his influence that he might be allowed the liberty of any beggar of travelling from town to town, or at least to London. There is something pathetic and yet noble in his plea that if the Earl could not get him these liberties, would he, if he was arrested again and committed to Newgate, get him the favour of a better prison, where there would be room to read and write. But there was no relief to be had from the noble Earl. It was this same year that the Second Conventicle Act was finally passed (1670), and the harrying of the Dissenters continued through 1671. In 1672 the Nonconformists had some relief. Charles, in his half-hearted struggle with Parliament, ruled through the 'Cabal', the name given to his ministers, Clifford, Arlington, Buckingham, Ashley, and Lauderdale. These ministers sought to aggrandize the Crown at the expense of Parliament, and persuaded the King to exercise his Royal Prerogative of ruling the Church by issuing a Declaration of Indulgence for all Nonconformists. They were to be allowed preaching licences sanctioned by the King, to preach in specified places with open doors; there was to be no seditious preaching, and no word said against the Anglican Church. The relief was welcome, but Baxter and his friends were suspicious that the Indulgence was chiefly for the benefit of the Papists. However, he applied for a licence on condition he could have it without the title of Presbyterian or Independent, but merely as a Nonconformist. The licence was granted him on his own terms, and for the first time in ten years he preached in a tolerated assembly in his own home in Totteridge, and was chosen to preach the Merchant's Lecture at Pinner's Hall in London. However, the King reckoned without Parliament, which assembled in 1673. With the concurrence of the Lords, they forced the King to withdraw the Indulgence, on the ground that 'Penal statutes in matters Ecclesiastical cannot be suspended but by Act of Parliament'. It is said that when the decision was told to the King, he tore the Great Seal from the Act in frustrated anger. Once more he had been forced to give way by his paymasters. The Cavaliers were not going to give up their hold on either King or Church.

The remainder of Baxter's life until the abdication of James II was one continual persecution. In common with other Protestant Dissenters, he was tossed about in the struggle between the King and Parliament, and between the Romanizing tendency of the Court and the opposition of the Anglican Church. The King himself was more or less a shuttlecock between his own tolerant nature, his desire to give some relief to Dissenters, particularly to the Roman Catholics led by his brother the Duke of York, and his own chronic need for money—money for his war with the Dutch, money for his favourites, and above all money for his rapacious mistresses. To get money, he had to go to his implacable Parliament, who by a judicious mixture of force and bribery bent him to their will and secured his assent to their acts of vengeance against the Dissenters. The only relief the Dissenters got was when Parliament became frightened at the Roman Catholic menace, or when the King tried to show his authority by defying Parliament. At these times they were able to breathe a little more freely, and preach the Gospel without immediate fear of arrest.

'IN PERILS OFT'

Baxter was frequently disturbed in his work. On one occasion six constables, four beadles, and many messengers watched his service for twenty-four consecutive Sundays, and although many of the London aldermen were unsympathetic to this persecuting policy, there were always some, such as Sir Thomas Davis, who were willing to do the will of the bishops, and grant a warrant against Baxter. In 1682 he was arrested for coming within five miles of a corporate town. Officers were sent to distrain upon him for £190 for preaching five sermons. They tried to drag him off to jail, and were only stopped by his physician, who appealed to the King, saying that Baxter was so ill he could not leave his bed. 'Let him die in his bed', said Charles, but the officers decided that, though they would have to leave him at home, they could take his bed, which they sold, with all his goods, to pay the fine. In 1684 he and a thousand others were sued. Six officers were sent to take him, and camped outside the door of his study, where he had fled from a sickbed to evade them. They stayed there all night, keeping him from his food and rest, and in the morning he had to yield to them. Though he was scarcely able to stand, they took him to the Sessions, where he was bound over to good behaviour in a bond of £400.

Charles died in 1685, and his brother James came to the throne, a convinced Roman Catholic, and determined to reinstate that religion in England. He recognized that the Protestant Dissenters were his greatest enemies, and soon found a ready tool in Judge Jeffreys to crush any opposition they might give to his policy. Baxter was now in his seventieth year and tired of controversy, asking only for a place to die quietly. He had used the moments when he was not too ill to write a paraphrase of the New Testament, which drew down on him an attack by Sir Roger L'Estrange, the champion of the bishops. He alleged that Baxter's book was seditious, and attacked the Anglican liturgy. Three weeks after James's accession, Baxter was committed on these charges to the King's Bench Prison, and appeared for trial in Westminster Hall on 14th May 1685. Outside in New Palace Yard stood Titus Oates in the pillory, and before him sat his judge, the loathsome, disease-ridden Jeffreys. The trial was a farce, and can be read in Dr. Powicke's excellent life of Baxter,[1] or in Appendix I of the *Autobiography of Richard Baxter*, in the Everyman Edition. But Baxter was not without his friends. Sir Henry Ashurst paid for counsel, and secured Mr. Pollexfen, afterwards Lord Chief Justice of the Common Pleas, as leader, with five other barristers. Dr. Bates, his brother minister, stood by his side. All were hopelessly browbeaten by Jeffreys. One counsel after another tried to speak for Baxter, but they were shouted down by the foul-mouthed judge. Hardly anyone in court believed that Baxter could be convicted, but Jeffreys knew his jury, who, like him, were the tools of the Government. Baxter was fined £340, and sent to prison until he paid, where he stayed for some eighteen months. But Jeffreys did not get all his own way: his desire that Baxter should be whipped through London at the cart's tail was overruled by the other judges. Possibly they thought that even the bishops would hardly stomach that to a man who had been twice offered a bishopric.

He was released on the mediation of Lord Powis on 24th November 1686, and given permission to live in London, notwithstanding the Five-mile Act. From 1687 to his death in 1691 at the age of seventy-six, he lived with his friend, Rev. Matthew Sylvester, in Charterhouse Yard. He preached as his health permitted, and had some happiness in writing when he could no longer preach. He died on 8th December 1691, and was buried in Christ Church, London, beside his wife, who had died in 1681. Although, like St. Paul, he was 'In perils oft', particularly from his 'own countrymen' from 1662 onwards, it would be a mistake to assume that his life was unhappy. The man who wrote the hymn, 'He wants not friends who hath

---

[1] F. J. Powicke, *The Reverend Richard Baxter Under the Cross, 1662-91* (Cape, 1927), pp. 142 ff.

Thy love' knew very well the source of true happiness, and found it in God. But he was also blessed by the companionship of a friend who comforted him and in a quiet way guided his life—that is, by his wife. He was singularly fortunate in his marriage, and although in his young days he thought that ministers ought not to marry, his own marriage spread a cloak of love around him and his home. His beautiful little book, *A Breviate of the Life of Margaret Baxter*, reveals to us the poignant and charming intimacies of his home, and makes us glad to know that the life of this brave outcast from the Church he loved was made more than bearable by the devotion of his wife.

Chapter VI

THE BISHOP OF NONCONFORMITY

IF a bishop is, beyond all others, the first teacher of his diocese, then Baxter fully deserves the title given him by some of his contemporaries—namely, that of 'The Bishop of Nonconformity'.[1] For all his life he was a teacher: a teacher of children when he was a reader and schoolmaster at Dudley; a teacher of families when as Vicar of Kidderminster he went from house to house catechizing his flock; a teacher of his own brethren when he led the group of associated ministers at Worcester; and lastly, when he left Kidderminster and its congenial tasks, a teacher of the whole Church through his books and tracts. These became for him, as for many of the Puritans of the previous century, a substitute for preaching by word of mouth when his preaching licence was taken away, and by his writings he would live though all else were forgotten.

So great was his reputation as a teacher that the name 'Baxterianism' was given to the beliefs and doctrines that he held. Eight years after his death we find Mr. Thomas Edwards (1652–1721) bemoaning the influence which Baxter's ideas still had among the ministers and laymen of the various Churches, 'poisoning the nation', as Mr. Edwards says, 'with his teachings'.[2] 'While we can understand a violent Sectarian or Prelatist bemoaning Baxter's influence (he was an uncompromising enemy to both), the unbiased reader will find in Baxter's writings a breadth and sanity not always found in the works of seventeenth-century divines. It was an age of fierce controversy often carried on in violent language, and while Baxter could speak plainly, and even with asperity to Crown or commoner, there is a balance and analysis in his works which must commend itself even to those who marvel that so much heat was raised over so much hair-splitting.

Baxter himself was conscious of the spate of books and arguments which he penned, and occasionally in the preface to one or other of his books he apologizes for writing so much. It is

---
[1] Florence Higham, *Faith of Our Fathers* (S.C.M. Press, 1939), p. 91.
[2] F. J. Powicke, *The Reverend Richard Baxter Under the Cross, 1662–91* (1927), pp. 142 ff.

quoted of St. Augustine that he once said that he spoke in order that it might not be said of him that he remained silent. It is a perfect description of Baxter. He wrecked the Worcester House Conference because his conscience told him that he must speak, although his fellow members wanted him to remain silent and let the first words come from the bishops. In the account he gives of this conference in his *Autobiography*, we can sense his reluctance to speak and almost feel the struggle in his own soul. He did a most unpopular thing, unpopular with the King, unpopular with the bishops, and unpopular with his own fellow representatives, but no one could charge him afterwards that he had not made his position clear. Again, in his Preface to his work, *On Justifying Righteousness*, he excuses himself for writing so much on the one subject in the words: 'And he that blameth me for writing so many Books of the same thing should be one that first considereth how many Books and daily Invectives and Censures of Men that never understood the cause, have called me to it and made it necessary.'[1] He was a man conscious of a message, and above all conscious of the little time he had to deliver it. If any Puritan lived as being always under his great Taskmaster's eye, then Baxter did. His great Taskmaster had given him his commission to maintain the pure Gospel against the errors of Prelatists, Papists, Anabaptists, Separatists, Socinians, Antinomians, and others, and since he could not teach by preaching he must do it by writing.

THEOLOGICAL POSITION

To reach some conclusion as to his place in the theological thought of his age, we cannot do better than examine his position with respect to two of the great controversies which occupied the minds of seventeenth-century thinkers—namely:

1. His relationship to Calvinism and Arminianism.
2. His attitude to the question of Justification and the conflict between Faith and Works.

The rivalry between Calvinism and Arminianism was one of the most hotly contested questions of his day. Generally speaking, at the Elizabethan settlement all the divines, whether Puritan or Episcopalian, were Calvinists. The Puritans had

[1] Richard Baxter, Preface, *The Substance of Mr. Cartwright's Exceptions Considered* (1675), p. 71.

remained faithful, more or less, to this theological standpoint, throughout the years, but the tendency in the High Church party had been to discard Calvinism for the milder doctrines of Arminius, so that the controversy between Prelacy and Presbyterian-Puritanism in the field of Church government was reinforced by the conflict between Arminianism and Calvinism. Now, as Baxter held a halfway position between Prelacy and Separatism, so he held a halfway position between Calvinism and Arminianism. Baxter's knowledge of the Scriptures and the Fathers, both ancient and contemporary, was prodigious, and may explain his moderating attitude. He knew so much, as it were, that he could see two sides to every question! Not that his omniscience prevented him from coming down heavily on the side that he considered right, but in certain questions of dispute he struggled manfully in page after page of closely-printed type to preserve a middle road, and to keep what he considered valuable in both sides.

HIS RELATION TO CALVINISM

Dr. Powicke points out that Baxter was not an Arminian in the sense that John Goodwin was, nor was he a strict Calvinist, though he applauded the Synod of Dort and the Westminster Assembly.[1] Baxter's position seems to have been well summed up by the Rev. Robert Baillie, one of the Scottish Commissioners to the Westminster Assembly, who accused him of being a disciple of Amyraldus (1596–1664)[2] and, with the candour of the Scotch Presbyterian, he deplored the fact. But Baxter seems to have arrived at Amyraldus's doctrine of the universal application of the redeeming work of Christ, as opposed to the strict Calvinist view that that work had reference only to the elect, long before he had read anything of Amyraldus's work. He had even written a book in support of this view as early as 1654. It is not surprising, therefore, that when he did become acquainted with the works of this particular divine that he considered him a very judicious person!

Amyraldus, a professor at Saumur, had made a study of Calvinism, and come to the conclusion that the normal interpretation of Calvinism was wrong. He therefore made it his

[1] F. J. Powicke, *The Reverend Richard Baxter Under the Cross, 1662–91* (1927), vol. 2, pp. 142 ff.
[2] ibid., vol. 2, p. 236.

life-work to rescue Calvinism from the degradation into which it had fallen at the hands of second-rate theologians. These, he contended, had failed to grasp that the master-thought of the *Institutes* was not 'predestination', but the 'purpose of God', God working His purpose out down the ages in a triumphant 'destiny' to establish that living thing, the Kingdom of God. If we can paraphrase Romans viii. 29, 'Whom he foreknew, them he purposed to be conformed to the image of his Son'. The emphasis is on the *kind* of destiny those would have whom God in his omniscience knew would persevere to final salvation, and not on predestination as it is normally understood—namely, the arbitrary act of God choosing some to salvation and some to damnation. The extraordinary thing about Calvinism is that, though the doctrine, as it is commonly understood, would seem to preclude any human action or effort in the scheme of salvation, because if men are elected by the fiat of God to salvation or damnation, what they themselves do about it does not affect the final issue, no other doctrine of the Church has acted as such an incentive to Christian living. Nothing could exceed the concern of the Calvinist Puritans about the state of their souls, and no movement in English religious history, save perhaps the Methodist Revival, has had such a dynamic behind it. A parallel case of apparent inconsistency can be observed in the energy of the Communist movement. Communist philosophy insists that the establishment of a classless society is inevitable, the dynamic of history, as it is interpreted dialectically, makes it so. If such a consummation is inevitable, then it would hardly seem to matter what Communists do or do not do. Yet no movement of modern times has been so concerned to 'co-operate with the inevitable' as that which springs from the teachings of Karl Marx. It is this peculiarity in Calvinism which leads us to think that perhaps Amyraldus was right in his interpretation of the doctrine, and that Calvinism is more profound than many have imagined.

But whether Amyraldus was right or not in his analysis of Calvinism, the result of his teachings was the formulation of what is called the double-reference theory of the Atonement, or *Hypothetical Universalism*. This theory may be concisely stated thus: God's purpose was to save men, and redemption through Christ was the carrying out of this purpose in the way necessitated by sin. Theoretically, the redemption is as wide as the purpose, and so is universal. Therefore the Gospel must be preached, and all men invited to repent and believe. But the universality of the redemption is hindered by the fact that some men die unrepentant, so the universal reference is hypothetical. It is the limited reference to those that are saved, i.e. the elect, that is real and practical. This was roughly Baxter's position, as Dr. Powicke points out, but only roughly. Where Baxter really differed from the Calvinists of his day was in the fact that he did not believe that God willed that anyone should be damned, but he thought that God did will that the elect should be saved, as a kind of extra grace, as it were. The elect were lucky, but many others would be saved as well, and those who were damned, were damned not because they could not be saved, but because they would not be saved.[1]

In *God's Goodness Vindicated* he asserts that it is not true that God decrees to condemn any man but for sin. Nor does He decree to condemn any for Adam's sin only, nor for any other sin that is not conjoined with final impenitency. Nor do His decrees or foreknowledge cause any man's sin. Nor does He will the permission of any man's sin. Indeed, God has actually given a great deal of mercy to them that perish, which had a natural tendency to their salvation. Christ died for all, and so pardon, justification, adoption, and the right to glory are for all on condition of acceptance. This is almost Arminianism, but Baxter retained what he thought was vital to Calvinism—namely, God's sovereignty and freedom to do what He would with His own. In *A Call to the Unconverted*, he explains this in his own way. God wills, he says, the conversion of those that never will be converted, not as abolute Lord, but somewhat in the same way as a prince could guard a murderer and so stop him from murdering and being hanged, but he does not do so; rather he appeals to the peoples not to be murderers. So God could convert all men by a simple act of His sovereignty, but He does not do so; He appeals to all to repent and be saved, even though in His omniscience He knows that some will refuse His call. It is not a very good analogy, as no prince is likely to be so omniscient as to know that a man is a potential murderer, and even if he did it is still more unlikely that he would allow such a man to roam about to the danger of honest citizens! Baxter goes on to argue that whereas God does call all to be

[1] Richard Baxter, *A Call to the Unconverted* (Orme, 1830), vol. VII, p. 357.

converted, if He does more for some men, for some special reason of His own, He is not bound to do so for all. In other words, God gives all men the chance to be saved, but if He has revealed that some will be so drawn to Christ that they will infallibly be saved, it is His own business and no one has the right to question it. It is the practical question that really matters to Baxter: Will you accept God's pardon and salvation? If a man is one of the elect or not, only God knows; meanwhile, here is the supreme choice of his life.

HIS RELATION TO THE DOCTRINE OF JUSTIFICATION

It was the same instinct that caused him to cross swords with those people whom he felt were treading the slippery slope of Antinomianism by emphasizing the all-exclusive necessity of faith without works, as the precondition of justification. Baxter's insistence on repentance, desire for Christ, prayer for pardon, and sincere obedience to God in the Christian, caused some of his opponents to say that he looked to works to obtain salvation.[1] Some even went farther, such as Dr. Tully and Mr. Cartwright, who said that faith itself is a part of those works to be denied as a means of justification. This seemed to Baxter to be very dangerous for Christian morals, because it reduced man to a cipher. This doctrine seemed to him to be the result of an ill-informed Calvinism. 'I shew', he says, 'that Faith alone is the Condition of Justification, and of right to Salvation and Glory, and yet that Works are also requisite as the Fruits of that Faith, and as making way for the actual enjoyment of Glory.'[2] Here again he tries to preserve a balance. He knows that man is justified by faith alone, and that even faith is a gift of God, but he also knows that good works are a necessity, if a man is to do the will of God. So he stands as a fencer fighting two opponents—the Papists, with their doctrine of merit, and the Antinomians, with their ridicule of good works.

HIS CONCERN FOR HOLINESS

The criterion Baxter had for every doctrine and form of Church order was whether it helped Christ to promote holiness in Christian life. Even as a youth, attracted to the worldly

---
[1] Richard Baxter, *On Justifying Righteousness* (1676) Postscript: (p. 70 in *The Substance of Mr. Cartwright's Exceptions Considered*, 1675).
[2] ibid., p. 150.

practices of his day, he revered character when he saw it in his Puritan neighbours, and Christian character became the touchstone of his labours. His passionate desire for discipline in the Church was just that the Church might be kept holy. In his first year at Kidderminster a wave of intellectual doubt engulfed him, and, true to his honest mind, he faced the temptation to doubt, re-examining the grounds of his faith. That which convinced him afresh of the validity of Christianity was character. 'And I saw', he says, 'that Christ did bring up all his serious and sincere disciples to real holiness and to heavenly-mindedness, and made them new creatures . . . it is not like that God will make use of a deceiver for this real visible recovery and reformation of the nature of man.'[1]

He got into trouble too because of this insistence on holiness—the same kind of trouble that came from his insistence that faith without works was dead. Some thought that he preached and taught mere morality, and did not give enough reverence to the doctrine of justification, and the imputation of Christ's righteousness to men. He answers them in his tract called *How far Holiness is the Design of Christianity*. In it he defines holiness and true morality as the same thing, pointing out that the object of holiness is God, and that the object of true morality is God,[2] and that our holiness therefore is that we should be peculiarly the children of God. Thus if people take morality or holiness to be only the love of ourselves and our neighbours, a disposition of mind and course of life, in which we live orderly, justly and charitably to all, and soberly to our own minds and bodies, and all this for the maintaining of the temporal prosperity of ourselves and others, or for the meriting of a prosperity in the life to come; but not at all referring this to God as the beginning, the guide and ultimate end of all; it is but analogically called either holiness or morality, and not in a proper or univocal sense, because the end is left out which must give being to all true holiness or morality. Baxter could sing with the Jesuit Francis Xavier:

> My God, I love Thee—not because
> I hope for heaven thereby,
> Nor yet because who love Thee not
> Are lost eternally.

[1] *Autobiography* (Everyman, 1931), p. 27.
[2] Richard Baxter, *Theological Tracts*, vol. I (1630), p. 9 of above tract.

> Not with the hope of gaining aught;
> Not seeking a reward;
> But as Thyself hast lovèd me,
> O ever-loving Lord.

The love of God was the inspiration of all holiness or morality, and a Christian loved his neighbours because, if he searched, something of God was to be found in them.

HIS DOCTRINE OF THE ATONEMENT

In the same work Baxter outlines his view of the Atonement. 'We believe', he says, 'that Christ dyed for our sins, as a sacrifice ransome, propitiation, attonement. And that his *own voluntry Sponsion*, and his *Father's will* were his *obligation:* And that our *sins* were the *occasion*, and the evil to be done away; And that (for the holy ends forementioned) he suffered for our sakes and in our stead, such a kind and measure of suffering, as was fit to attain the ends of our Creator—thus far our sins may be said to be imputed to him, in that he dyed for them; Though properly he undertook the punishment only; but never the sin itself; His nature and holy will abhorring such an undertaking.'[1] As for Christ's righteousness being imputed to sinners for their pardon, he could not hold that it was at all possible for the same individual righteousness that was in Christ to be in itself and really given to us. He stands by the Scholastic idea of substance and accidents, Christ's righteousness was an 'accident' pertaining to Himself, and an accident cannot be removed from one 'substance' to another, for to remove it is to destroy it. Christ's righteousness cannot be given to us, but His habitual perfection, with His active righteousness, and His sacrifice or sufferings, all set together and advanced in value by their conjunction with His divine righteousness, were the true meritorious procuring cause of our pardon, justification, adoption, sanctification, and salvation. Thus Christ's righteousness is imputed to us not immediately in itself, but in the effect and fruits: 'As a Ransome is said to be given *to a Captive* because it is given *for him*; though strictly the *Ransome* is given *to another* and only the fruits *of it to him*.'[2]

PHILOSOPHICAL OUTLOOK

Baxter was equally at home in discussing the niceties of natural religion, as he was in distinguishing the various strands of

---
[1] cf. *Tracts*, p. 16.   [2] cf. ibid., p. 17.

revealed truth. In his philosophical outlook he had many affinities with the Cambridge Platonists, particularly in his insistence on the prime importance of the human reason, which, far from being an expression of human weakness as Luther thought it was, is, as he says, our natural excellency and the image of God in our nature. The thing that strikes one when reading Baxter is his scientific mind, if we use scientific in the sense of getting to the bottom of an argument. His analysis is ruthless and precise, if a little verbose, and reminds one of the methods and system of the greatest of the Schoolmen, St. Thomas Aquinas. There is something superb in the intellectual honesty of both these men who will not endure false analogies or unbalanced arguments. Baxter is more prolix than St. Thomas, partly because he had more knowledge, and partly because he wrote against time. But they are much alike in the way they dig at the roots of things, and get at the basic facts to lay as a foundation for their edifice of knowledge. In common with the great medieval theologian, he held that the existence of God could be proved by the light of natural evidence, and that 'a Philosopher and yet an atheist or ungodly, is a monster; one that most readeth the book of Nature and least understandeth it'.

Baxter is still in the scholastic tradition as to the approach he makes to the philosophy of Christianity, but in him the tradition had been modified along the line of the Cambridge Platonists, for whereas Aquinas quotes Aristotle chiefly—the Philosopher, as he calls him—Baxter's preference is for Plato and Plotinus. Again his initial approach to the problem of God's existence is different, although they both argue from the known to the unknown. St. Thomas, in the *Summa Contra Gentiles*, uses the argument from motion derived from Aristotle,[1] and in the *Summa Theologica* he uses the celebrated five proofs:

1. The argument from motion.
2. The argument from the nature of the efficient cause.
3. The argument from possibility and necessity.
4. The argument from the gradation found in things.
5. The argument from the governance of the world.[2]

Baxter, on the other hand, starts from what he considers the nearest truth—namely, his own existence—and ascends in a

[1] Aquinas, *Summa Contra Gentiles* (Burns, Oates & Washbourne, 1924), ch. 3.
[2] Aquinas, *Summa Theologica* (Burns, Oates & Washbourne, 1924), p. 24.

certain order until he proves that he is a 'living Wight having—Power—understanding—and—Will'. From there he goes on to discuss 'Man as related to things below him', and then 'Men as mutually related to each other', and, lastly, 'Man and other things as produced by their first cause'.[1]

He then goes on to analyse the nature of the First Cause, which he calls God.

One thing Baxter does at the very outset of his argument is to face the problem of Solipsism. This is a problem that all Christian philosophers must face—that is, whether one can rely on the judgement of the senses to give a real picture of the world. He faces it in the only way in which it can be faced—namely, by asserting as an axiom that the senses can be trusted, and that men do not live in a 'continual delusary dream', but that their apprehension of a world outside themselves is the apprehension of a real world. 'If any would perswade me', he says, 'that I *feel not* when I am sick or wounded, or *see not* when I see, or *taste not* when or what I taste; yet must I be perswaded that fallible or infallible, this sense must be used, and serve for the ends to which it is given me.'[2] Like Dr. Johnson, who asserted the reality of the external world by kicking a stone and feeling the pain, so Baxter asserts that the senses are trustworthy, and that man is not a prisoner alone and abandoned in a sensuous cage.

Baxter can take his place, not only with the best theologians of the seventeenth century, but also with the best philosophers. Had not his natural bent taken him into the fields of churchmanship, he would have made an accurate and admirable scientist. In his attitude to the teachings of Nature, he could echo the words with which Newton closes his *Principia*: 'The Master of the Heavens governs all things, not as being the soul of the world, but as Sovereign of the Universe. A God without Sovereignty, without Providence, and without object in His works would be only destiny or nature. Now from a blind metaphysical necessity, everywhere and always the same, could arise no variety, all that diversity of things according to places and time—could have been produced by the thought and will of a Being who is The Being existing in Himself and necessarily.'[3]

---

[1] Richard Baxter, *Reasons for the Christian Religion* (1667), p. 4.
[2] ibid., p. 2.   [3] cf. ibid., pp. 28–29.

HIS LAST TREATISE

While we are considering Baxter's position as a teacher, we must consider a small treatise which he wrote when he was seventy-six, a month or two before his death. It is entitled *The Poor Husbandman's Advocate to Rich Racking Landlords*, and signed, '18 October 1691, Moriturus G. Salvianus', the name Baxter had used earlier for himself when writing *The Reformed Pastor*. It is said that when a man dies his thoughts turn to the days of his youth and the things that really interest him, as Falstaff on his death-bed 'babbled o' green fields', and Pitt muttered: 'I would like one of Bellamy's veal pies.' So Baxter having run the gamut of theological controversy, philosophical wanderings, arguments about Church government, returns on his deathbed to the things that really mattered to him: religion and its moral demands. The treatise is a passionate cry to the rich to aid and relieve the distress of the poor. Not the poor in general, but a particular class of poor, the poor husbandman, among whom he had been brought up as a child. The poor husbandman of Rowton, High Ercall, and Wroxeter. True to his lifelong conviction that 'good works' are necessary if faith is to be effectual, so he pleads that religion is nothing if it does not issue in justice and mercy. Once more the cry of St. Paul, 'Woe is me if I preach not the Gospel', is urgent in his heart. Before it is too late he must speak a last word to the rich, and even though his attitude to the relief of poverty is medieval rather than modern, the basis of his appeal is Scriptural and Christian, and takes its inspiration from the parable of Judgement in Matthew xxv, a parable which made a great impression on him when, many years before, he had occasion to note it while writing *The Saints' Everlasting Rest*.

This treatise was unearthed from the manuscripts in Dr. William's library by Dr. Powicke, and published in 1926, with a Foreword by the late Professor Unwin of Manchester University.[1] Professor Unwin in this Foreword points out Baxter's keen social observation, sharpened as it were by sympathy, in signalling out the husbandman from the freeholders and tenant-farmers. For as the latter were profiting by the new order, i.e. the transition from an agricultural to an industrial society, so the former were becoming more impoverished. Professor Unwin

[1] *Bulletin of John Rylands Library* (Manchester University Press, 1926), vol. X.

also commends Baxter's diagnosis of the causes of this poverty—namely, rack-renting. Rent of arable land had risen from one shilling an acre to six shillings an acre with the rise in the price of wheat, from the Reformation to the Civil War. Since the Civil War the price of wheat had fallen, but rents had not fallen in proportion. The maintenance of economic rents was being made possible by improvements in agricultural methods, and by the prosperous condition of industry, but the class least able to adapt itself to these new conditions was that of the small tenant-farmer, 'left stranded on the margin of cultivation'.[1] Baxter calls them enslaved, 'for none are so serviley dependent (save household servants and ambitious expectantes) as they are on their Landlords'.[2]

Baxter's solution is that the rich should retrench their needless superfluities, and fleshly lusts, and get to know the poor, for this would move them to charity more than mere hearing would do. Lawyers and physicians, too, should spare the poor in their fees and charges, and ministers and landlords should keep them from law-suits by composing their differences. He does not spare the rich in his castigation of their selfishness and waste, which may possibly be the reason why this treatise has so long lain unknown, though it must have been known to Matthew Sylvester, who had charge of Baxter's manuscripts after his death. Yet Baxter knows in his heart that this appeal will fail with most landlords, and so he closes his treatise with advice to 'poor Tenants that can get no redress frō man'. He advises them to avoid the temptations to discontents, uncharitable thoughts, and unlawful ways of getting rich that their sufferings will bring them. He begs them to count their blessings because their poverty brings them nearer to Christ, and rids them of the constant temptation to fleshly lusts; above all, they can take comfort from the fact that their daily labour was so necessary that they might call it an acceptable service to God.

True to his scholarly nature, he tells them: 'Whatever shift you make be sure you teach your children to read',[3] and if they can only get one book, to get *The Poor Man's Family Book*, which contains all their soul's concern from the hour of conversion to the hour of death. For though they are poor they should not flatter themselves with the thought of a long life, but spend

---

[1] *Bulletin of John Rylands Library*, vol. X, 1926, p. 168.
[2] ibid., p. 185. [3] ibid., p. 217.

every day in preparation for death. 'In all your business', he says, 'remember where you are going and where you must dwell forever.'[1] He spared neither rich nor poor in his analysis of their sins and opportunities. With neither did he seek popularity, nor fear criticism. He would have gained the approval of the Superintendent of a northern Methodist Church who gave as his report at a Sunday School anniversary the one sentence: 'We teach the children here to fear God—and nobody else.'

BAXTER AND GEORGE HERBERT

Baxter will be remembered, however, not for his works on philosophy, nor for his treatises on Church government, but for two books which stand out in the history of Christian literature, *The Saints' Everlasting Rest* and *The Reformed Pastor*. Both books have influenced many people, *The Reformed Pastor* particularly in the eighteenth century. The Rev. Samuel Wesley and the Rev. John Wesley were much indebted to it in their pastoral work. John Wesley, when giving advice on pastoral work to his preachers, says that each leader in society should instruct the people from house to house, quoting Baxter as an example of this form of teaching, and Baxter's tract, *Gildas Salvianus*, as well worth a capable perusal.[2] John Fletcher of Madeley, Samuel Rutherford, and many others also profited by Baxter's teaching on the work of the pastoral office.

It is surprising therefore that Baxter, who did so much to resurrect the pastoral work of ministers, never mentions George Herbert's work on the same subject, entitled *The Country Parson*. This is still more surprising when we remember that Baxter had a high opinion of Herbert himself and particularly of his poems. Also, Herbert's mother and Baxter's mother were near neighbours as children at High Ercall in Shropshire, and so the families must have known something of each other. In passing, we may mention that Baxter never mentions John Bunyan nor Milton, though he must have heard of both, and yet if Baxter had read *The Pilgrim's Progress* it is impossible not to think that he would have commented on it. However, to return to Baxter and Herbert, although there is no evidence that Baxter had read *The Country Parson*, yet there is something in common between Baxter's book, *The Reformed Pastor*, and Herbert's classic, apart

[1] ibid., p. 218.
[2] *Baxter: The Reformed Pastor*, edited by J. T. Wilkinson (1939), p. 40.

from the subject matter. The two styles, of course, vary considerably, as J. T. Wilkinson points out in his excellent introductory essay to his edition of Baxter's book. Herbert's style is simple, easy, and plain, whereas Baxter's style is like a torrent, but a torrent that is clear and refreshing. The thing that is common to both these men is their high sense of the pastoral office. The High Churchman and the Nonconformist believed firmly in the dignity, authority, and holiness of their vocation. Just as Baxter says, 'It is God by His Spirit, that makes us overseers of His Church',[1] so Herbert says, 'The Country Parson is in God's stead to his Parish',[2] and though the words are different, the underlying thought is the same. So both insist that the Parson must exercise discipline in the Church, and that the Parson must be holy, for he is called to a holy work.[3] Both of them enlarge on the importance of catechizing the people, and both insist on the necessity of the Parson being charitable and going to the poor particularly. Both Baxter and Herbert believe in Hell, but little is said of its torments; Hell to both of them means banishment from God.[4] True to the tradition of the seventeenth century, both ministers exalt preaching. This is readily understandable of the Puritan Baxter, but is equally true of the High Churchman Herbert, who says: 'The Country Parson preacheth constantly, the pulpit is his joy and his throne.'[5] In commenting on the method and manner of the preacher, Herbert feels that a sermon of one hour in length is sufficient, because 'all ages have thought that a competency'. It says much for the power of concentration of Herbert's rustics, as compared with that of modern-day congregations, that they were able to stand an hour's sermon. Or is it that in those days it was easier to lead the people 'as lambs to the slaughter'?

Another point of similarity between the two divines is that both held that parsons should, if they were able, practise medicine among their people, or at least, according to Herbert, the parson's wife should do so.[6] If none in the parson's family is

---

[1] *The Reformed Pastor*, p. 119.

[2] G. H. Palmer, *Life and Works of George Herbert* (Hodder & Stoughton, 1905), p. 263.

[3] cf. J. T. Wilkinson, op. cit., p. 163, and G. H. Palmer, op. cit., p. 224.

[4] cf. Florence Higham, *Faith of Our Fathers* (1939), p. 132, and G. H. Palmer, op. cit., p. 75.

[5] G. H. Palmer, op. cit., p. 223.   [6] ibid., p. 275.

competent, then he should see that there is kept a physician in the village or town. Baxter, as we know, gained some renown as a physician among his people, and gives that as one reason why they were ready to hear him in the pulpit. A bottle of physic, no doubt, would compensate some for an hour's sermon! Later, when his work had grown too great for him to spare the time for the practice of medicine, he obtained a physician for the town. In the next century John Wesley showed the same concern for the bodies of his people as well as their souls, and wrote a book of medicine for their use.

Enough has been said here to show the similarities between Baxter's conception of the minister's work and duty, and Herbert's conception. Neither of them believed that the work of a minister was merely to preach and to administer the Sacraments. The work of a minister, as each taught his separate followers, was, in addition to the above, to be a spiritual father to his people, whether this people was a congregation or a village society. Nothing in the lives of their people was too small for their notice, and nothing must hinder them from 'keeping God's watch', to use Herbert's phrase, among their people. These two men were the most renowned pastors of their age, and although one lived quietly in the Church, and died peaceably in his country living, while the other was in the forefront of the theological controversies of the day, and was finally outcast from the Church which he loved, when it comes to the work for which they were ordained, we find that one might easily have been substituted for the other without any loss to the efficiency or character of their holy office. It is hard to believe that the controversies which divided them were of great importance, compared to the real work of saving and safeguarding souls. And it is not too much to say that if the love which they both preached and exemplified had had as comfortable a lodgement in the hearts of others as it had in them, there would have been no split in the seventeenth-century Church which might not have been adequately healed.

Chapter VII

BAXTER'S DOCTRINE OF THE CHURCH

1. *The Church Universal*

DOES NONCONFORMITY BELIEVE IN THE CHURCH?

THE foregoing chapters have shown us that although Puritanism sprang from various motives and emotions, the thing which gave the movement a purpose and kept it together through a century and a half was a particular view of the Church and ministry. It was this view of the Church and the ministry which brought down upon it the wrath of Elizabeth, and the opposition of James, because they both felt that the triumph of Puritanism would mean the curtailment of the Royal Prerogative. We have also seen that Nonconformity was, in a large part, the opposition given by the inheritors of the Puritan tradition to the attempt by a section of the Church to fix the government of the Church by diocesan bishops as of divine right and therefore unalterable. We have seen also that Baxter was in this tradition, that he was a Nonconformist, not because he was indifferent to the Church, but because he was dominated by a love for it. His great desire was to see the Church one, holy, and catholic, truly worshipping God, and bringing souls to salvation and holy living. He hated to see the Church made the pawn of politicians, or the plaything of Prelatical bishops, and he refused to identify himself with those who would turn the Church of England into an established sect, although he was given ample opportunity of joining them, and indeed offered considerable inducements.

Few of the writers on Baxter have troubled to see this aspect of his religious life. Most of them have been content to interpret his Nonconformity by the individualistic pietistic religion popular in the Dissenting Churches of the nineteenth century, and have forgotten, or never knew, the pit from whence Baxter and Nonconformity were digged—namely, the vigorous ecclesiastical conviction that lay behind the Puritan movement of Elizabeth's day, and the seventeenth century. Even such a scholar as Dr. Shaw calls Baxter a 'Latitudinarian and eclectic',[1] thereby implying that Baxter viewed the government, creeds, and cere-

[1] Dr. Shaw, *History of the English Church during the Civil War and Commonwealth* (Longmans, Green, 1900), vol. II, p. 152.

monies of the Church as something indifferent. No judgement could possibly be wider of the mark, except perhaps that of A. R. Ladell, another of Baxter's biographers, who errs even more, confusing not only Baxter's mind, but also Puritanism as a whole! 'Baxter's position and teaching', he says, 'were Puritan in the best sense, strangely self-centred, yet wholeheartedly sincere, aiming at and striving for the convincing and conversion of the individual. Baxter had no conception of the Church as a society or even as a family, his vision was focused upon the soul naked and responsible before its creator.'[1] While not denying Baxter's intense evangelistic piety, it is a complete misreading of his religious convictions to assume that he had no conception of the Church as a society—in fact, we shall see in this chapter that he specifically calls the Church 'a society', and it was his concern with the government and organization of this society that made him a Nonconformist.

Before we go on to discover Baxter's doctrine of the Church, it will be well to remind ourselves that Nonconformity is the outcome of a particular doctrine of the Church and ministry. The late Bernard Manning, in his *Making of Modern English Religion*, makes this clear. Here he points out that the Nonconformists did not separate from the Church from malevolence or stupidity, but to gain an inheritance, an inheritance which is twofold, 'The evangelical passion that comes whenever Luther's experience is repeated, and the ecclesiastical conviction that comes whenever Calvin's doctrine possesses a man'.[2] This is very true of Baxter. He had the evangelical passion which Manning associates with Luther, and the ecclesiastical conviction characteristic of Calvinism. Calvin's concern was with the Church, the saved society, rather than with the salvation of the individual soul, and Baxter inherited this concern from the Puritans. He worked, wrote, and prayed with dogged persistence that the Church in England should be holy, united, and ruled as nearly in accordance with God's revealed will in the Scriptures as is possible for frail, sinful men.

THE DIVINE SOCIETY

There is no formal, logical statement of his doctrine of the Church to be found in Baxter's writings. His view is stated

[1] A. R. Ladell, *R. Baxter* (S.P.C.K., 1925), p. 66.
[2] Bernard Manning, *Making of Modern English Religion* (S.C.M., 1929), p. 104.

piecemeal as the exigencies of argument draw it out of him. All his life he was occupied in one controversy or another. Now with Tombes over the question of Infant Baptism, now with the Roman Catholics 'To open the Juggling of the Jesuits', or, again, with the Anglicans on the true nature of the ministry. But behind it all is a real love of the Church and a firm view of her necessary place in the scheme of Salvation. To Baxter the Church was not an amorphous collection of Christians with no proper form or structure, but the Mystical Body of Christ, the Divine Society, peculiarly the possession of the Lord Jesus Christ, 'Who hath purchased it with his blood'.[1] He says: 'Remember that by a Church is meant not a mere company of Christians anyhow related to each other, but a society consisting of an ecclesiastical head and body, such as we call a political society.'[2] This Church is the universality of baptized visible Christians headed by Jesus Christ himself,[3] a definition he takes from the Epistle to the Ephesians iv, 4–7, 16.

All the Christians in the world, he says (in particular Churches or out), make up one catholic or universal Church. This Church is 'Mystical and Invisible in that:

1. The Faith of men's minds is Invisible,
2. and Christ is Invisible to us Mortals now he is in Heaven;

but it is also Visible:

1. In respect of the Members and their outward Baptism and Profession,
2. and because that Christ the Head was once Visible on Earth and is still Visible in Heaven to the Glorified part (as the king is to his Courtiers, when the rest of the Kingdom seeth him not), and

will visibly appear again to all.'[4] All Christians, those who are on earth and those who are in Heaven, make up the Church as a Divine Society headed by Jesus Christ the Redeemer. This Society is so united and conjoined, that the Church on earth has constant communion with the angels, and with the holy souls now with Christ. When

[1] Richard Baxter, *Key for Catholics* (edited by J. Allport, 1839), conclusion, p. 527.
[2] W. Orme, *The Practical Works of Richard Baxter* (1830), vol. 5, p. 254.
[3] ibid., p. 281.
[4] Richard Baxter, *Treatise of Episcopacy* (First Edition), p. 42; cf. Orme, vol. V, p. 281.

Christians meet together for worship they must enter the holy assembly reverently and without superstition.[1] They must remember also that when they draw near to God in His holy worship, they are part of 'The same society with those blessed spirits praising him in perfection'. In his book, *Christian Ecclesiastics*, Part 3, Chapter 10, from which the above is taken, he gives twenty-two directions about our 'Communion with the Holy Souls departed and now with Christ', and in Chapter 11 he gives thirteen directions about our 'Communion with the Holy Angels'. In fact, the Church as it is represented by the glorified part is the 'Noblest part of the body of Christ and family of God of which you are inferior members; and therefore that you owe them greater love and honour than you owe to any saints on earth'.[2] He complains of the neglect of our duty to the souls of the blessed now with Christ. This neglect 'Doth much harden the Papists in their erroneous excesses hereabouts'.[3] So Christians must pursue their communion with the inhabitants of the Kingdom of God, and not neglect it because the Papists abuse it, for 'error is an ill way of confuting error'.[4] With many quotations from Scripture, he shows how Christian communion with the Church above will benefit the Church on earth and give honour to God in honouring them. Thus the Church is firstly the whole society of redeemed Christian people visible and invisible, on earth and in Heaven, headed by Jesus Christ. Another clue as to what Baxter means by the Church is to be found in the conclusion of his book, *A Key for Catholics*, where he states: 'Let the three attributes of *Holy*, *Catholic*, and *Apostolical*, be still affixed to the Church; and be practically considered; and those considerations issued in *The Communion of Saints*.'[5]

THE CATHOLICITY OF THE CHURCH

These are three of the classic attributes of the Church. The fourth is 'Unity', about which Baxter has a good deal to say. In fact, after his Kidderminster ministry he devoted himself to trying to heal the broken unity of the Church. In emphasizing these attributes he is in direct line with the tradition of sound Christian scholarship, concerning the nature of the Church, which has come down from before the days of Augustine. Where

---

[1] Orme, vol. V, p. 216. [2] ibid., p. 223. [3] ibid. [4] ibid.
[5] Richard Baxter, *Key for Catholics* (edited by J. Allport, 1839), p. 525.

he differed from the Laudian party, and from those pillars of Nonconformity, the Roman Catholics and the Dissenters, is in his interpretation of these attributes. But that he believed the Church to be one holy, catholic and apostolic is without shadow of doubt. These attributes were approved by him to be a true description of the Reformed Churches. Not that he would have unchurched all and every Roman Catholic. For he held that the Catholic Church is not confined to Protestants, nor to Greeks, much less to Roman Catholics only, or to any other party whatever; but it comprehends all the members of Christ; and as visible, it contains all who profess the Christian religion by a credible profession. To the objection that he leaves no room for the Church of Rome, he answers: 'Not as Papists; as such they can be no members of it. But if with any of them Christianity be predominant and prevail against the infection of Popery, so that it practically extinguish not Christianity, then as Christians they may be members of the Church, and be saved too, but not as Papists.'[1]

This gives us an excellent insight into Baxter's conception of the catholicity of the Church. 'All Christians as Christians are the Catholic or Universal Church',[2] irrespective of the type of Church to which they belong. 'As all sincere heart-covenanters make up the Church as regenerate, and mystical or invisible; so all that are Christened, that is baptized and professing consent to all the essentials of the baptismal covenant, not having apostasized nor being by any lawful power excommunicated, are Christians, and make up the Church as visible.'[3] So to know which is the true catholic or universal Church is but to know who are baptized, professed Christians.[4] Our relation to this universal Church is stricter and more indissoluble than to any particular Church.[5] 'But first remember you are members of the universal Church, and as such, in mental communion with the whole, present yourselves and services to Christ; and next as members of your Particular Church.'[6] So powerful is this membership in the universal Church that there is none 'That can excommunicate any man out of the universal Church; and such usurpation would be a treason against Christ, whose prerogative it is'.[7] On the other hand, if a man deserves to be excommunicated

---

[1] *Key for Catholics.*   [2] Orme, vol. V, p. 252.   [3] ibid., p. 248.   [4] ibid., p. 249.
[5] Richard Baxter, *Treatise of Episcopacy* (First Edition), p. 32.
[6] Richard Baxter, *Life of Faith* (1670), p. 525.   [7] Orme, vol. V, p. 250.

from one particular Church, he deserves to be excommunicated from all 'If it be upon a cause common to all; or that nullified his Christianity'.[1] The excommunication must begin in the particular Church and excludes the person from that Church, and not from the universal Church. This latter only Christ can do; therefore excommunication is an exercise of local Church discipline, confirmed if necessary by successive particular Churches. Baxter takes his stand on the assertion that there is one universal Church, whose head is Christ alone. 'No power on earth, Popes, Council or Prince hath power to make Universal Laws to bind the whole Church of Christ on Earth, because there is no Universal Head or Sovereign but Christ.'[2]

THE HOLINESS OF THE CHURCH

But it must not be deduced from this that it is therefore immaterial to what particular Church we belong. The universal Church is made up of particular Churches, and these are joined together in certain ways, i.e. those in England are united in the national Church; those particular Churches which adhere to Rome form an imperial Church. But these organizations, while they may be equivocally called Churches, are man-made, human institutions. There is, therefore, a great difference in the purity and soundness of the individual parts of the universal Church, some being more orthodox and holy, and some defiled with so many errors and sins as to make it difficult to discover whether they do not deny the very essentials.[3] His view is that the Reformed Churches are the soundest and purest,[4] and that, while a man may be saved in one as well as another particular Church, only the purest give him the best advantage for his salvation. In his work on *Christian Ecclesiastics*, Part 3, Question 1, Prop. 26, he gives directions on what makes up the fitness of that particular Church we should prefer to choose for our ordinary personal communion.

It is following on this that we can discuss what he means by the holiness of the Church, for it is in true holiness that the various parts of the Church differ. In *A Key for Catholics* he discusses the question of sanctity in the Roman Church and their contention that the Reformed Churches cannot be holy as they have no canonized saints. The argument itself does not

[1] ibid.   [2] Richard Baxter, *Treatise of Episcopacy* (First Edition), p. 43.
[3] Orme, vol. V, p. 251.   [4] ibid.

concern us here, but in it we find these words: 'We make it our care to admit none but saints to our church communion, though we preach to others to prepare them for it; for we believe that the Church is a holy society, and find Paul calling the whole churches to which he writes by the title of "saints"; and we believe that it is "the communion of saints" which is there to be held.'[1] Again, in *Christian Ecclesiastics* he says: 'The Church is a society dedicated or sanctified to God, by separation from the rest of the world . . . the Church is a holy people and therefore a separated people.'[2] The holiness of the Church is to be found in the holiness of the lives of the people forming the Church. Baxter held that the parish churches of England that had true ministers were true Churches of Christ.[3] But he refused to believe that everyone in the parish should be admitted to Communion, let alone forced to it.[4] His attitude is summed up in these words: 'If you say, as the Quakers do, that yet the most among us are ungodly; I answer, that those among us who are known to be ungodly and scandalous are not owned by us, nor are members of our Church, nor admitted to the Lord's Supper, in those congregations that exercise discipline, but are only as Catechumens whom we preach to and instruct, if not cast out.'[5]

Thus we see that all the baptized in the parish are entitled to the benefits of the Church, but to Baxter only that section which are admitted to full Church communion can strictly be called a Church. The controlling factor is Church discipline. Those who are not admitted to full Church communion are in the position of being instructed by hearing the Word in church, and by personal visits and exhortations by the minister. Those who are 'cast out' are under stricter discipline for their own conversion back to the fold. Their exclusion is not ultimate in the Popish sense, but temporary until they reform. One of Baxter's complaints about the sentences of excommunication executed by the bishops' courts was that they were not reformative, but punitive, in the same sense as the secular courts.[6] His desire was to see the restoration of Church discipline for the preservation of the holiness of the Church and the reformation

[1] Richard Baxter, *Key for Catholics* (edited by J. Allport, 1839), p. 247.
[2] Orme (1830), vol. V, p. 162.
[3] Richard Baxter, *Treatise of Episcopacy* (First Edition), p. 41.
[4] *Autobiography* (Everyman, 1931), p. 116.
[5] Richard Baxter, *Key for Catholics* (edited by J. Allport, 1839), p. 262.
[6] Richard Baxter, *Treatise of Episcopacy* (First Edition), p. 10.

of sinners. It was to this end that Baxter claimed the right and the necessity of exercising Church discipline. Discipline he says, 'Is needful to the honour of God our Creator, Redeemer and Sanctifier, that He may be declared Holy in the Holiness of his Church. . . . It is needful for the Honour of Holiness itself which will be vilified if we difference not the precious from the vile.'[1] In the same treatise he points out that 'Excommunications and Absolutions in public are not only, nor chiefly, for the external Order of the Church, but for the preserving of the people's souls from sin, and for the warning of others, and for the preserving in their minds a due esteem of the holiness of our Religion and the necessity of holiness in us, and to convince those without that God's Laws and Ways and People are more holy than those of the world'.[2] Holiness in Baxter's mind is essentially a moral quality and not a sacerdotal one. In fact, in *The Life of Faith* he tells us what holiness is not:

'1. The Papists take it for Holiness to be very observant in their adoration of the supposed transsubstantiated Host, to use their reliques, pilgrimages, crossings, prayers to Saints and Angels, anointings, Candles, Images, etc., . . . to be a state of perfection.

'2. Others think that holiness consisteth much in being rebaptized and in censuring the Parish Churches—and in avoiding forms of prayer, etc.

'3. And others (or the same) think that more of it consisteth in the gifts of utterance, in praying and preaching than indeed it doth; and that those only are godly that can pray without book (in their families or at other times) and that are most in private meetings, and none but they.

'4. And some think that the greatest parts of Godliness are the spirit of bondage to fear, and the shedding of tears for sin, or finding that they were under terrour before they had any spiritual peace, and comfort or being able to tell at what Sermon, or time, or in what order, and by what means they were converted.'[3]

Baxter was no friend to mere formal religion, whether Papist or sectarian. 'Holiness is the true morality',[4] he says, 'it is God's Image in us.'[5] 'It consisteth in:

'1. Our resignation of ourselves to God as our Owner, and submission to his Providence.

---
[1] ibid., p. 187. [2] ibid., p. 75. [3] Richard Baxter, *Life of Faith*, p. 369.
[4] ibid., p. 365. [5] ibid., p. 346.

'2. And our subjection to God as our Ruler; and obedience to his Teachings and his Laws.

'3. And in Thankfulness and Love to God as our Chief Good efficiently and finally.'[1]

Love is the final and perfective act implying and embracing all the rest; it is the fulfilling of the law and the true state of sanctification. Even our ultimate end and perfection is but our perfect love to God maintained by our perfect vision of Him with reception of His love to us. 'True Morality, or the Christian Ethics, is the love of God and man stirred up by the Spirit of Christ through Faith, and exercised in works of Piety, Justice, Charity and Temperance, in order to the attainment of everlasting happiness in the perfect vision and fruition of God.'[2] The Church is the training school of this love, and therefore is holy and must be kept holy. He did not deny that certain people and things might be holy from the nature of their office and use. Ministers of Christ are sanctified in their ordination; places and utensils may also be sanctified. In fact, every Christian is dedicated to a holy state in his baptism. As such all the baptized are sanctified and holy. But this external sanctification in baptism must be internally adhered to, and issue in holy living when the baptized reaches years of reason.[3] But all this depends on the holiness of the Church, which in itself is to be found in the lives and practice of the members. Its final definition is to be found in the love of God to man, the love of man to God and to his fellow men. The holiness of the Church is the practice of perfect love.

THE UNITY OF THE CHURCH

Because Christian people neglect the practice of love, and prefer their own sins and lusts, the outward unity of the Church is broken. In a beautiful passage in the *Christian Directory*, Baxter apostrophizes this holy love. 'The spirit of love is that one vital spirit which doth animate all the saints. The increase of love is the powerful balsam that healeth all the churches' wounds. Though loveless, lifeless, physicians think that all these wounds must be healed by the sword. And indeed the weapon-salve is now become the proper cure. It is the sword that must be medicated, that the wounds made by it may be healed. The decays of love are the churches' dissolution, which first causeth

[1] Richard Baxter, *Life of Faith*, p. 364.   [2] ibid., p. 366.   [3] ibid., p. 362.

fissures and separations, and in processus crumbleth all to dust; and therefore the pastors of the church are the fittest instruments for the cure who are the messengers of love, and whose government is paternal and hurteth not the body, but is only a government of love, and exercised by all the means of love.'[1] If all Christians had this holy love, then the body of Christ would not be marred by disunity. For unity in the universal Church and in particular Churches is very necessary. 'Understand', he says, 'and consider well the reasons why Christ so frequently and earnestly presseth concord on his Church, and why he so vehemently condemneth divisions.'[2] With quotations from Scripture, he shows why Christians will hate divisions as they hate drunkenness, lying, or perjury, because all are equally forbidden in the Word of God.

Unity brings great benefits to the Church. It is necessary to the life of the Church, for as Christ is the head and principle of the life of His Body, unity is necessary for the conveying of that life to the members. It is necessary for the strength and safety of the Church. As unity proceeds from love, so it cherishes and increases love. 'Concord is the womb and soil of love, although it be first its progeny. In quietness and peace the voice of peace is most regarded.'[3] Concord and unity is the Church's beauty, and greatly conduces to the success of the ministry and the propagation of the Gospel. But despite all this he recognizes that full unity in the Church is almost too much to ask for. True unity in the Church is conditional on the absence of sin, and the presence of holiness. Because of this, he regrets that 'You may now see how little hope there is that ever the church should have any such peace on earth as we desire. If unholiness be the hindrance, and the greatest part of the world are so unholy, and so our unity is likely to rise no higher than our piety, you may see then how much unity to look for.'[4] But he justifies his pleas for unity and the conversion of all at once to holiness as a prelude to unity, on the ground that 'An high motion, when reasonable, may be serviceable to lower hopes'.[5] If you aim high enough, you are bound to hit something. Yet all desired unity and every party had their own solution for healing the wounds in the Body of Christ. 'One thinks we must be united in the Pope and another in a General Council; another

[1] Orme, vol. V, p. 186.   [2] ibid., p. 169.   [3] ibid., p. 172.
[4] *Catholic Unity* (Orme), vol. XVI, p. 444.   [5] ibid.

Saith we shall never have unity till the magistrate force us all one way; and yet they would not be forced from their own way.'[1] But Baxter felt it was almost impossible to achieve unity by any ecclesiastical or politico-ecclesiastical method. For unity is primarily a moral and religious problem. 'Our unity is in God and we lost it by departing from this Centre of unity;—so have we still a natural desire after unity in itself considered; but God who is our unity is little known or desired by the most.'[2] As the only way to God is through Christ, so 'We can never be perfect in union and agreement among ourselves till we are perfect in union and agreement with Christ'.[3] This can never come about until we are perfectly holy. 'When we are perfect in love, and perfect in humility, and meekness, and patience, and perfect in self-denial, and all other graces, then, and never till then, shall we be perfect in our union and agreement among ourselves.'[4] This perfection is only to be found in heaven; therefore it is only in heaven we shall be united and agree perfectly. As we have not perfect light and knowledge here on earth, then, where our differences are merely about matters of opinion, we should be guided in our attitude by love and faith. It is this lack of love which causes people to erect into principles what are only in Baxter's view matters of opinion. 'Poor people think that it is the want of uniformity in certain ceremonies of man's invention, that is the cause of our great divisions and distractions, when alas! it is the want of unity in matters of greater consequence, even of faith and love and holiness.'[5] However, not all the things about which Churches and parties quarrelled were matters of opinion to Baxter. He would not and did not concede that Prelacy was a matter of opinion. He was far from being a Latitudinarian in some things. He took his stand on Holy Scripture, for whatever was in Scripture was the revealed will of God. Ceremonies and beliefs not to be found there were indifferent if not sinful. At the end of *A Key for Catholics*, he quotes certain sayings which have delighted him; one of them sums up his attitude to this and all controversies: '*Servanda in Neccessaries Unitas; in non-necessaries libertas; in utrisque charitas.*' Many of the controversies which divided the Church were about non-necessary things, and in them there should be liberty of opinion.

---

[1] *Catholic Unity* (Orme), vol. XVI, p. 380.   [2] ibid., p. 379.   [3] ibid., p. 329.
[4] ibid., p. 330.   [5] ibid., p. 373.

Although from some of his arguments it would seem that there was no unity in the visible Church, and little possibility of achieving it, yet he maintained that there was a basic unity of belief and practice in the Church, even though 'It is only the sanctified that have true Christian unity'.[1] The Papists claimed to be the true Church on the ground that they only had true unity—namely, their adherence to the See of Rome. But Baxter asserts that 'In all the essential matters of Christianity there is as true a union among all the differing sorts of Christians as there is among Papists; or any one sect—enough to make us of one Christ'.[2] Indeed, the members of the Catholic Church are united in all these following respects: They have but one God, one Head, Redeemer, Saviour, Mediator, even Jesus Christ. They have one Holy Ghost dwelling in them, they are animated by this one Spirit. The Church is one as to its principal and ultimate end. The same God is their end who is their beginning. They have one Gospel to teach them the knowledge of Christ. It is one kind of faith that by this one holy doctrine is wrought upon their souls. There is one new disposition or holy nature wrought by the Spirit of God in every member of the Catholic Church. The affections which are predominant in all the members of the Church have one and the same object: sin is what they hate, the displeasure of God the chief thing that they fear, and God in Christ is the prime object of their love. They have also one rule or law to live by: which is the law of faith, of grace, of liberty, of Christ. Every member is devoted to God in the same covenant—namely, baptism. Every member of the Catholic Church has instrumental founders of his faith under Christ, Apostles and Prophets infallibly inspired by the Holy Ghost. Every member of the Church is related to the body as a member of it. Every member has an habitual love to each particular member of the same Church. Though occasionally there are bickerings and quarrellings upon misunderstandings, if they knew more of the truth of each other's Christianity, they would love each other more. Every member has a special love of the whole and a desire after the Church's welfare and prosperity. Every member has a special love to the more noble sort of members, i.e. those who have most of Christ in them. All members have an inward inclination to hold communion with fellow members, so far as they discern them to be members

[1] ibid., p. 383.   [2] ibid., p. 330.

indeed. There is in every true member an inward inclination to the instituted means of grace, i.e. the Lord's Supper, prayer, confession, the praises of God, etc. So every member has in the main the same holy employment, i.e. the service of God. Every member has an inward enmity to that which is destructive of itself, i.e. sin, divisions, etc. Lastly, they shall all at the end of their course obtain the same crown of glory, and be united perfectly in Jesus Christ.[1]

In other words, the Churches were all trying to do the same thing: to worship God and to enjoy Him for ever. They were doing this in different ways and with more or less success, according to the purity and holiness of the different sections. Fundamentally, they were all united in the Baptismal Covenant, which contained potentially the purposes and promises of God. The unfortunate divisions between the Churches are caused by sin, which is caused by lack of love. 'Were it not for Love,' he says, 'the church would be crumbled into malicious Sects that would spend their time in prating and militating against each other—Yea, their own Sects would turn to dust and atoms, if Love, which is there confined, did not soder them together, when it is dead in them as to all others or as to the most.'[2] If men would practise perfect love then there would be no divisions. 'Remember that Love is the bond and life and interest of the Church and of the world.'[3] With sure eye, he saw the way sin had destroyed the outward unity of the Church, and yet he worked and prayed with fierce passion to save what was possible from the wreckage. With an ardour unquenched by hatred, lies, stupidity, and physical illness, he strove for a broad, united, single national Church. And when conferences failed, he 'Lay in tears, in deepest sorrow when our overturners had done their work'.

THE APOSTOLICITY OF THE CHURCH

Lastly, we have to consider what Baxter means when he applies the word 'apostolical' to the Church. It is usual to use the word 'apostolical' in relation to the Church in describing the ministry of the Church. And certain sections of the Church, i.e. the Anglican, Orthodox, Roman, etc., claim to be true Churches partly on the ground that their ministry is in direct

---
[1] Richard Baxter, *True Catholic*, p. 293.
[2] Richard Baxter, *Life of Faith*, p. 541.   [3] ibid.

succession to the Apostles. The Apostles ordained bishops, who in their turn ordained bishops in continuous succession down to the present time. These bishops ordained in each generation presbyters or priests to exercise certain powers in the Church, powers dependent on, but inferior to, the power of the bishops. This is the Apostolical Succession, and is said to guarantee sound doctrine in the Church and the correct transmission of priestly and episcopal orders. The question we have to ask ourselves is, 'Did Baxter consider the Apostolic Succession necessary to the being of a true Church?' This can only be adequately answered when we have discussed Baxter's views on two questions:

1. What is the true nature of Episcopacy?
2. What is the nature and what the necessity of succession in the ministry of the Church?

The question of the nature of Episcopacy will be dealt with in a later chapter. It will be sufficient to say here that Baxter, following Bishop Usher, considered bishop and presbyter to be of the same order and the terms interchangeable.[1] Consequently, if the power of Ordination is by definition a part of the bishop's office, it must be of the office of presbyter too. 'He who is ordained,' says Baxter, 'according to the Apostles' directions or prescript in Scripture has the true apostolical ordination, but so are we ordained; therefore the Apostles never confined ordination to Prelates, much less to those Prelates who depend on the Pope of Rome; the Bishops to whom the Apostles committed this power are the same who are called Presbyters by them; and they were the Overseers or Pastors but of one single church and not of many churches. And such are those who ordain among us now.'[2] So much may be said also for ordination. If ordination in direct succession from the Apostles is necessary, then the Reformed Churches had it. Whether such ordination is necessary to the being of the true Church and ministry can be left to a later chapter, in which chapter will be discussed also the nature of 'Succession'. But we can anticipate and say that Baxter did not consider the Apostolic Succession as defined above as necessary.

However, he still uses the word 'apostolical' to describe the Church, but he uses it in the sense of Ephesians ii. 20, 21: 'We are

[1] Richard Baxter, *Key for Catholics* (edited by J. Allport, 1839) ('Orders'), p. 239.
[2] ibid., p. 239.

built on the foundation of apostles and prophets, Jesus Christ Himself being the chief corner stone.' The Apostles and Prophets are under Christ the instrumental founders of the faith of every member of the catholic Church. It is that faith, which He delivered to the Apostles and Prophets, which the Church believes and preaches now and therefore the Church is rightly called apostolical.

We thus see that Baxter, far from ignoring the Church in his theology and practice, views it as a divine, supernatural society, one holy, catholic, and apostolic. It was raised by God for His own delight and for the promotion of true worship and holy living. In the world, but not of it, separated by a divine act of redemption wrought in and by its only Head and Saviour, Jesus Christ.

2. *Particular Churches*

THE TRUE FORM OF THE CHURCH

We have seen above that Baxter had an exalted conception of the Church as a divine society. But yet he did not conceive of every organization called a Church by Roman, Greek, or Protestant Christians as of divine institution. 'There is', he says, 'a church form of God's own institution and there is a superadded human polity or form. There are two sorts of Churches or Church forms of God's own institution. The first is the universal church considered politically as headed by Jesus Christ; this is so of Divine appointment, as that it is an article of our Creed . . . and secondly there is another, subordinate church form of Christ's institution; that is, particular churches, consisting of pastors and people conjoined for personal communion in God's worship.'[1] The first is God's act—namely, Christ and redeemed, baptized Christians. In this Church all true Christians are to be found. The second is Christ's act—namely, the setting up of these Christians in particular Churches under pastors separated from among them. All Christians need not necessarily belong to particular Churches, though where possible they must do so,[2] but they all belong to the universal Church.[3] The relation of particular Churches to the universal Church is as

---
[1] Orme, vol. V, p. 163.
[2] Richard Baxter, *Five Disputations of Church Government and Worship* (1659), pt. 2, ch. 1, sect. 1 (All that have opportunity).
[3] cf. Orme, vol. V, p. 370.

particular corporations to a kingdom.¹ Now, both these Church forms are of divine institution and unalterable. But he goes on to point out that besides these two sorts are allowable associations which some call Churches. 'God hath required these particular churches to hold such communion as they are capable of for promoting the common ends of Christianity: and prudence is left to assemblies, councils, and correspondencies according to God's general rules. If any will call their councils or associations engaged for special correspondencies by the name of churches, I will not trouble any with a strife about the name.'² Thus to Baxter the Anglican Church, organized as under Archbishops, bishops, deans, etc., or the Methodist Church, as organized in a Conference under a President, chairmen of districts, superintendents of circuits, etc., or the Roman Church, organized under the Pope, cardinals, bishops, etc., are not of divine institution. In fact, the Churches might equally well be organized as a football team, full-back, threequarter-backs, half-backs, etc., in ascending, hierarchical order, or in soviets, as far as the being of the Church is concerned, for these forms have nothing to do with it, being merely human superstructures erected on the divine foundation. This foundation is the universal Church headed by Jesus Christ, whose members are organized in partticular Churches headed by pastors. This was one of Baxter's main reasons for refusing the *Et cetera* Oath in 1640, because this oath settled the government of the Church by archbishops, deans, archdeacons, etc., as of divine law. 'I found', he says, 'that I must also swear that it ought so to stand [i.e. the government of the Churches as defined above], which could mean no less than by a Divine Law, when Man's law may not alter it.'³ For the same reason, he disagreed with the Latitudinarians and involuntary conformists, 'Who plead that no church-government, *as to the form*, is of divine institution, they [the Nonconformists] answer, this is to condemn themselves and say "Because no form is of God's institution, therefore I will declare that the episcopal form is of divine institution." For this is one part of their subscription or declaration, when they profess assent and consent to all the things in the Book of Common Prayer and ordination.'⁴

¹ Orme, vol. V, p. 164.   ² ibid.
³ Richard Baxter, *Treatise of Episcopacy* Introduction (First Edition).
⁴ *Autobiography* (Everyman, 1931), p. 185.

BAXTER'S DEFINITION OF A PARTICULAR CHURCH

We have seen in a previous chapter what Baxter means by the universal Church, so it is now open to us to see what he means by a particular Church. Now, firstly, any accumulation of Christians does not make a particular Church. Such a Church is a society of Christians conjoined with a pastor in a certain relationship. Both together make up a spiritual entity of Christ's appointment. 'And it is no particular church', he says, 'in a political sense, but only a community, if they have not their pastors to be under Christ, their spiritual conductors in the matter of salvation.'[1] He compares this to the fact that there is no school which is not constituted of teacher and scholars. He justifies his view that both pastors and people are necessary to the being of a particular Church from Holy Scripture. He quotes such texts as 'They ordained them elders in every church' (Acts xiv. 23), and others from Titus, Thessalonians, Hebrews, Corinthians, etc., showing that such a form is laid down and commanded in Scripture. In his *Treatise of Episcopacy* he defines more fully what he understands by a particular Church. 'A particular church of Christ's Institution by his Apostles is a sacred society consisting of one or more Pastors and a capable number of Christian Neighbours consociate by Christ's appointment and their own consent for personal communion in God's publick worship and in holy living.' In this definition:

'1. The Genus is "a sacred Society" so called, to distinguish it from a meer community or unbodied company of Christians, and to distinguish it from Civil and prophane societies. (For the Genus is subalternate and the species of a superior Genus.)

'2. The constitutive parts are Pastor and People.

'3. I say "Pastors" as distinguishing it from all other societies as headed by Officers and Rulers; As Kingdoms by Kings, Colleges by their Governors, Schools by Schoolmasters, Families by Parents, etc. For Societies are specified by their Governours.

'4. I say "one or more" because it is *the office in some person* that is the constitutive part, the number being indifferent as to the Beings, though not as to the well-being of the Society.

'5. The People being the other material part of the Society, I call them "Christians", that is Baptized, Professing Christians,

---

[1] Orme, vol. V, p. 164.

to distinguish them from all Infidels who are uncapable to be members.

'6. I call them "Neighbours" because the Proximity must be such as rendereth them capable of the Ends of the Society, For at an uncapable distance they cannot have Church-communion.

'7. I put in "a capable number" because too few or too many may be utterly uncapable of the Ends: One or two are uncapable defectively; such multitudes as can have no Church-communion are uncapable through excess (of which more after).

'8. The form is the relative Union of Pastor and People in reference to the Ends: Which I mean by the word "consociate".

'9. The foundation or prime efficient is "Christ's Institution".

'10. The condition *sine qua non* is "their mutual consent".

'11. The end or terminus is their "communion".

'12. The matter of this communion is both "God's publick Worship and a holy life"; which distinguish them from such as associate for civil ends or any other besides these.

'13. The proper species of this holy communion is that it be "Personal" by which I mean such as Pastor and People may ordinarily exercise in "presence" to distinguish it from that sort of communion,

'1. which we have only in spirit, in faith, judgement and affection with Christians in all parts of the world:

'2. from that external communion which several Churches hold together by Messengers, Delegates, or Letters.'[1]

We see therefore that a particular Church form is defined by 'The Relative Union of Pastor and People'. Now, a minister at his ordination receives an office in the universal Church and is still a minister if that office is not exercised,[2] but a congregation is not a true Church of God's institution unless it is in a certain relation to a pastor. For in the form of a particular Church there are two constitutive parts, the '*Pars gubernans and the Pars gubernata*',[3] the governing part and the governed part, the pastor and the flock. 'And where either of them are notoriously wanting, it is notorious that there is no true Church.'[4]

---

[1] Richard Baxter, *Treatise of Episcopacy* (First Edition), p. 33.

[2] Orme, vol. V, p. 295.

[3] Richard Baxter, *Treatise of Episcopacy* (First Edition), p. 125, and Orme, vol. XVI, p. 303.

[4] *Christian Ecclesiastics* (Orme, vol. V), p. 266.

It is important for us to understand how much store Baxter set by this relationship. A particular Church, as he understood it, was not defined by a dull, lifeless office dispensing grace to those who came as one might go to a shop for a pound of goods, nor was it a company of like-minded, clubable people secure in their spiritual aristocracy. It was a living fellowship between pastor and people. The pastor must know his people, must teach and govern them; they must know him, and submit to his leadership in all things lawful. It was the failure of diocesan Prelacy to fulfil this relationship which helped to turn his thoughts to examining what was intended in the Early Church by the office of bishop. He is fond of quoting Ignatius of Antioch to the effect that 'There is to every church one Altar, and one Bishop with the Presbytery and the Deacons',[1] and emphasizing that Ignatius meant this not of some one Church, nor yet as an accident proper for the times, but of all Churches. This relationship was 'Of the Notes of every church's Individualism'. It was what distinguished a particular Church from a secular society, and gave effect in concrete existence to the purpose and calling of the universal Church. The relationship between pastor and people was of mutual consent[2] freely exercised, and of mutual obligation freely recognized.

THE OBLIGATION OF A CHRISTIAN FLOCK TO ITS PASTOR

While we can leave the pastor's obligation to his flock until a later chapter, we can now inquire into the obligation of the flock to its pastor. For a Christian flock has definite and inviolable obligations; all the duty was not on the side of the minister, it was equally on the side of the people.

In his treatise on *Christian Ecclesiastics*, Vol. V, Baxter has a chapter entitled, 'Directions to the People concerning their internal and Private Duty to their Pastors and the Improvements of their Ministerial Office and Gifts'.[3] In it he opens out under fifteen particulars the 'True ground, and nature, and reasons of the ministerial office'. By this the people 'May also see the nature and reasons of your obedience to your pastors'.[4] He then enumerates the reasons of their obedience which may be summarized thus:

[1] *Treatise of Episcopacy*, pt. 2, p. 21.
[2] Orme, vol. V, p. 289.
[3] ibid., p. 107.
[4] ibid., p. 110.

BAXTER'S DOCTRINE OF THE CHURCH

1. God has sent His messengers to them as their pastors and Christ has said that he that heareth them heareth Him, and he that despiseth them despiseth Him and Him that sent Him.

2. The pastors have authority by their commission and ability by their qualifications.

3. Lastly, as the people have reason to obey their natural parents, or those who offer them gold or riches which they want, or who offer a pardon from their King, how much the more therefore have they reason to obey their pastors as they come to them from Christ, their king.

But the authority of their pastors is not coercive, absolute, or lordly, but ministerial. 'Therefore', he says, 'you have no more excuse for your disobedience than for refusing his help that would pull you out of the fire or water when you are perishing. You see here that your pastors cannot command you what they list nor how they list: they have nothing to do with the magistrates' work; nor can they usurp the power of a master over his servants, nor command you how to do your work or worldly business (except in the morality of it). In the fifteen particulars before mentioned their work and office do consist, and in those it is you owe them a rational obedience.'[1]

We notice that he says, 'A rational obedience', and not a blind obedience, for later in the chapter he points out what kind and measure of obedience they owe to their pastors.[2] It is commensurate to the kind of his office and work. It is as their teachers and guides in the matter of salvation that the people must obey them. Not as prophets or lawgivers to the Church, but as stated officers of Christ to open and apply the laws that He has given. 'Not as those that have dominion of your faith, or may preach another Gospel, or contradict any truth of God which by Scripture or nature he hath revealed, or can dispense with any duty which he hath commanded, but as those that have all their power from God, and for God and your salvation and the good of other men's souls; to edification only and not to destruction.'[3] The pastors are not the keepers of the people's consciences, nor their spiritual overlords, but their guides and leaders whose power is exercised by love and reason. What God has revealed in Scripture or Nature is a control outside of which no man may go to introduce new doctrines unknown to Scripture or contrary to reason.

[1] ibid., p. 112. [2] ibid., p. 131. [3] ibid., p. 132.

Yet this obedience does not conclude the duties of the people to their pastors. Their fellowship together is much more intelligent and much more lively than even rational obedience could produce by itself.

The people must get to know their own pastor and hear him when he delivers the Word as a minister of Christ. This applies to all pastors, 'But to your own pastor you are bound in a peculiar relation, to an ordinary and regular attendance upon his ministry. . . . Your own bishop must in a special manner be obeyed.'[1] Because he is over you in the Lord, 'Watching for your souls as one that must give account'.[2] The flock must piously and reverently join with him every Lord's Day at least in the public prayers and praises of the Church, 'And not ordinarily go from him to another'. They must receive the Sacrament of the Body and Blood of Christ from him. They must have recourse to him in private, especially for the resolution of weighty doubts. 'You must hear your bishops and repent, when in meekness and love they convince and admonish you against your sins, and not resist the Word of God which they powerfully and patiently lay home to your consciences, nor put them with grief to cut you off as impenitent in scandalous sins from the communion of the Church.'[3] When any of the flock have been brought under the censure of the Church after scandalous sin, they must go and humble themselves by penitent confession, and crave absolution and restoration to the communion of the Church. They must deposit their public alms in the bishop's hands. They must send for him in sickness to pray for them. They must use their pastor as their leader and champion against all heretics, infidels and subtle adversaries of the truth. 'It is for your own benefit and not for theirs that you are required in all these works of their office to use them and readily obey them.'[4]

Again, the flock must not only give their pastors a rational obedience in all things lawful, but they must seek to understand 'How Christ doth authorize and send forth His ministers'. For the first part of what he calls 'The art of wolves' is to draw the flock away from their pastors. These wolves are, on the one hand, the leaders of sects who obtrude themselves on the Church as teachers, and 'Creep into houses and lead people captive';[5] on the other hand, they are the Papists, particularly the Jesuits, whose principal work against the flock is to try to make them

---
[1] Orme, vol. V, p. 113.   [2] ibid.   [3] ibid., p. 114.   [4] ibid., p. 115.   [5] ibid., p. 115.

believe that their pastors are no true pastors, because they have not the Apostolical Succession. Consequently, Baxter would have them know the true nature of ordination that they may save themselves from heresies and defend their pastors from malicious slanders.

They must also recognize the validity of ministerial acts when the minister is qualified (in his abilities and call), though he himself be weak and have personal faults which prove his own destruction. But while God can if He will use such a man, He ordinarily 'Worketh morally by means, and fitteth the means to the work He will do by them'.[1] Therefore the wise man will strive to live under an 'able, Godly, powerful ministry though he part with his worldly wealth and treasure to attain it'. Also he will understand what measure of belief he owes to his teachers, so that his incredulity hinder not his faith in Christ nor his overmuch credulity betray him into heresies. Here Baxter outlines a précis of what true Christians may expect to be asked to believe by the aforesaid able, Godly, powerful minister.

The flock must look on their pastors as the officers of Christ, and see not only their natural but their ecclesiastical persons. For 'If they teach you his Word or deliver you Christ and his benefits in the sacraments, it is Christ Himself that doth it by them as by His instruments'.[2] So they must use their pastors' help in private, 'As the use of a physician is not only to read a lecture of physic to his patients, but to be ready to direct every person according to their particular case'.[3] By their holy lives and their effort to convert the ungodly, instruct the ignorant, convince the unbelieving, they must all preach and be helpers of the ministers of Christ. Lastly, they must not forsake their faithful pastors to follow deceivers, for it is for their sake that their ministers bear the slanders and contradictions of the wicked and 'lead the way in the fiery trial'. 'It is perfidious ingratitude to forsake them in every trial, that must lose their lives and all the world, rather than forsake you or betray their souls: or to grudge them food and raiment that lay by the gainful employments of the world, that they may attend continually on the service of your souls.'[4]

It is typical of Baxter that, in describing the duties of the flock to the pastor, he exhorts them to use the spiritual privileges which are theirs, leaving the question of food and raiment until

[1] ibid., p. 119. [2] ibid., p. 132. [3] ibid. [4] ibid., p. 134.

the last. This is how he behaved in his own life. The monetary considerations of his office were always secondary, and for years he was content to live on the stipend of a lecturer, doing the work of the Vicar of Kidderminster and yet allowing the incumbent the fruits of his office. To Baxter what a minister needed was, as the hymn says, 'Enough, but not too much to long for more'. Even when in 1647 the living of Kidderminster was pressed upon him, he refused it. 'Though I had been offered many hundreds of pounds per annum elsewhere', he says, 'I was willing to continue with them in my old lecturer's place which I had before the wars, expecting they would make the maintenance a hundred pounds a year and a house, and if they promised to submit to that doctrine of Christ which as his minister I should deliver to them I would not leave them.'[1] Actually, he arranged that the increase should not come out of tithes and so be no additional burden on them. Even then they only paid him £80 or £90 a year and the house-rent of a few rooms at the top of another man's house. This he never bothered about, but was much more concerned that they, as a flock, should obey Christ and His Laws. This Church life was very precious to Baxter when it functioned properly, both pastor and people conjoined in holy worship and holy living. There was nothing dull or tedious about it. In it was true happiness to be found, for Baxter knew that none are so happy as those who are 'In Christ'. In one of his treatises entitled the *Right Method for a Settled Peace of Conscience* he commends a 'Bright and boyant spirit to those who sought good health and a quiet mind' in these words: 'Keep company with the more cheerful sort of the Godly; *there is no mirth like the mirth of believers.* . . . Converse with men of strongest faith, that have this heavenly mirth.'[2] Because he knew, from his own experience as Christian and pastor, that mental and spiritual health, and often physical health, are to be found in their fullness only in those societies which derive their strength from the Lord of all life.

THE PLACE OF THE CONGREGATION IN THE APPOINTMENT OF ITS MINISTER

We have seen how much store Baxter sets by the duties, privileges, and obligations of the congregation, and how he exhorted them in his writings to stir themselves up to holiness

[1] Orme, vol. V, p. 100. [2] *Autobiography* (Everyman, 1931), Preface, p. xxxvi.

of life by the right use of the dignity that was theirs as the redeemed of the Lord Jesus. But besides the privilege and obligation which Church members had of using every means open to them for the pursuit of personal holiness, and the conversion of the world, the congregation of a particular Church also had certain rights in the appointment of the person who should be their pastor. Baxter expounds his view in the *Christian Directory* when he deals with the question, 'Whether the people are bound to receive or consent to an ungodly, intolerable, heretical pastor, yea, or one far less fit and worthy than a competitor, if the magistrate command it, or the bishop impose him?' In his view there is a treble guard at the door of the Church, which tends to its security, and preservation from the great evils that intruders may introduce.[1] This treble guard consists of the magistrate, the pastors or ordainers, and the people, and they function in the following way:

1. The magistrate is authorized by God to govern ministers and Churches, according to the orders and laws of Christ (and not against them), but not to ordain or degrade, nor to make ministers or unmake them nor to deprive the Church of the liberty settled on it by the laws of Christ.

2. The bishops or ordainers are authorized by Christ to judge of the fitness of the person to the office in general, and solemnly to invest him in it, but not to deprive the people of their freedom and exercise of the natural care of their own salvation, or of any liberty given them by Christ.

3. The people's liberty in choosing or consenting to their own pastors, to whom they must commit the care of their souls, is partly founded in Nature . . . and partly settled by Scripture, and continued in the Church above a thousand years after Christ, at least in very many parts of it.

He goes on to explain that the people's consent is not necessary to the general office of a minister, but, seeing that the work of the ministry is teaching, and that nothing can be done for people against their wills, it is necessary that in some way or other their consent be obtained before the minister is appointed to their particular Church. This is all the more necessary since, by definition, a Church is a society voluntarily conjoined for holy worship and living. Each of the three parties mentioned above have their proper function in admitting men into the ministry,

[1] Richard Baxter, *Five Disputations of Church Government and Worship* (1659), p. 253.

and their several functions are not allowed, ordinarily, to overlap. The right of the people is to 'Discern and consent', but the people should not insist on their choice. 'If the Ministers to whom it belongeth, do disallow the person, and take him to be unmeet, and refuse to ordain him: because obedience in such cases is their duty, and a duty that cannot tend to their loss: at least not to so much hurt to them as the contrary irregular course may prove to the Church.'[1] But, to safeguard the rights of the people, neither the magistrate nor the ministry should hinder the people from their choice, where the person nominated is fit, for the people's consent is of necessity—in fact, it is impossible to do the work of the ministry without it.[2]

THE PLACE OF THE CONGREGATION IN CHURCH ORGANIZATION

We notice from this view of the relative functions of the magistrate, the ministers, and the people in the government of the Church that Baxter was in direct succession to the Puritans of the preceding century. They laid great emphasis on the duties of the Christian magistrate, but tried carefully to safeguard the freedom of the Church, and at least a certain amount of popular control. But it was not any modern idea of the value of the democratic principle that induced Baxter to insist on a certain measure of popular authority in the government of the Church, but the consciousness he had of the supreme importance of the spiritual welfare of the congregation. God had ordained that man should, as his first concern, fit his soul for the presence of God, therefore it was only just that he should have some say in the appointment of his pastor, who would be the shepherd and bishop of his soul.

On the other hand, he was careful to safeguard the unity of the Church against the Separatists' doctrine.[3] He did not approve of single pastors of particular Churches ordaining successors or a colleague, though he would not deny that a man so ordained was a minister, but it was better that ministers from neighbouring Churches, who held communion with the particular Church, should join with the pastors of the church in the ordaining. Ordination was part of the office of a minister, and not a function of the congregation, it marked out a man

---

[1] Richard Baxter, *Five Disputations of Church Government and Worship* (1659), p. 256.
[2] Orme, vol. V, p. 271.
[3] cf., on the whole discussion, *Five Disputations*, ch. 9, pp. 252–71.

to an office in the universal Church and not merely to the pastorate of a particular Church. Therefore he did not agree that ruling elders of a particular Church should take part in the ordaining, as was the custom of the Separatists, though, as he said, 'I make no great matter of it'. He agreed that there should be ruling elders in a Church, associated with the minister in the discipline and oversight of the Church, but could not agree that Scripture taught that they had the authority to ordain. The point is that ruling elders are what he calls 'Humane creatures', that is, they are not of divine appointment, in the way the ministry is. They come into the Church organization, not by ordination, but by election. In other words, there may be something to be said for elders elected by the congregation to help in the discipline of the Church, but they were not ministers of Christ in the specific sense of receiving His Prophetic, Priestly, and Ruling functions.

In his *Treatise of Episcopacy* he gives a description of how he organized the Parish of Kidderminster with respect to the overseeing and ruling of the Church. The three Godly justices of the peace of the town held their monthly meeting with the ministers and deacons of his church, in order to emphasize the discipline of the church by holding the magistrates' court there. Besides the four ancient, Godly men who held the office of deacon, he had above twenty seniors of the laity, who without pretence of church office, met with them in their monthly meeting to see that they did the church and sinners no wrong. He associated the laity in the government of the church, but without giving them autonomous power or separate office, from the ministers. Deacons he would have because that was an office, which the laity could occupy, specified in Holy Scripture. When this system was proposed to the parish, of about 3,000 persons only 600 consented to the discipline, the rest refusing to do more than hear him preach.[1]

SUPERIOR GRADES IN THE MINISTRY

Before we conclude this study of Baxter's view of universal and particular Churches, there is one point worth our notice. We know that the only form of Church government that he would admit as being of divine institution was the universal Church headed by Jesus Christ, organized in particular Churches

[1] Richard Baxter, *Treatise of Episcopacy* (First Edition), pt. 2, p. 185.

headed by pastors. But he did not rule out the possible benefits of superior grades in the ministry of the Church. In his *Treatise of Episcopacy* he mentions this problem. 'Whether God himself', he says, 'hath appointed another sort of Bishops who may be better called Archbishops, as Successors of the Apostles in the Ruling part of their Office; and whether these have not a Power above particular Church Pastors in Ordinations, and in the oversight of the Pastors themselves and in the Care of many churches, I have long ago confessed is a Case of too much difficulty for me to determine.'[1] On the whole he seems to think it likely, but, as he is not certain whether it is of divine right or not, he says: 'I resolve not to contend against any such order, nor to disobey any just commands of such, nor to reproach the customs of the churches.' Even if these men are given some of the magistrates' power of Church government by the sword, are called bishops and made barons and endowed with lordships, he will not reproach this order, or deny any just obedience to any such officers of the King. Even if they are affirmed to have a 'superior power of the keys' to the ordinary pastors (provided that it is recognized that the pastors of each church have the whole pastoral office and power of the keys) and have the decision of controversies that arise in particular churches between pastors and people, even if they have power to censure particular bishops (or pastors), to ordain ministers, remove them and depose them as there is just cause (by bare sentence and the people's consent), and all this as successors to the Apostles, he will not contend against any of this, being uncertain of the thing in question. But if he is asked to subscribe that all this is true, as an article of his faith, the same uncertainty would forbid him. In regard to Church government, the one thing that he is certain of is that God instituted the Church as the universal Church headed by Jesus Christ, and organized in particular Churches headed by pastors.

[1] Richard Baxter, *Treatise of Episcopacy* (First Edition), pt. 2, p. 36.

Chapter VIII

THE MINISTRY

1. *Its Origin and Development*

THE FOUNDING OF THE CHRISTIAN MINISTRY

WE have seen from the last chapter that Baxter did not rule out the possible benefits to the Church to be derived from superior grades in the ministry of the Church. Indeed, he was prepared to go a long way in conforming to the form of Church government established in the Church of England, provided it was not made an article of faith as being of divine institution. We have also seen that what distinguished a particular Church from a secular society was the spiritual relationship between pastor and people. We can now examine Baxter's doctrine of the ministry, for as we shall see it was his doctrine of the ministry that caused him finally to refuse the *Et cetera* Oath (which was mainly concerned with the ministry of the Church), and started him on his Nonconformist path.

In the fourth chapter of his *Treatise of Episcopacy*, he gives a rationale of the foundation of the ministry, by comparing the institutions of magistrates and ministers, the twin pillars, according to him, upon which ordered society rested. The office of magistrate, he argues, is grounded in the law of Nature, which, of course, in these days is itself delivered up to Christ, but has its origins in pre-Christian days. But the office of the sacred ministry is 'Much of Grace and Institution and less of Natural original than Magistracy'.[1] And while proofs for the magistrates' authority and obligation can be fetched from the Mosaic magistracy, no such proofs can be fetched for the ministry, from the ministry of the Mosaical Church, 'because the Law of Moses is abrogate and indeed never did bind the Gentiles'. Therefore he says we cannot bind ourselves to do as the Mosaic Church did in point of pure institution, when God himself took down their institutions and set up new ones. Thus while Christ merely added new laws for the magistrate (in a Christian society) to carry out, i.e. to promote Christ's Instituted Doctrine, Worship and Discipline, he instituted a new ministerial office, 'as to

[1] ibid., p. 29.

the species and great essentials of the office'. Christ changed both the instituted Mosaical Law and the priesthood, and 'did begin himself in his own person as the Great Prophet, High Priest and King of his church, to exercise his office in the Jewish Nation'.[1] But because He was not to continue corporally and everywhere on earth, He designed that the Holy Ghost should be His agent internally and the sacred office of the ministry His agent externally in the 'Teaching and Governing of His Redeemed Ones in a holy order and in conducting them in holy worship, in a Ministerial subordination to his Prophetical, Regal and Priestly Office'.[2]

As Christ officiated among the Jews, so He first placed this ministerial power in twelve chosen men and seventy assistants, with some relation to the twelve tribes and seventy elders of Israel, to whom He sent them. But during His life these men were pupils and learners. They were not yet authorized openly to declare Christ to be the Messiah and Saviour, but only to prepare men for that belief. 'Because those works were not yet done which must be the Evidences of their Doctrine and the Instruments of men's Conviction, viz. Christ's Death, Resurrection, Ascension, and His sending the miraculous gift of the Holy Ghost.'[3] When Christ was risen and before His Ascension, He perfected their commission, both as to their work and province; 'But appointed them to stay till the descent of the Holy Ghost upon them (as the sealing and delivery of it, giving them full ability for their work) before they set themselves to the solemn performance of it.'[4]

As He enlarged their commission to all the world, so He added Paul by a voice from Heaven to the number of the Apostles. Paul was especially made an Apostle to the Gentiles to show the rest they were no more confined only to the twelve tribes of Israel. These Apostles were not only entrusted with the Gospel, but were endowed with the Holy Ghost to lead them infallibly into all truth. They were also the eye- and ear-witnesses of the life, miracles, Resurrection and doctrine of Christ. But they spoke not of themselves, but as the Holy Ghost inspired them. For it was He who wrought their miracles, settled the Churches and indited the Sacred Scriptures. The Apostles being His instruments, others were also employed as

---

[1] Richard Baxter, *Treatise of Episcopacy* (1681 Edition).
[2] ibid., p. 30.   [3] ibid.   [4] ibid.

their assistants in propagating the Christian Faith and so had the same Spirit, though in several measures and gifts. And so far as they had the Spirit, He was the seal of their doctrine. These Apostles and their assistants converted and baptized multitudes and settled them in Churches. By the authority of Christ and the Holy Ghost they ordained others to the sacred office of the ministry; the same office as their own for preaching, teaching the Gospel, worshipping, and guiding the Churches by holy discipline, which things are the common essentials of the sacred ministry;[1] but not the same in respect of the Apostles' extraordinary endowments as eye- and ear-witnesses, infallibly delivering the will of Christ.

While in the nature of the office all Christ's ministers have the same power, all are not called equally to exercise all these parts. Some were indefinitely employed in an unfixed course in converting men and gathering Churches where they came. Others were fixed in the stated relation of pastors to particular gathered Churches, yet with the obligation to convert unbelievers as they had opportunity. These unfixed officers were called ministers in general, stewards of God's mysteries, and evangelists. But the fixed officers were especially called bishops, pastors, and elders.[2] Sometimes these titles were interchangeable according as each did some of the others' work. We see therefore that Baxter understands the ministry of the early Church to have been twofold:

1. The itinerant ministry of the Twelve, the Seventy, and others such as Barnabas, Silas, and Timothy.[3]

2. The fixed ministry of bishops, pastors, and elders over particular gathered Churches.

The difference was one of function and not of order, and the unfixed ministry had power of ruling and preaching, presumably in conjunction with the fixed ministry in any Church to which they came.[4] 'The Apostles', he says, 'settled in every particular Church one or more with the Pastoral power of the Keys, to teach and govern that Church, and to lead them in publick worship. And every such Body should still have one or more Pastors with such power.'[5] Naturally, the Apostles would have a special interest in those Churches which they had been special

---

[1] ibid., p. 31.   [2] ibid., p. 11.
[3] Richard Baxter, *Five Disputations of Church Government and Worship* (1659), p. 26.
[4] ibid.   [5] Richard Baxter, *Treatise of Episcopacy* (First Edition), p. 33.

instruments in gathering.¹ They might even have settled down in them, where, of course, they would have the respect due to the spiritual fathers of the Church.²

Thus to Baxter the origin of the ministry is to be found in Christ's intention to continue His Prophetical Regal and Priestly office in a new community to take the place of the old community of Israel. This is evidenced by His placing His authority in the Twelve and the Seventy. They were to go first to Israel, later just before His Ascension, He enlarged their commission to the whole world. This commission is to gather Churches by preaching and baptism, and then to teach and guide them.³ We can thus see the movement; the preaching of the Good News creates the Church as men are converted and baptized. The Apostles then organize the Churches as they are gathered and as they move on ordain someone from the Church to be the overseer of the flock. So he concludes that bishops, elders, pastors, or presbyters are fixed ministers of one particular Church, and that the general ministry of the Apostles did not take away the governing power from fixed presbyters of particular Churches.⁴ Another conclusion he draws is that bishops, as fixed bishops of this or that diocese, are not successors of the Apostles, who were general unfixed officers,⁵ but are only successors in the sense that the early fixed pastors of the Church were successors. Whether the Apostles had successors in their particular, unfixed ministry, we see from above and from the *Five Disputations on Church Government and Worship*⁶ that he thought likely, although difficult of proof. But he was uncertain as to what power they had by divine institution over other fixed pastors. What he was quite certain of was that the Apostles were not bishops of dioceses, but that their commission was to the whole world.

THE EVIDENCE OF *THE DIDACHE*

This view of the organization of the Church in early days seems to be borne out by *The Didache*, or the *Teaching of the Twelve Apostles* (unknown, of course, to Baxter). In this ancient document we have evidence of a loosely-constructed ecclesiastical order similar to that which Baxter discovered in the New

---

[1] Richard Baxter, *Five Disputations of Church Government and Worship* (1659), p. 25.
[2] ibid., p. 25.   [3] Richard Baxter, *Treatise of Episcopacy* (First Edition), p. 31.
[4] Richard Baxter, *Five Disputations of Church Government and Worship* (1659), p. 26.
[5] ibid., p. 26.   [6] ibid., p. 22.

Testament. The people for whom the book was written are bidden to appoint to themselves bishops and deacons, whom they are ordered not to neglect, 'For they are the ones who are honoured of you together with the prophets and teachers'.[1] At the same time instructions are given to them on how to behave towards, and how to recognize, the true travelling Apostles and prophets.[2] The possibility of a travelling Apostle or prophet settling down in the local Church is envisaged, and instructions are also given on how to treat him, for if he is a true prophet then he is worthy of his support. This again supports Baxter's view of the interaction between the fixed and travelling ministry. Their differentiation is one of function and not of order. There is no hint in *The Didache* 'of a bishop as distinguished from a teaching elder; and apparently there was in each congregation a plurality both of presbyters (or elders) and of deacons'.[3] While this is true of *The Didache*, it is interesting to note that when the Apostolic Constitutions came to be written (some hundred years later, according to Hitchcock and Brown, from whose edition of *The Didache* the present notes and quotations are taken) the position had altered. For in the Apostolical Constitutions, the passage corresponding to that on 'Bishops and Deacons' in *The Didache* quoted above, is found as 'Bishops, presbyters and deacons'.[4] Now it is to this differentiation of the ministerial office into bishops and presbyters, as distinct and virtually different orders in the Church, that Baxter traces the decline in holiness and discipline subsequently to be found in the Church. We shall see how he seeks to substantiate this as we trace his view of the growth of Diocesan Prelacy.[5]

THE GROWTH OF EPISCOPACY

In the third chapter of the first part of his *Treatise of Episcopacy* he gives a brief summary of how this differentiation gradually took place and its effect on the office of bishop. The subject is more fully treated in the first and second chapters of his *Church History Abbreviated*. He gives five reasons for the gradual elevation of one pastor over the rest in a particular Church, but confesses that 'We cannot prove that this fixed Episcopacy was either set up by the Apostles, or countenanced by them, nor yet that it

[1] *The Didache* (Hitchcock and Brown's Edition, 1885), ch. 15.
[2] ibid., ch. 11. [3] ibid., note on ch. 15. [4] ibid.
[5] See also Dr. Streeter, *The Primitive Church*, on the fluidity of the early ministry.

was begun or in being in their days; yet it could not be long after their days that it begun; And if Hierome mistake not, it began at Alexandria some years before the death of St. John the Apostle'.[1] Nor can he bring any documentary proof to show this differentiation actually coming about, for, to quote Lightfoot, 'In the mysterious period which comprises the last thirty years of the first century, and on which history is almost wholly silent, episcopacy must, it is true, have been mainly developed. But before this period its beginnings may be traced, and after the close it is not yet fully matured.'[2] Baxter's arguments are *ad hominem*, and bear a resemblance to passages in the works of St. Jerome,[3] although he does not quote the saint. It will be sufficient if we indicate briefly the reasons he gives.

1. His first argument arises from the Apostolic disapproval of litigation among Christians before secular courts. But men being what they are, and disputes being bound to arise, they would naturally have to be taken to the pastors for settlement. And as it would be necessary for one to be umpire and have the deciding vote, one man would then gain the pre-eminence over the others.

2. The second reason is a similar one in connexion with the rise of heresies. (Jerome gives the same reason, only with him it is the removal of schism.)

3. The third reason he gives for the pre-eminence of one pastor over another is that of natural ability.

4. The fourth reason he gives arises from the probability of squabbles arising among the clergy as to which of them should have the pre-eminence among themselves. This he thinks would make the clergy and the people pick one man to rule the others, one who was wisest and best, rather than let each man be the judge of himself and the rest.

5. The fifth reason he suggests is that, owing to the scarcity of fit persons, one man would be appointed over a gathered Church who, when others were appointed to help him, would have to consent to their ordination so that, 'Because they came after him, and that by his Will if not Ordination, it must needs follow that he would usually have the pre-eminence'.[4]

---
[1] Richard Baxter, *Treatise of Episcopacy* (First Edition), p. 15.
[2] Lightfoot, *The Christian Ministry* (Macmillan, 1901), p. 38.
[3] Jerome on Titus xv; cf. Lightfoot, op. cit., p. 39.
[4] Richard Baxter, *Treatise of Episcopacy* (First Edition), p. 14.

Thus, Baxter thought that, owing to the natural frailty of human nature, the necessity of having some arbiter in disputes, and the general desire of people for order and good government in the Church, the title of bishop would be given to the one who became the prime overseer of the whole Church, both people and elders. All this while 'the Bishop was not supposed to be of a distinct office, or species of Ministry (now called An Order), but only an Overseer and chief of persons in the same Office with him'.[1]

As for the unfixed, itinerant ministry, Baxter thought it probably ceased owing to the sloth and selfishness of pastors. He did not hold, as some did, that it ceased of necessity with the death of the Apostles. It was the purpose of the Apostles that the fixed bishops should do their part in both evangelizing infidel countries and ruling gathered Churches. But as they found too much work in their own Churches, and the duty of converting infidels too arduous by reason of the labour and danger, the itinerant ministry fell out of use.[2] *The Didache* gives other reasons for the passing of the itinerant ministry. We noticed that described in this work were not only bishops settled in the Church, but also travelling Apostles and prophets. Now the faithful are given instructions on how to distinguish the difference between true and false prophets when they come to the Church. For instance, when the prophet comes he is to be entertained one day or possibly two, but if he stays three days he is a false prophet. Again, the true prophet will only ask for bread when he leaves, but if he asks for money, then he is a false prophet. Or again, if the travelling prophet orders a meal in the spirit, and eats it himself, then he is a false prophet.[3] It is easy to picture the little Church, small, struggling, devoted, entertaining the travelling preacher as their fathers had entertained the Apostles themselves, only to be charged excessive expenses at the end of the visit! Or perhaps giving him board and lodging for a few days out of their meagre funds, only to find that after, possibly, weeks he seems to make no effort to move on, finding the living and little work much too pleasant.

This is not to suggest that all the itinerant apostles were frauds, but the very fact that *The Didache* finds it necessary to devote a chapter to these warnings shows the problem they raised in the very early Church. In fact, the section of *The*

[1] ibid., p. 15.   [2] ibid., p. 16.   [3] *The Didache* (1885), ch. 11.

Didache which deals with the ministry might be called 'A plea for the Settled Pastorate, rather than an Itinerant Ministry', although the writer has not quite got to the stage of refusing the travelling preacher. However, they have to be carefully watched. At least it is easy to see why the people would rely more and more on their settled ministers, whom they had learned to love, or at least over whom they had more control. At any rate, *The Didache* gives evidence, not only of a travelling ministry, but that all was not well with the travelling ministry; while such abuse as is presupposed there would certainly help to bring such a ministry to an end.

THE EXTENSION OF EPISCOPAL AUTHORITY

Baxter then goes on to explain how it was that the bishop, who was overseer of one Church, gradually obtained authority over several Churches. He quotes the *Epistles of Ignatius* as evidence that in his day 'Every church had but One Altar, and One Bishop with his Fellow-Elders and Deacons as the note of its Unity; or Individuation. For so many people as had personal Communion at One Altar, with the Bishop or Elders were the constitutive parts of the Churches.'[1] Thus, he says, it continued in the days of Justin, Tertullian, and Cyprian, 'No Bishop having more than one Church or Altar, without any other formed self-communicating Church under him, but only Oratories in City or Country.'[2] The first to break this order were Rome and Alexandria, where converts multiplied to a greater number than could conveniently meet for Communion. So sub-assemblies were formed with their presbyters, who communicated distinctly by themselves, though he points out there is no evidence that they communicated there in the Sacrament for a long time after they met for preaching and prayer. He mentions that in Epiphanius' time, about 370 years after Christ, it is noted by him as a singularity in Alexandria 'that they had distinct Assemblies besides the Bishops'.[3] So he concludes that the Apostolic order was subverted and the relationship of one Church assembly—one bishop, was changed to a form where one bishop ruled over many Churches, and kept their sub-presbyters as their curates to officiate in their various Churches.

This process was enlarged when the Church began to organize

[1] Richard Baxter, *Treatise of Episcopacy* (First Edition), p. 17.   [2] ibid.   [3] ibid.

itself according to the model of the civil government. Under Diocletian the provinces of the Empire were rearranged and grouped as 'Dioceses'. This arrangement was eventually followed by the Christian Church. The bishop of the Church in the city of the Imperial Diocese, in which the Governor resided, became the head of all the bishops of the district.[1] On the accession of Constantine, the whole position of the Church was changed. From being merely tolerated, Christianity became one of the official religions of the Empire, not without great secular benefits to the Churches and particularly to the clergy, but with a consequent decline in holiness among Christians. In particular, he confirmed the authority of bishops to try Christians for secular offences in their own courts.[2] It was the custom for Christian disputants to seek arbitration from their own bishops (as Jews do today in the Beth Din). Constantine legalized this, and enacted that no civil judge should compel any Christian to his bar. The result was the corruption of the Church, and such an increase in the bishop's work that it became almost impossible to exercise discipline in the Church, even with the use of the sword.

BAXTER'S VIEW OF EPISCOPACY

This description of the growth of Episcopacy served Baxter in contrasting the true nature of the ministry, from its later development. It also aided him in pointing out that diocesan bishops were unable to perform their true office because of the multiplicity of their work. For it was not 'Episcopacy in general, but (the Popish and) the English species of Prelacy, which our Judgments cannot approve and which we cannot swear to as approvers'.[3] He saw the lack of discipline in the Church, and for a time assumed that it was due to the neglect of the work by the bishops. But when he came to examine, more closely, the question of Episcopacy, he began to see that the very frame of diocesan Prelacy itself excluded the proper exercise of discipline.[4] He describes in his *Autobiography* how at the time of the *Et cetera* Oath the ministers of the county met at Bridgenorth to debate the business. Some were for and some against the oath. 'This put me', he says, 'upon deeper thoughts of the point

---

[1] cf. Whitham's *History of the Christian Church* (Rivingtons, 1920), p. 163.
[2] Richard Baxter, *Treatise of Episcopacy* (First Edition), p. 19.   [3] ibid., p. 5.
[4] *Autobiography* (Everyman, 1931), p. 17, ll. 15–19.

of Episcopacy, and of the English frame of Church Government, than ever I had before; and now I had the opportunity of seeing some books which I never had before. . . . And though I found not sufficient evidence to prove all kind of Episcopacy unlawful, yet I was much satisfied that the English diocesan frame was guilty of the corruption of churches and ministry, and of the ruin of the true church discipline, and substituting a heterogeneal thing in its stead.'[1]

The office of bishop then had changed since its inception by the Apostles. Instead of being that of a pastor over a single communicating Church, it was now the office of a ruler over many churches and ministers. Neither was it any longer a purely spiritual office, but was encumbered with a multitude of secular duties. So much so that some of the spiritual duties claimed to be exercised only by bishops were handed over to laymen. For example, while the lay work of granting probate of the testaments of the dead and granting administration of goods to the next of kin was claimed by the bishop, the trial of heretics, a spiritual work, was judged by the lay chancellor, a civil lawyer, who even wrote out the writ of excommunication in the bishop's name.[2] This mixing up of spiritual and temporal affairs caused great confusion, and defeated the ends of the Church as a holy society. Baxter points out that 'The supposed offenders are no otherwise dealt with to bring them to true Repentance, than in as Civil Courts by other Lay Judges. They that appear not, and they that pay not the Fees of the Court and Officers are Excommunicate, and they that obey not the Orders of the Court.'[3] This kind of thing made a farce of Church discipline and subverted the purpose of true Church order, which was to gather together in holy worship and discipline the redeemed of the Lord Jesus Christ.

The problem of exercising Church discipline presented itself to Baxter under two heads:

1. If diocesan bishops were to do the work, then there were not enough of them. There were in England 26 or 27 bishoprics, and, according to Speed's calculation, 9,725 parish churches at least.[4] It was therefore impossible for any bishop to oversee every Christian in his diocese.[5] To do so properly would mean

[1] *Autobiography* (Everyman, 1931), p. 19.
[2] Richard Baxter, *Treatise of Episcopacy* (First Edition), p. 8.
[3] ibid., p. 8.   [4] ibid., pp. 5, 150.   [5] ibid.

a bishop to each parish church (which was Baxter's desire).[1] At least he desired that the full power of Church government, much of which was reserved to the bishop, might be restored to the Church pastors.

2. And this was the second part of the problem. Parish pastors were not true pastors in the New Testament sense because of this usurpation by the bishops. They were merely sub-presbyters, or bishops' curates. And such they are in the Church of England today. When an Anglican priest is inducted into his living, the bishop asks him to receive the '*Curam meam et tuam*'. It is the bishop who is the pastor of each church, and the priest-in-charge is merely the instrument of the bishop without the full pastoral power. This to Baxter was wrong, not only because it subverted the institution of Church pastor as laid down in the New Testament, but also because it did not make the work of church discipline easier, but harder.

We can now sum up Baxter's attitude to Episcopacy, and enlarge his statement quoted above: 'it is not Episcopacy in general but (the Popish and) the English species of Episcopacy, which our judgments cannot approve'. After a long dissertation in his *Church History Abbreviated* on the corruption brought into the Church by Episcopacy, he says: 'Yet Bishops . . . must not be worse thought of than they deserve. . . . There is an Episcopacy whose very constitution is a crime, and there is another sort which seemeth to me a thing convenient, lawful, and indifferent, and there is a sort which I cannot deny to be of Divine Right.'[2] He goes on to define these three different sorts of bishops, and to explain, in short, why one sort is of the '*Esse*' of the Church, another sort may be for the '*Bene esse*' of the Church, and another sort for the destruction of the Church. The sort of Episcopacy which is of divine right is the New Testament and Early Church species, where bishop and presbyter are two names for the same thing. So that each communicating church had its own bishop. This condition would be satisfied in the Church of England if each parish priest enjoyed the full power of the keys, to rule, discipline, and guide in worship. The sort which he considered lawful and indifferent was the sort described by Jerome: 'When among many Elders in every single church, one of most wisdom and gravity is made their President,

---

[1] ibid., pt. 2, p. 11 ('Nay, what one Considerable Parish, etc.').
[2] Richard Baxter, *Church History Abbreviated* (1680), p. 22.

yea, without whom no Ordinations or great matters shall be done.'¹ This he considered a natural development of the Church to avoid divisions, and that it was received universally, and without any considerable opposition, even before emperors became Christians. The sort which he considered to be a crime was the sort obtaining in the Church of England and the Roman Church of his day, the sort whose growth and development has been before described. Even so, in the sort he thought lawful and indifferent there was some work of the bishop which he would agree to if it made for the Church's peace, some he definitely objected to, and some, as he puts it, 'He would rather be without'.²

WAS BAXTER A PRESBYTERIAN?

His own view has certain points in common with the people who were called Presbyterians. And although others called him a Presbyterian, he always denied the name—in fact, he bridled somewhat at the charge. In the Preface to the *Treatise of Episcopacy* and also in his *Autobiography*, he recounts how he came to publish the *Treatise*: 'Upon Mr. Dodwell's provocation', and in answer to the requests of some bishops to state the Nonconformists' case. In the *Treatise* he challenges them with the words, 'Why and with what front do you call us all Presbyterians, who offered Bishop Usher's Model to the King and you in 1660?'³ The subtleties of Baxter's arguments, distinguishing him from the Presbyterians, may have passed over the heads of less acute men, but he evidently saw such a distinction himself. The distinction seems to be this. The Presbyterians were for congregational, or parish bishops, as of divine right, and Baxter agreed with them.⁴ But they stopped there, and the President of their Classis had no superior authority than merely presiding over the Classis. But Baxter seems to have thought that there should be in the Church an order of men corresponding to the itinerant order in the Early Church, successors to the Apostles in an unfixed, general ministry, who might be called archbishops. These would have an authority superior to the parish bishops, not '*In specie*', but '*In gradu*'

---

¹ Richard Baxter, *Church History Abbreviated* (1680), p. 23.
² Richard Baxter, *Five Disputations of Church Government and Worship* (1659), p. 18.
³ Richard Baxter, *Treatise of Episcopacy* (First Edition), pt. 2, p. 88.
⁴ Richard Baxter, *Five Disputations of Church Government and Worship* (1659), p. 348.

(cf. the chapter on Particular Churches, p. 115). Thus he thought of himself as occupying a mid-place between the men in the Church who wanted a Presbyterian form of Church government and the Episcopal party. So he says: 'When the King came home I accordingly used my Endeavours as a Reconciler with the Ministers here called Presbyterians, who seemed mostly of the same mind. And how little an alteration of the Church Government in the King's Declaration of Ecclesiastical Affairs did we receive with thankfulness, and it would have been with conforming joy, but that we knew the leading Men that treated with us too well to hope that they had any intention to continue it, but to use it . . . they knew to what, till they had done their work and got this Act of Uniformity.'[1]

This may possibly be the real reason why he refused the offer of a bishopric from Charles II. The circumstances of the offer were these: The Presbyterians, in company with Baxter and others, were very active in promoting the return of the King,[2] particularly after the Declaration of Breda. In fact, Baxter was very proud of this, and even went to great lengths to insist that 'It was a Parliament of Episcopals and Erastians, and not of Presbyterians, who first took up Armes in England against the King'.[3] So it was no wonder that the Presbyterians were forward in arranging his return. When the King was settled, he called a conference to settle the affairs of the Church at Sion College at which Baxter, Calamy, Reynolds, and others represented the section called Presbyterians. The King brought a chosen few of the Episcopal side. Eventually a Declaration was drawn up and submitted to the King. In the interval Baxter was offered the Bishopric of Hereford, Calamy was offered Coventry and Lichfield, and Reynolds was offered Norwich. Baxter, while advising Reynolds to take Norwich, but strictly upon the terms of the Declaration, refused his own offer. He did so for various reasons, one of which was: 'I feared that this Declaration was but for a present use, and that shortly it would be revoked or nullified.'[4] He feared it might be a temporary means to draw them on, till they came up to all the diocesans desired. Baxter was proved right, for although the Declaration was agreed upon, the Episcopal party soon forgot its terms, and shortly

[1] Richard Baxter, *Treatise of Episcopacy* (First Edition), Introduction.
[2] ibid., pt. 2, p. 211.   [3] ibid. (and pt. 1, p. 88).
[4] *Autobiography* (Everyman, 1931), p. 156.

afterwards the Act of Uniformity was passed, which caused about 2,000 Nonconformist ministers to leave the Church. Whether this offer of a bishopric was in genuine recognition of Baxter's merits, or whether it was a bribe to the Nonconformist leader, no one will ever know. Baxter himself is very charitable in his judgement of the Episcopal men.[1] But if it was a bribe, then how sadly they misjudged their man, for worldly advancement had little temptation for him. All he wanted was to be restored to his beloved people at Kidderminster, where, if in wordly title he was only a reading vicar's curate, in the eyes of God and of the people he was truly '*Episcopus Gregis*'.

2. *Its Authority and Succession*

BAXTER'S ORTHODOXY

We have seen in the previous chapter that Baxter traced the origin of the ministry to a specific intention of Christ to continue His own ministerial office in a new society—namely, the Church. This is, of course, the traditional and orthodox view of the founding of the ministry, and he held it in common with the Presbyterians, Episcopalians, and Roman Catholics. Baxter was far removed from many modern Nonconformists who often dispute the fact that Christ founded a Church at all, and certainly disagree that He founded a ministry with specific rights and authority in the Church which did appear. We can quote one of the greatest modern Nonconformist scholars, Professor Peake, who says: 'Jesus Himself created no organization, . . . the appointment of the Apostles was not the institution of a fixed order destined to permanence.'[2] Two types of ministry were necessarily present in the Church, he says: the ministry of teaching and the ministry of administration; but both of these gifts were in the first instance charismatic—that is, the right to exercise them depended on the possession of spiritual gifts. His view is that such offices as minister, presbyter, deacon, evangelist, and teacher arose out of the need for order in the Church, and not from the institution of 'orders'.

A slightly more conservative view is expounded by another great Nonconformist scholar, the Rev. Dr. R. Newton Flew, in his book, *Jesus and His Church*. He shows that our Lord was

[1] *Autobiography* (Everyman, 1931), p. 158.
[2] Professor A. S. Peake, *Commentary on the Bible* (T. C. & E. C. Jack, 1919), p. 645.

working with a definite idea of an *ecclesia*, and in that *ecclesia* there must be, of necessity, some kind of form,[1] but he too finds that the idea of the ministerial office possessing a *character indelebilis*, and also a governmental authority over the Church, is not proved by the New Testament evidence. Baxter would have agreed with these two scholars that the ministerial office is charismatic, in the sense that ministerial authority and power comes direct from God, and not from man, but he would have disagreed with them on the question of the governmental authority of the ministry, simply because he believed that the ministry inherits the 'kingly' authority of Christ. He would have heartily approved of Dr. Flew's quotation of the sentence in the *Mishnah*, 'He who is sent by a man is as he who sent him',[2] as determining the meaning of Christian apostleship, for it concedes all that Baxter would ask for; he who is sent by Christ has in some measure our Lord's Regal, Priestly, and Prophetical authority, even if that authority is not fully explained or mentioned in the New Testament! Baxter's approach to these problems was, of course, different from that of our modern scholars, who, besides having a better technique, also have more knowledge to work on. He approached these problems from inside a tradition, and sought to compare that tradition with the manuscripts. Whether it is possible to discard tradition and dogma and approach the Bible with the detachment of a biologist facing the corpse of a rabbit for dissection is a moot point. It is another moot point whether it is desirable. There is a great danger in reducing everything to the least common denominator, as some scholars do, and taking the residium as the pure, unadulterated Gospel.

However, these problems of Biblical criticism were not so radical in their analysis in the seventeenth century as they are today; possibly the Germans were not so well educated! All parties agreed to the broad fundamental idea that Christ instituted, through His Apostles, a ministry in the Church. Where the parties differed was in these respects:

1. What was the function of a minister?
2. How was the ministry propagated?

---

[1] R. Newton Flew, *Jesus and His Church* (Epworth Press, 1938), p. 186.
[2] ibid., p. 109.

MINISTERIAL AUTHORITY AND FUNCTION

In his *Five Disputations of Church Government and Worship*, Baxter discusses the true nature of the ministerial function, and the true nature of the reasons for ordination, and at the outset he defines what he means by a minister. 'A Minister of the Gospel is an Officer of Jesus Christ, set apart (or separated), to preach the Gospel and thereby, to convert men to Christianity, and by Baptism to receive Disciples into his Church, to congregate Disciples, and to be the Teachers, Overseers and Governours of the particular Churches, and to go before them in publick worship, and to administer to them the special Ordinances of Christ, according to the word of God; that in the Communion of Saints, the members may be edified, preserved, and be fruitful and obedient to Christ; and the Societies well ordered, beautified and strengthened; and both the Ministers and People saved; and the Sanctifier, Redeemer and Father Glorified and Pleased in his People now and for ever.'[1] He goes on to point out that a man may be a minister in the sight of God, but not in the sight of the Church and *vice versa*, but that Christians must take many men as true ministers to them, who yet before God are sinful invaders of the ministerial office. He does not hold that ministerial functions are dependent on holiness of life, though it is the duty of Christians to find an able, competent minister if they can.

As the minister is an officer of Christ, he receives his authority from Christ and can have none but what he receives. Therefore it follows that he has no sovereignty or lordship over the Church, for that is Christ's prerogative, nor does he receive any part of his authority from man, though man may be the instrument by which he receives it. But as a minister his ministry has a double objective:

1. The world, as that matter out of which a church is to be raised.
2. Believers called out of the world.

Thus the first part of the ministerial office is to preach the Gospel to unbelievers for their conversion. So in order of Nature a man is a preacher of the Gospel in general before he is a pastor of a particular Church.

The second part of the ministerial office is concerned with believers merely converted, whom they yet have power to

[1] Richard Baxter, *Five Disputations of Church Government and Worship* (1659), p. 130.

dedicate to God—that is, to invest them in the rights of a Christian, by baptism in solemn covenanting with God the Father, Son, and Holy Spirit.

The third part is concerned with the baptized, to congregate them into particular Churches for Holy Communion in God's worship. The fourth part of the work of a minister is about particular Churches, as the ministers are pastors of them. In this the minister subserves Christ in all parts of his office. Under Christ's Prophetical office, the minister teaches the Church; under His Priestly office, he is to stand between God and the people, 'and speak to God on their behalf and in their name, and to receive their Publick Oblations to God, and to offer up the Sacrifice of Praise and Thanksgiving on their behalf, and to celebrate the Commemoration of the sacrifice of Christ upon the Cross; and in his name to deliver his Body and Blood, and the Sealed Covenant and benefits to the Church'.[1] While under His Kingly office—a paternal kingdom, as Baxter is careful to qualify—he is to proclaim His laws, govern all the flock as overseer of it, and to reprove, admonish, censure, and cast out the obstinately impenitent, confirm the weak, approve the confessions of penitents and to absolve them, by delivering to them pardon of their sins in the name of Christ.

Such, then, are the functions of a minister. A true minister inherits all the offices of Christ, in so far as a human being can inherit them, and if any Church limits these functions, or any part of these functions, to any one section of its ministry, then those that are excluded cannot be considered true ministers of Christ. As we have seen in the previous chapter (p. 127) on the growth of the ministry, Baxter's objection to the Anglican ministry was that only the bishops could be considered as true ministers; the parish ministers were only what he called 'sub-presbyters', because they were denied part of the pastor's authority by the bishops.

It is interesting to note also that Baxter considered that the receiving of confessions and the absolving of penitents was a part of the governmental or 'kingly' function of the ministry, and not a part of the priestly function. Possibly this was because these works of a minister were related in his mind primarily to the Church, and not to the individual soul. Only Christ, who knows the hearts of men, can receive confessions and absolve in any absolute sense; the minister has to deal with these aspects

[1] ibid., p. 138.

of the Christian life in relation to his duty of keeping the Church of Christ pure and holy. This emphasizes what we have pointed out in a previous chapter (p. 94), that Baxter viewed excommunication and absolution as disciplinary acts and not priestly ones.

THE POWER OF THE KEYS

It is in this sphere that Baxter really crosses swords with the Episcopalian party. He discusses the question of Church discipline and the governmental function of the ministry under the term, 'The Power of the Keys'. For him this is a crucial point in determining the extent of his conformity with the national Church. His claim was that 'The office of Presbyters instituted by the Holy Ghost containeth an Obligation and Authority to guide by Doctrine, Worship and Discipline the flocks committed to their care'.[1] This authority and obligation is the power of the keys. It is not a question, as he says, of governing the Church by the sword, which authority belongs to the King, and is extrinsic to the pastoral office. This is the proper work of the magistrate, and does not belong to the office of bishop or presbyter as such. All the question is of the power of the keys of admission, conduct, and exclusion, of judging who shall have the Sacraments and Church Communion with Church assemblies. 'The keys are to Let in and put out',[2] he says.

We see that an essential feature—indeed, we can go so far as to say, one of the fundamental features—of the conflict between Baxter and the Prelatists was the same as that between Cartwright and Whitgift, and the same as that which wrecked the Hampton Court Conference when Dr. Raignolds put forward the request that parish ministers should have power to confirm, and when James I 'smelled whereunto that tended', that there should be a bishop in every parish, which he did not like. It arose out of the question whether bishop and presbyter were the same office. Baxter and Cartwright approached this problem from different angles, but came to the same conclusion. Cartwright reached the conclusion that bishop and presbyter are the same office direct from his study of the New Testament, as we have seen from the first chapter of this thesis (p. 15), while Baxter came to it from his concern for the exercise of discipline in the Church, and particularly after his study of what was the office of bishop in the Church when the *Et cetera* Oath was imposed. In a sense,

[1] Richard Baxter, *Treatise of Episcopacy* (First Edition), p. 101. [2] ibid., p. 118.

Baxter's cry is like that of Whitgift: 'Tell us not what we may do on sufferance, but what we may do of right,' but from the point of view of a conscientious parish minister, who saw that Church discipline was not properly exercised in the Church, and felt that the power to do this work was denied him by the bishops.

THE ERROR OF THE BISHOPS

The error of the bishops (indeed, Baxter considered it a sin) was that they took from the presbyter the essential obligation and authority of his office.[1] In general, he says, the bishops affirmed that the governing power in the Church did not belong to the presbyters, although the Church of England publicly notified her judgement that Church government, discipline, and the power of the keys was not something alien to or above the order of presbyters.[2] But the Prelatists asserted that presbyters were but bishops' curates,[3] and they meant by this that, not only did the bishops rule them, but that the bishop taught his diocese *per alios*, even by his curates. Thus they had altered the words of the Litany from 'Bishops, Pastors, and Ministers of the Church' to 'Bishops, Priests, and Deacons', lest the priests be supposed to be pastors, but the collect for bishops and curates had not been altered.

Thus Baxter asserted that what the presbyter did in the *person* of the bishop and as his instrument, he did not do in the distinct person of a presbyter, and therefore, because of this, parish priests in the Anglican Church were not true ministers, but merely the servants and instruments of the diocesan.

In Chapter 16 of the second part of his *Treatise of Episcopacy*, he gives twenty instances in which the presbyters' power is taken away from them. An analysis of these disabilities is very interesting:

1. Five of the instances are concerned with the administration of the Sacrament of the Lord's Supper.

2. Three are concerned with the act of excommunication.

3. Two with the Sacrament of baptism, the power of absolution, and the preaching of the Gospel.

4. One each with the ministerial power in the burial of the dead, the rebuking of sinners, the churching of women, confirmation, the reading of the Scriptures in the church, and the public prayers of the Church.

[1] ibid., p. 126.   [2] ibid., p. 111.   [3] ibid., p. 126.

The point about his complaint is that in all these instances the minister had no power to decide himself whether he should exercise his ministerial calling, the only person who had the right to decide, even in individual cases, was the bishop of the diocese. We can see the sort of disability that Baxter is referring to if we examine two of the instances he gives. Let us take first of all the question of baptism, which Baxter considered the first and foremost exercise of the power of the keys. He points out that 'No Presbyter hath power to judge whom he shall *Baptize* or whom to refuse; but is to Baptize all without exception that have Godfathers and Godmothers, who will but say the words of the book'.[1] It seems rather an academic point, but apparently he had difficulty about it in his own ministry. His complaint was that, supposing these conditions are agreed to by the greatest heathen, the minister must baptize the child. He described to the bishop how a notorious infidel boasted to him that he would bring his child to be baptized and say the words of the book, and see who dared to refuse him. The bishops answered that there was no scruple if the child had godfathers. Baxter felt that to give the Sacrament under such conditions was to make a mock of a holy thing, or to treat it in a superstitious manner, and that the only one who could rightly judge whether to refuse to baptize or not was the minister of the parish, who knew the religious life of the people concerned. It is interesting to note that the tendency in High Church clergy today is to refuse to baptize the children of non-churchgoers, whether they will say the words of the book or not.

We will take as our second instance the authority of the minister in the burial of the dead. The presbyter, he says, has no power to judge, so far as to the performing or restraining of his action, whether the deceased is to be pronounced blessed or not. There were three sorts of people to whom he must deny Christian burial:

1. Those who die unbaptized.
2. Suicides.
3. Those who were excommunicate, even if it was for such a paltry reason as not paying their fees.

On the other hand, thieves, murderers, drunkards, scorners of Christ, blasphemers, perjurers, who never professed repentance, so long as they were brought for burial, must be pronounced

[1] *Treatise of Episcopacy*, p. 126.

saved, in the words: 'That God in mercy hath taken to Himself the soul of this our dear brother.' In an ironical aside, he compares the difference in holiness between the Church of Rome and his own Church: the Roman Church, he says, canonize one saint in an age, but the Church of England canonize as many as are buried by the priest. And, indeed, if canonization means that the soul of the deceased is certainly with God, then he was right. This seemed to him to be nonsense, and arose from the fact that the presbyter had no power to judge and discern who were, or were not, deserving of the Christian ordinances.

We can now see why Baxter was so elated when he read the text of the King's Declaration concerning Ecclesiastical Affairs in 1660, for in all the instances he cites, where necessary acts of jurisdiction, excommunication, absolution, and ordination were to be performed presbyters were to be associated with the bishops in advice and assistance. It proved to him that the King, whose return he had helped to accomplish, and those who counselled him, did not think that these works were alien to or above the office of presbyter. On these terms, he says, he and the others with him were ready to conform and unite with the Prelatists. We can also see, more clearly, why he refused the *Et cetera* Oath and in later life the Oxford Oath, for these oaths were expressly formed to deny to him, and to the people who thought like him, the opportunity and the right of reforming the Church according to their view of the authority and function of the ministry.

But not only did Baxter differ from the Prelatists as regards the authority of the minister, but he also differed as to how this authority was transmitted from generation to generation.

THE PRELATISTS AND ORDINATION

The Prelatical bishops, whose views triumphed in the Church after the Restoration, claimed that the right to preach and the right to administer the Sacraments (or at least, the Lord's Supper) depended upon a right ordination, only to be had from a bishop whose power to ordain was said to be derived through an unbroken line of bishops from Christ and His Apostles. Thus men ordained otherwise than by bishops were not true ministers of Christ, and all they did as ministers was in vain, and the Churches they formed or served were Churches in name only. This was the unequivocal position taken up after the Convocation of 1661, and it marked for Baxter the vital difference between the Church before and the Church after the Act of Uniformity. Baxter's contention was that though Episcopal ordination was the customary rule of the Church, and had been for about a thousand years, it was not the exclusive rule. He elaborates this in his book, *Baxter's Answer to Dodwell*,[1] where he claims that no responsible divine before 1661 spoke of such ordination as a necessity. He cites Dr. Stillingfleet's quotation of Cranmer's position, that such an ordination was not of necessity to the being of a true minister, nor even was an uninterrupted succession from the Apostles necessary. Neither Hooker nor Whitgift considered such an ordination necessary, and even Bancroft, who did so much for the consolidation of Episcopal authority, did not go as far as to consider Presbyterian ordination invalid, though no doubt it was the logical conclusion from his view of Episcopacy. This view of the necessity of Episcopal ordination rose and fell with the Laudian party, and was revived again on the rehabilitation of the bishops on the return of Charles. What amazed Baxter was the arrogance and stupidity of these prelates who unchurched all the Reformed Churches, and by so doing made the national Church of England schismatic, because they so defined the Church as to exclude true Christians.

BAXTER'S VIEW OF ORDINATION

Baxter, however, was not content to show that such a view of the necessity of Episcopal ordination was new in the Church, but he insisted that it was wrong both theologically and historically. He discusses the question very fully in his 'Second Disputation on Church Government'.[2] In three successive chapters he:

1. Analyses the nature and ends of ordination.
2. Discusses whether ordination is of necessity to the being of the ministry.
3. Argues that an uninterrupted succession of regular ordination is not necessary.

He opens his analysis of the nature and ends of ordination from the philosophic analogy that, as there is no power in the world but from God, the absolute sovereign and first cause of

[1] Richard Baxter, *Baxter's Answer to Dodwell* (1681), p. 26.
[2] Richard Baxter, *Five Disputations of Church Government and Worship* (1659).

power, so there is no Church power but what is from Christ, the sovereign King of the Church. As the will of God is the cause of all things, 'and nothing but the signification of it is necessary to the conveying of meer Rights', so in the making a man a minister of the Gospel there is needed no other principal efficient cause than the will of Jesus Christ, nor any other instrumental efficient, but is of use to the signifying of His will; all other things are but in the nature of signs.

The duty of doing the work of a minister originates in a command from Christ: thus Christ's command to us to do His work makes us ministers. God's command to Paul to preach and do the other works of a minister gave him authority to do them, and God's command to the people to hear and submit makes this authority a power as to them. The nature and ends of the work commanded are such as prove a benefit to the Church by bringing them the Gospel ordinances. All this is comprehended in the imposition of the duty on the minister. Therefore the duty of the Church in making ministers is to find out on whom Christ imposes the duties of Church ministration, and by what signs of His will the person himself, and the Church, may be assured that it is the will of Christ, that a certain man shall undertake the doing of these works.[1]

Now, certain things are already given and may not be altered by anyone. God has laid it down in Scripture that:

1. There shall be a ministry.
2. The gospel shall be preached.
3. Churches shall be congregated for worship.
4. The Sacraments shall be administered.
5. The Scriptures shall be the constant universal rule.
6. Qualified persons shall desire, and seek, and be admitted to the work of the ministry.
7. The people shall desire such pastors and seek for them and consent to their choice.
8. Magistrates shall encourage and protect them, and set them in their office by their authority.

The ordainers have nothing to do with these things, and if any man shall forbid any of these works of the Law of Christ, then he is not to be obeyed. All that the overseers of the Church have to do is to *call* men to the work, *approve* them, and *invest*

[1] cf. ibid., p. 141.

them in the office, which three acts are called ordination. Yet even here the ordainers are not the only discerners; the person himself, the people, and the magistrates have some share in the work, and God goes before them all to give His graces in the realm of ministerial ability, particularly in knowledge and utterance and a desire after the work, in the man himself.

WHO GIVES THE MINISTERIAL POWER?

Having shown what the ordainers may or may not do, Baxter approaches the crux of the matter in answering the question: Is the ministerial power given by the bishops or ordainers to the candidate? That is, is there some grace inherent in the bishop's office which is, as it were, transferred in ordination to the candidate? He answers with a decisive, No! 'The Ordainers do not give the power as from themselves to others, nor doth it pass through their hands. They are but the occasions and Instruments of Inauguration or solemn possession when their interposition is due. *It is the standing Act of Christ in His Law that giveth the Power immediately, I say immediately, as without any mediate receiving and conveying cause, that is directly efficient of the Power itself,* though not so Immediately as to exclude all Preparations, and perfecting Instruments, accidental causes and other means.'[1] He cites what he considers to be parallel cases in marriage and the power of the magistrate. It is, he says, the woman's consent that designates the man as her husband, but it is not this consent that gives him the power of a husband over her. This is done directly by Christ in that Law by which He constitutes the husband to be the head of the wife. So also in the case of the power of the magistrate. Men only choose the person who shall receive the magistrate's power, the power itself is of God. As for him, he will 'never consent to any side that will needs give more to men (whether Presbyters, Prelates, or people) in making a Minister than in making a King. All power is of God; the powers that be are ordained of God'.[2]

Hence the argument of the prelates, *Nemo dat quod non habet,* is vain, for it falsely supposes that the ordainers are the givers of the power. This he thinks is the master error of the Prelatic view of Church government. Christ has the power, he says,

[1] Richard Baxter, *Five Disputations of Church Government and Worship* (1659), p. 146 (italics mine).
[2] ibid., p. 146.

and Christ gives it. Men do not give it, though some have it: for they have it to use and not to give. This is true, not only of Episcopal ordination, but also of congregational ordination. As it is not the bishop who gives the power, neither is it the people, in either case they choose the man and God gives him the authority.

IS ORDINATION NECESSARY?

Having shown what are the nature and ends of ordination, Baxter then discusses whether ordination is necessary to the being of the ministry, and concludes that it is not. However, it is a thing to be had where it may, and anyone who refuses it, for any reason save that of conscience, commits a grave sin. This position naturally follows on from his definition of ordination. If the ordainers' duty is to call, approve and invest a candidate, who will receive his power from God, it follows that God may give that power without the accompanying ordination. His argument is that ministerial offices must continue in the Church for that is Christ's command, but the obligation to be ordained may cease for some persons. This he proves by instancing certain cases, such as if all the bishops turned heretic, as happened in some parts of the world in the Arian revolt. In such cases where ordination is not to be had, Church ministries are valid without it. Ordination as such is no more necessary to the ministry than coronation is to a king, or solemn investiture is to a judge. Just as a man may be a Christian before baptism, as even the Papists admit, so a man may be a minister before ordination, but if ordination is to be had, he sins greatly if he neglects it, for as baptism is the open badge of a Christian, so ordination is the open badge of a minister.

The governing consideration is whether the work of God is to be done or not—that is, the work of saving men's souls. If a man cannot have ordination by just seeking it (assuming he is otherwise qualified), then he must work without it, even if it brings disorder into the Church. 'It is better that men be disorderly saved than orderly damned.'[1] This argument was, of course, aimed against those who tried to extract political oaths from ministers at their ordination, oaths which had nothing to do with their work as ministers, and it justified for Baxter the continuance of nonconforming ministries and Churches.

[1] *Five Disputations*, p. 165

IS AN UNINTERRUPTED SUCCESSION OF REGULAR ORDINATION NECESSARY?

Baxter answers this question in the negative also, on the ground that as ordination itself is not necessary to the being of the ministry, but only to the well-being, then an uninterrupted succession must be less necessary. Apart from this, it is quite impossible, he says, to prove a regular succession from the Apostles. He claims that it is not sufficient for his opponents to say that such a succession is probable, for that is not certainty, and indeed there is every reason to be suspicious that there have been many errors in ordination in the past.

He cites the fact that in his village, when he was young, there were five men who went into the ministry. One was an old Reader, whose original could not be reached, another was his son, whose self-ordination was much suspected. The others had letters of orders, two of them suspected to have been drawn up by the former minister, and one that was suspected of having ordained himself. Two of them were proved to have counterfeit orders after they had been long in the ministry. Such cases, he claims, were not exceptional in the Church. To prove his point that there was no certainty of a regular succession, he quotes Bellarmine, the great Roman Catholic scholar, as saying that there was no absolute certainty, but only a *moral certainty*, but he is careful to point out that Bellarmine gives no ground even to conjecture at any such probability.

Thus he thought it a grave wrong for men to make this rule of Episcopal ordination a necessity for ministerial orders, when there was not even a reasonable probability that it had ever been considered so in the history of the Church.

BAXTER'S ORDINATION

Baxter's ordination has been much discussed by those who have studied his life. All we know is that he was ordained deacon by the Bishop of Worcester in 1638, and his account of it is that he felt himself engaged thereby to God *durante vita*, in a perpetual office. The reviewer of Dr. Powicke's *A Life of Richard Baxter*, in *The Times Literary Supplement* for 8th January 1925, cites the fact that in the Diocesan Registry at Worcester there is a certificate of the ordination of a 'preaching presbyter' for the parish of

Bradley, done with prayer, and fasting, and the laying on of hands by the Associated Ministers of Warwickshire, and conjectures that Baxter was probably so ordained. Dr. Powicke, in answering him in the next issue, doubts whether Baxter would have consented to a second ordination, seeing that he always objected to re-ordination, and considered his ordination as deacon as something indelibly sacred and binding. But Baxter did not consider deacons and ministers to be of the same order. He specifically says so in the 'Second Disputation on Church Government and Worship'. He has been defining what he means by a minister, and says: 'This Ministry before described (whether you call it Episcopatum, Sacerdotium, Presbyteratum or what else is fit) is but one and the same Order (for Deacons are not the Ministers defined by us:).'[1] Baxter was fond of quoting the saying, attributed to Ignatius of Antioch that deacons are the 'hands, ears and eyes of the Bishop' so that, while they are in the orbit of the sacred ministry, they are not ministers. Thus, either Baxter took the second step and was ordained presbyter at the hands of some association of ministers during the Commonwealth period, or, what is more probable, he considered that God had given him sufficient authority to practise all the works of a minister, even the celebration of Holy Communion, when he entered into the cure of souls at Kidderminster. Even such a 'High Churchman' as Sir Ralph Clare was quite prepared to take the Communion at his hands if he could have it kneeling and on a particular day, and Baxter was quite prepared to give it to him if he would consent to live under discipline. Again, when he was offered a bishopric there was no mention made of re-ordination. Unfortunately, we look back on these problems after nearly three hundred years of controversy, during which 'Holy Orders' in the Anglican Church and in the Roman Church have come to mean specifically bishops, priests, and deacons, forgetting that for hundreds of years before the Reformation 'Holy Orders' embraced a multitude of people who never exercised purely ministerial functions, and that while the three orders existed in the Church, the real division was between clerical and lay, pastors and people. All we can say of Baxter is that he considered that there was a distinction between ministers and people, and that he was in the ministerial orbit, and entitled to do all the works of a minister.

[1] ibid., p. 140; and *Treatise of Episcopacy*, p. 34.

Chapter IX

THE WORD OF GOD

IN an earlier chapter (p. 10) we have pointed out that what really united the Puritans was a special devotion to Holy Scripture, and a desire that the whole of Church life, both doctrinally and ecclesiastically, should be based on the Word of God. Some of the Puritans went so far as to insist that what was not commanded in Scripture was unlawful, in respect of faith, morals, and Church order, and all the Puritans of the Separatist variety extolled the Scriptures as the supreme and sole revelation of God's will.[1] It now remains for us to examine how far Baxter, as a Nonconformist and in the Puritan tradition, agreed with this view of Scripture.

We have already pointed out in Chapter V in what way Baxter differed from Dr. Owen, for whereas Dr. Owen claimed that no man could know God to salvation by any other means than Scripture, Baxter was quick to point out that this was not strictly true. The promise of salvation, he said, was given to them that believed, and not to them that know Scripture, for Christ was savingly preached before the New Testament came to be written. He enlarges on this in his *Christian Directory* when answering the question, 'May not a man be saved that believeth all the essentials of religion, as coming to him by verbal tradition and not as contained in the Holy Scriptures, which perhaps he never knew?'[2] He reiterates the fact that 'He that believeth shall be saved', whichever way he comes by the belief, though, of course, those that are ignorant of the being of the Scriptures have a great disadvantage to their faith. He then enumerates four sorts of people who may be saved without a knowledge of Scripture. These are:

1. All Christians who lived before the New Testament came to be written.

2. Those in ignorant countries where the Bible is rare.

3. Children who may be taught the Creed and Catechism before they understand what the Bible is.

[1] cf. Dr. Peel, *The First Congregational Churches* (Cambridge University Press, 1920), p. 18.
[2] Orme, vol. V, p. 533.

THE WORD OF GOD

4. Lastly, there may be many thousands of Papists saved where the priests keep the Scriptures from the people, and teach them only the articles of faith and the catechism.

These four sorts of people not knowing the Scriptures still could be saved.

He would even go farther than this, for he strongly objected to those divines who said that all were damned who were not Christians. Baxter was sure that those who had not the Gospel were not put into a worse state by Christ's Incarnation. They might be saved on the same terms as before His birth, if they lived up to the best light that was in them. He commended Aquinas and the Schoolmen who said that salvation was incomparably more common to Christians than to any others, as their light, and means and helps were more, but who still refused to damn all the rest. He held that in every nation, those who feared God and worked righteousness were accepted by Him. Thus we see that to Baxter a knowledge of the Bible was not of absolute necessity even to a Christian for salvation, for there is no more essential to the Christian religion than what is contained in the baptismal covenant: 'I believe in God the Father, Son and Holy Ghost and give up myself in covenant to him, renouncing the flesh, the world and the devil.'[1]

It follows therefore that even for Christians it is not necessary to believe that every book or verse in Scripture is canonical, or written by the Spirit of God. For the Roman Catholic canon is larger than that owned by the Protestants, so that if the Protestant canon prove defective in any one book, it does not follow that they could not be saved for want of sufficient faith. All Holy Scripture is not so necessary that a man may not be saved if he does not believe it all. Some parts of it are more necessary than others, and even a man who believes that Scripture has mistakes or errors may be saved. 'He that thinketh that the prophets, sacred historians, evangelists, and apostles, were guided to an infallible delivery and recording of all the great, substantial, necessary points of the Gospel, but not to an infallibility in every bye-expression, phrase, citation or circumstance, doth disadvantage his own faith as to all the rest; but yet may be saved, if he believe the substance with a sound and practical belief.'[2] It is not therefore the words or form of Scripture that matters, it is the revelation contained therein that has saving power.

[1] *Autobiography* (Everyman, 1931), p. 138.   [2] Orme, vol. V, p. 561.

SCRIPTURE AND TRADITION

We see, therefore, from the above that Baxter was prepared to concede something to tradition, for the only two means of revelation that are left to us are Scripture and tradition,[1] though tradition is the 'more weak and uncertain' of the two.[2] In *Christian Ecclesiastics*, Part 2, Chapter 3, he gives fourteen reasons why he thinks Scripture to be the more certain and tradition the weaker way of knowing God's revealed will, which, as he says at the outset, is the object of belief. He starts off by maintaining that it is our duty to believe the revealed will of God, but only such parts as are necessary to the keeping of the covenants God has made with men. So that a man may be saved, though he should not believe many things which he is bound by God to believe. This sounds rather Irish, but he goes on to explain that a man can only be excused these beliefs through ignorance of the matter, or ignorance of the divineness of the testimony. This doctrine, which it is necessary to believe in order to be saved, has not always been the same, but has differed according to different covenants and administrations. The doctrine which is now necessary was not so before the Fall, and what is necessary since the coming of Christ was not so before His coming, because that which was not revealed cannot be the object of faith. In an interesting aside, he suggests that what may be of absolute necessity for us to believe may not be so for Indians or Turks.

God has made the substance of Scripture doctrine thus necessary, and has revealed it to us with sufficient grounds and arguments to testify to the truth of the doctrine, and to the divineness of the testimony. The study of the natural creation, while revealing some things of God, does not reveal all that is necessary to be believed. But the full revelation has been given by God immediately, by writing, as on the Mosaic tablets of stone, or by informing angels who may be His messengers, or by inspiring some choice, particular men. Few, therefore, have received that revelation immediately, and the revelation which has been given is handed down to us in Scripture or in tradition. Now, the more immediate the revelation the more sure it is, for the more hands it passes through, the more uncertain it is. So when we receive the revelation of God in writing, as it were, there is less danger of corruption than when it is delivered to us

[1] Richard Baxter, *The Saints' Everlasting Rest* (1866), p. 140. [2] ibid., p. 131.

in the words of men, because men are notably fallible, and there is more possibility of the expression varying if the revelation is not written. So God has been pleased, when He ceased immediate revelation, to hand down His will written in a form of words which should be His standing law by which to try all other men's expressions.

Baxter was struggling with the fact that our knowledge of Christ and of God's covenant with us is the outcome of tradition. The Scriptures themselves are tradition, for before they came to be written they must have been handed down by word of mouth. On the other hand, he saw what reliance on tradition had made of the Roman Church. He saw that many things which to his mind were hardly credible, and even superstitious, were held in that Church simply because they were traditional in the Church. Thus it seemed to him that the Scripturalists and the Traditionalists were both wrong, for it is not Scripture or tradition in themselves which must be believed, but certain things of which the record is in the Bible, and therefore in tradition. The Bible, which may be called crystallized tradition, is the corrective of tradition, and indeed the governor of tradition, because it was written by the Apostles and first eyewitnesses, and from these writings current in the Church a selection was made under the guidance of the Holy Spirit, which should be the canon or rule of traditional belief. Thus other beliefs and practices must be tried by Scripture. This makes the Bible the supreme authority on matters of faith, morals, and Church order for Christian people. But even the Bible must not be so used that its use becomes idolatrous.[1] The Bible is the touchstone by which the life of men, and the living witness of the Church, is to be regulated.

HOW FAR ARE THE SCRIPTURES A PERFECT RULE AND LAW FOR MEN?

Now, the question arises of how far the Bible is a perfect rule for men, if it is the supreme authority for Christian living? He maintains that the Bible is a perfect rule in its kind, and to its proper use. Because it is the most direct form of God's revelation to us, it is a perfect rule for faith and morals, and, being in direct descent from the Puritans, he would also include Church order. It contains all the essentials, and integral parts, of the

[1] Orme, vol. V, p. 488.

Christian religion, so that nothing is of itself any part of the Christian faith which is not there. We can illustrate his point by taking the vexed question of how one should partake of the Lord's Supper. He contends that while Scripture lays it down that all Christians should eat of the Lord's Supper, it does not lay down any rule as to whether the elements should be eaten sitting or kneeling, nor whether they should be put in people's hands or that the people should take them.[1] Therefore, to make these actions into regulations is to add to the faith, and tends to dethrone Christ from His sovereignty by a man-made rule. This was the error of many Separatists, and also of the Papists, who claimed that the Church could and should make such rules. The Bible is therefore an instrument in which the essentials of the faith are contained, and it is only the essentials that matter.

His attitude to the Bible reminds us of Luther's famous phrase, 'The Bible is the crib in which the Christ-child is laid, but there is much straw in the crib', and if Baxter's estimate of the amount of straw in the crib was probably less than Luther's, the principle underlying their respective attitudes was the same. But though Baxter differed from many of his Nonconformist brethren in his attitude to the Bible, he was one with them in the strictly Puritan tradition that God has revealed in Scripture the form of Church government—namely, that form which we have described in previous chapters. The Bible, he says, 'Instituteth the form of His Church universal which is called his body; and also of particular holy societies for His worship'.[2]

On the other hand, the Bible is no particular rule of natural sciences, such as physics and metaphysics, nor any rule for the 'arts for medicine, music, arithmetic, geometry, astronomy, grammar, rhetoric, logic; nor for the mechanics, as navigation, architecture'.[3] Nor is it a full rule for all those political principles which are the ground of human laws, such as whether a kingdom shall be monarchical, aristocratic, or democratic. Thus it is unlawful to add anything to Scripture, or to say that anything is a sin which is not stated to be a sin there. His general rule is that there is such a distance between God and man, and even the highest men are so dependent on God, that we should be very unwilling to vie with the authority of our Maker in belief or practice. While men stick to Scripture they are safe, because it is the most direct and immediate revelation of God's will to men.

[1] Orme, vol. V, p. 513. [2] ibid., p. 503. [3] ibid., p. 504.

While we must distinguish the uses to which Scripture must be put, some uses being legitimate to its proper end, and some not, we must also distinguish in Scripture itself the universal law of Christ which is binding on all His subjects, at all times and in all places, and those local, personal, and alterable laws which need not now be observed. The universal laws are those which result from the foundation of the universal and unalterable nature of persons and things, and those laws which God has revealed as constantly suitable to all. The local or temporary laws are those which result, either from the particular or alterable nature of persons or things, or those laws which God enacted only for some particular person or time. For instance, everyone is not to abstain from wine, as the Rechabites did, merely because it is mentioned in Scripture, for that rule was appropriate for a particular class of person, but not necessarily for all; nor must everyone go forth to preach Christ in the garb which He prescribed for the Seventy; nor has everyone to administer or receive the Lord's Supper in an upper room, in the evening, with eleven or twelve only; nor is it necessary that Christians should salute each other with a holy kiss, or use love-feasts in their sacred Communion.[1] All these are examples of the use of local and temporary customs for spiritual ends. Another example of a temporary law would be the practice of baptism by immersion, for this was suitable for a hot climate, but in a cold climate would be destructive of health. What God commands universally is a humble, reverent adoration of Him by mind and body. Now, the adoration of the mind is the same in all ages and among all peoples, but the bodily expression may vary according to custom.

THE SCRIPTURES AND WORSHIP

Similarly, the Scriptures are a guide and rule for worship, and what is of universal obligation must be distinguished from what is temporary and mutable. His unalterable conviction was, 'As men are within, so will they incline to worship God without'.[2] Outward worship is but the expression of inward worship, and he thought that if all those who contended about the outward form of worship could be helped to the inward light, life, love, and experience of holy, serious Christians, they would find enough in themselves and their experiences to decide con-

[1] ibid., p. 33.   [2] ibid., p. 19.

troversies of this kind. 'It is very observable', he says, 'in all times of the Church, how in controversies about God's worship the generality of godly, serious people, and the generality of ungodly and ludicrous worshippers are ordinarily of differing judgements, and what a stroke the temper of the soul hath in the determination of such cases.'[1]

His directions for worship follow his usual method, starting from the nearest which he knows and working outward, that is from the interior life of the soul to outward worship. First of all, we are to be sure that we faithfully and seriously practise that inward worship of God in which the life of religion consists.[2] Then we must be diligent in all those parts of the outward worship of God in which all sober Christians are agreed, being warned not to differ from the common sense of the most faithful and Godly Christians, without great suspicion of our own understanding, and keen examination of the case. The judgement of men, even the holiest, should only be taken in subordination to the will of God and the teachings of Jesus Christ, and even then we should not condemn in others that which we should not do ourselves. The worship we should offer to God is revealed in His Word, and can be found by all who care to read, nor dare we offer to God worship which is contrary to the true nature and operations of a rational soul. 'Say not', he says, 'as blind lovers do, I love this, but I know not why, . . . let not your tongues lead your hearts, . . . the heart was made to lead the tongue, and the tongue to express it, and not to lead it. Therefore speak not to God the words of a parrot which you do not understand, . . . but first understand and feel what you should speak, and then speak that which you understand and feel.'[3] But one thing it is very necessary to understand—namely, how far Christ has given a law and rule of worship to His Church in the Scriptures. If we think that there is no rule of worship there, we will deny a principal part of the office of Christ as king and teacher of His Church. On the other hand, if we think that Scripture is a rule of worship more particularly than Christ intended it to be, we will involve ourselves in endless controversies and scruples over nothing. The same rule is to apply here—namely, the distinction between what is universal and obligatory and that which is local and temporary. All Christ's laws are expressed in Scripture, but all Scripture is not Christ's law.[4]

[1] Orme, vol. V, p. 19. [2] ibid., p. 18. [3] ibid., p. 26. [4] ibid., p. 28.

THE INTERPRETATION OF SCRIPTURE

This leads us on to the problem of the interpretation of Scripture, which may be stated thus: given the authority of Scripture in matters of faith and morals, who is to decide how the words and sense of Scripture are to be interpreted? There were two answers to this question which Baxter criticizes and rejects.

1. The Roman Catholic claim that the Roman Church alone can interpret Scripture.

2. Those who said that the Scriptures must be tried by the Spirit.

The Papists used this problem, Baxter thought, to confuse what he calls 'poor unlearned persons' who, when in their ignorance they could find no answer, were confronted by the claim that the only authority that could interpret Scripture was the Church, either through a general counsel or through the Pope, and that their decisions were infallible. Baxter answers this claim by stating that there is no universal Church governed by a mortal head, consequently there is no power set up by Christ to be the infallible judge of Scripture, for Christ only has the right to interpret infallibly His own laws. But, he claims, true bishops or pastors in their own particular Churches are authorized teachers and guides in expounding God's Word, and the people are bound to respect their teaching, and not to contradict it without true cause. Yet no such pastors are to be absolutely believed where God's Word is discerned to be against them, for all the people, as reasonable creatures, have a judgement of private discerning, to judge what they must receive as truth, and to discern their own duty by the help of the Word of God and their teachers.[1] Similarly, lawful synods have the same power of discerning judgement over their several flocks. Every Christian believes in the essentials of Christianity by a divine faith, and not by a mere human belief of his teachers, though by their help and teaching his faith is generated, confirmed, and preserved. 'Therefore no essential article of Christianity is left to any obliging decision of any Church, but only to a subservient obliging teaching.'[2] If the Pope or his Council were the infallible interpreters of God's Word, then God would have enabled them to do it by an infallible commentary which all

[1] ibid., p. 312. [2] ibid., p. 313.

men should be obliged to believe. And the Pope and his Council would be the most 'treacherous miscreants on earth, that in so many hundred years would never write such an infallible nor governing commentary to end the differences of the Christian world'.[1]

Over against this view of the interpretation of Scripture were the people who claimed that Scripture should be tried by the Spirit. They claimed that it was only the Holy Spirit in the hearts of believers which opened up the Scripture, and testified to the truth contained therein. Just as Baxter could not agree that it was the Roman Church which had the right to interpret the Bible, neither could he agree that the Spirit's testimony in the individual was the appropriate instrument of interpretation. It is true, he argues, that the Spirit in Himself is infinitely more excellent than the Scripture, for the Spirit is God, while the Scriptures are only the work of God. But the operation of the Spirit in the Apostles was more excellent than the operation of the same Spirit in us. Therefore, since the Scriptures are the infallible dictates of the Spirit in the Apostles, and are more perfect than any of our apprehensions which come by the same Spirit (which we have not in so great a measure), we must not try the Scriptures by our own spiritual apprehensions, but our own spiritual apprehensions by the Scriptures. This trying of the Spirit by the Scriptures is not to put the Scriptures above the Spirit, but is a trying of the Spirit by the Spirit, as He was manifested in the Apostles and the founders of the Church.

THE AUTHORITY OF SCRIPTURE

We see therefore that neither the Pope, nor the testimony of the Spirit in the heart of the believer, is a sufficient guide to interpret the Scriptures to men. Each Christian has a judgement of discerning, which he must exercise under the authoritative teaching of the ministers of the Church. But we may ask: If the Pope or the testimony of the Spirit in the heart of the believer are not the means of interpreting the Scriptures, are either of them then the authority which tells us that the Scriptures are the Word of God? If the Scriptures are the true and chief Word of God, then this is their authority, but how do we know that the Scriptures are the Word of God? Neither the attitude of St. Augustine, who said that he would not have believed the

[1] Orme, vol. V, p. 313.

Scriptures unless the Church had told him to do so, nor the attitude of Luther, who relied on the testimony of the Holy Spirit, satisfied Baxter. Yet he believed that the Scriptures were the infallible Word of God, and held that this could be proved without the pronouncements of the Pope or the recourse to the testimony of the Spirit. Not that he repudiated altogether the testimony of the Spirit, but he held that the purpose of the Spirit's testimony was not to convince us that the Scriptures are God's Word, but to remove our natural enmity to the truth and our prejudice against it. 'I say to affirm that the Scriptures cannot be known to be God's Word, without such a testimony of the Spirit . . . is in my judgement a justifying men in their infidelity, and a telling them that there is not extant any sufficient evidence of Scripture truth, till the Spirit create it in ourselves, and, withal, to leave it impossible to produce any evidence for the conviction of an unbeliever who cannot know the testimony of the Spirit in me.'[1] The view which he here contradicts assumes that all men who feel they believe that the Scriptures are the Word of God, have therefore the testimony of the Spirit. Yet even unregenerate men can believe in Scripture in the way that the Devil does, and yet have not a saving faith, simply because they have not allowed the Holy Spirit to illuminate their minds so that they may live out the commands of Scripture. Thus the authority of Scripture as God's Word is capable of proof by reason, and has not to be accepted merely on the authority of the Church or the special revelation of the Spirit. Before we go on to analyse Baxter's arguments to prove by reason that the Scripture is the Word of God, we must say something of this view of faith.

THE NATURE OF FAITH

Faith, he claims, is not contrary to reason, but is indeed an act of the reason,[2] or else it is a brutish act and not a human one. The strongest faith is that faith which has the strongest reasons to prove the testimony, and the truest faith is that faith which has the truest reasons, truly apprehended and used. Faith always implies a knowledge,[3] and the knowledge usually of the matter, and the author of the testimony. But although faith is an act of the reason, we must distinguish between the assent of

[1] Richard Baxter, *The Saints' Everlasting Rest* (1866), p. 131.
[2] ibid., p. 139. See note.   [3] ibid., p. 135.

the understanding to the truth of an axiom, when it is only silenced by force of argument (which will be stronger or weaker as the argument seems more or less demonstrated) and that deep apprehension and firm assent which proceeds from a well-established, confirmed faith, backed by experience. His view is that 'reason rectified is the eye of the soul, the guide of life; the illumination of the spirit is the rectifying it. No small part of our sanctification lieth in the rectifying of our reason, and thereby the will, and thereby the life. . . . Without Scripture or Divine Revelation, and the Spirit's powerful illumination reason can never be rectified in spirituals.'[1] Since faith is an act of our reason the truth of Scripture must first of all be demonstrated to our reason, and when our reason is convinced that Scripture is the Word of God, it is open to the Spirit to remove our natural enmity to the truth, and illuminate our minds and wills to apprehend and live by this truth.

BAXTER'S PROOF THAT SCRIPTURE IS THE WORD OF GOD[2]

We can now examine Baxter's arguments to prove by reason alone that Scripture is the Word of God. They are set out in *The Saints' Everlasting Rest*, and can be summarized under four heads:

1. Those writings, and that doctrine, which were confirmed by many and real miracles must needs be of God.
2. If the Scriptures are neither the invention of devils nor of men, then they must be of God.
3. Those writings which have been owned and fulfilled in several ages by apparent and extraordinary providences of God, must needs be of God.
4. Either the Scriptures are the written Word of God, or there is no such extant in the world.

1. *The Argument from Miracles*

Only God can work real miracles, for miracles imply a use of the laws of Nature in such a manner as can only be done by Him who is the author and controller of Nature. So Baxter first of all disposes of such objections as that Anti-Christ will come with lying wonders, or that God will allow false prophets to work miracles to try the world. He then faces the more serious

[1] *The Saints' Everlasting Rest* (1866), p. 139. See note.   [2] ibid., p. 145.

objection that miracles no more prove Christ to be the Son of God than they prove Moses or Elijah to be, for they worked miracles too. His view is that miracles are wrought to extol God and not the instrument which God uses to perform them. Christ's miracles did not prove Him to be the Son of God, but proved His testimony to be divine and therefore true, in which testimony was His claim to be the Son of God.

But he knows that the real assault will come, not against the interpretation of the miracles of the Bible, but against the possibility of such miracles being wrought at all. Here he takes care not to argue in a circle, proving the doctrine to be of God by the evidence of miracles, and then proving that the miracles were wrought by the divineness of the testimony. In fact, he joins hands with the modern school of historical criticism, and claims to use the testimony of Scripture as a purely historical testimony of matters of fact. He first lays down the two following propositions:

1. There is so much certainty in some human testimony, which may exclude all doubt.
2. We have such a testimony of the miracles of Scripture.

His arguments have a strangely modern ring about them, for he proceeds by analogy from the way in which we accept statements of fact, many of which we cannot verify for ourselves, on the testimony of others. Many of the things we believe, he says, we believe on purely human testimony, such as that there is a city of Paris, or a land of America, though we may never have been, or are ever likely to go to these places. But all reasonable men believe that these places exist because those they trust have testified to their existence. Similarly, we believe that Caesar or Alexander actually lived, though we could not have known them personally. Again, we trust the testimony of others. The same method is applicable to the Scriptures; we believe them because we trust those who have handed them down to us, in the same way as they trusted those who handed the Scriptures down to them, and so on right back to the Apostles. He claims that the fact that there is a certainty about some human testimony can be proved by reason. For if the first witnesses knew a fact of history infallibly, because they were eyewitnesses, and had an infallible method of transmitting that fact, or the knowledge of it, to posterity, and had no intent to deceive, then their testimony may be an infallible testimony. He then proceeds to prove the foregoing propositions, and when he has proved them he applies these rules which govern historical criticism to the facts of Scripture history, and claims that there is sufficient evidence to prove that miracles did happen and that they testify to the truth of the Divine Word.

Argument 2

In his second argument he proves that the Scriptures are the work of God, by proving that neither devils nor men could have written them, and that therefore God must have done so. He falls back first of all on the argument from miracle again. Devils, he says, could not work miracles to confirm the Scriptures, nor does it stand with God's sovereignty over them, or with His goodness, wisdom, and faithful government of the world, to allow Satan to make laws and confirm them with wonders, and obtrude them on the world, in the name of God. Or, again, it is impossible to believe that Satan would speak so much of God, or seek His glory as the Scripture does. Would he, for instance, show men their danger and direct them how to escape it? He cites Origen's statement that he many times asked Celsus, who asserted that the miracles of Scripture were no different from the wonders worked by local magicians, and therefore no evidence of the divine inspiration of Scripture, that if magicians by evil powers could work miracles, would they do them to lead men from sin and on to holiness of life? Such a method would eventually defeat the ends of Satan, and therefore the Scriptures could not be his work.

As for uninspired men, if they were the inventors of Scripture, they must have been either good men or bad men. Now, good men would obviously not have fathered a lie on the world, even to promote goodness, and if it is said that bad men wrote the Scriptures, then the same argument which served to show that Satan could not write something to defeat his own ends proves also that bad men would not do it. Indeed, it is impossible to think that men were the sole authors of Scripture from the very mixture of divine truth and human infirmity that exists therein. For the Scriptures were not written with the help of extraordinary human learning, yet the greatest philosophers could never reach to it in their own works. The very infirmity of the words testify to the fact that the truth they contain must be of God. 'The words are merely the dish to serve up the sense in; God is content that the words should not only have in them a savour of humanity, but of much infirmity, so that the work of convincing the world may be furthered thereby.'[1] Baxter's argument reminds us of Boccaccio's story of the Jew who visited Rome during one of its most immoral periods, and came back a convert to Christianity. His explanation to his friends why he had turned Christian after seeing the evil of the Papal Court, when the arguments of holy Christian men had formerly left him unmoved, was that any organization which could persist in spite of such moral depravity must be sustained by some supernatural power, the evil of Christian lives, and yet the persistence of the Christian Church had convinced him of the truth of the Christian claim to be the Church of God. So Baxter feels that since the Bible contains such sublime truths in such infirm language it must be God who indites the truths.

Argument 3

In his third argument he first lays down the proposition that those writings which have been owned and fulfilled in several ages by apparent extraordinary providences of God, must needs be of God. He then proceeds to prove that God has owned the Scriptures by such providences, by an appeal to history. He first deals with the providences that went to the propagating of the Gospel and the raising of the Church; then to the defence and the continuance of the Church, and, lastly, the improbable ways in which these have been accomplished. His argument in this section is analogous to his argument in his second proof—namely, the absurdity of supposing, on mere human reasoning, that a few ignorant men, such as were the Apostles, could have succeeded in turning the world upside-down, unless they were sustained and assisted by God's power. Despite all the obstacles of ignorance, human sin, and the natural enmity of men, the Church was raised, and persisted. He contrasts the spreading of Christ's Kingdom by love, and suffering, and reason with the spreading of earthly kingdoms by the sword.

These providences extend not only generally to the universal

[1] *The Saints' Everlasting Rest*, p. 167.

Church, but also to particular Churches and persons. Churches and Christian cities have been miraculously preserved in times of danger and trial, and there is no Christian who records faithfully the providences of God to himself who cannot show some strange and unusual mercies which testify to 'A divinity that shapes our ends, rough-hew them as we will'. The workings of God upon the souls of His people are so strange and clear, that one may trace a supernatural causality through them all, and as with individuals so with cities and civilizations which are built on God's Word. If the Scriptures were not the Word of God, there would have been as many wonders of Providence for the disgracing of it, as there have been for the defending of it. 'Can any man believe that God is the just and gracious Ruler of the World, (that is that there is a God) and yet that He would so long suffer such things to be published as his undoubted laws, and give no testimony against it, if it were not true?'[1]

Argument 4

And so we come to his fourth argument, that either the Scriptures are the written Word of God, or else there is none extant in the world. This argument is the most difficult of the four, partly because it is so involved, and partly because it rings strange on modern ears by reason of the assumptions in the proof. He says that he has two things to prove:
1. That God has such a written Word in the world.
2. That Scripture is this Word.

He claims that if he proves the first, then the second will be granted. He first of all turns the problem round to the following statement: that it is necessary for the honour of God and the welfare of man that there be some further revelation of God's will than is to be found in Nature, because if man has a happiness or misery to partake of in the life after this, and no sufficient revelation is given in Nature, then it is necessary that he has some other revelation of such a life which is sufficient. So Baxter is reduced in the end to proving that there is a future life for the soul. Since the conditions of such a life are not revealed in Nature, they must be revealed especially in Scripture. Therefore, Scripture is God's Word or revelation to man. To prove

[1] *The Saints' Everlasting Rest*, p. 176.

that there is a future life for man, he divides the proposition into three parts:
1. That there is a future state of happiness or misery for man.
2. That it is necessary he know it, and the way to be happy.
3. That Nature does not sufficiently reveal it.

He takes it for granted that there is a God, because Nature reveals Him, and passes over the arguments from God's righteousness and justice to prove the variety of man's future conditions because they are well known. He confines his argument to sense itself, because he says that works best with sensual men. His first point is that if the Devil is very diligent to deceive men of that happiness, and to bring them to that misery which he has mentioned, then there must be a happiness or misery in store for them. Anyone who doubts this must doubt the very existence of the Devil; therefore it is necessary to prove that there is such a being, and that he seeks our eternal undoing. If he can do this then he thinks that the rest will follow.

The arguments which he uses to prove the personality of the Devil have little validity to this age, which has been successfully persuaded by the father of lies that he does not really exist, but they have an antiquarian interest in that they open up to us the beliefs of one of the acutest thinkers of the seventeenth century, on a subject which even many Christians have discarded into the limbo of superstition and credulity (though the publication of Mr. C. S. Lewis's *Screwtape Letters* may possibly help to change the minds of Christian thinkers on this theme). Baxter, however, tries to prove his case with four arguments:
1. By the temptations of the Devil.
2. By the phenomena of apparitions.
3. By the phenomena of Devil possessions.
4. By Satanic contracts with witches.

'I hope', says Baxter, 'these are palpable discoveries', as if he was a little uncertain himself! His arguments drawn from the testimony of credible men seek to show that in all these manifestations Satan is concerned to draw men into sin, which itself implies that there will be a different future, as between sinners and righteous men, in the hereafter, since the difference is not always obvious in this life. This in its turn implies that there is a future state of misery or happiness for men, and this proves his point that somewhere there must be a special revelation concerning that life. Since the Scriptures claim to be this revelation and reveal the mysteries of God in such a sublime manner, then they must be the Word of God.

We have examined Baxter's arguments to prove that Scripture is the Word of God at length for two reasons. The first is that, in common with all the Reformed Churches, Baxter's final authority for Faith and morals is the Scripture, and in common with his Puritan predecessors his final authority for Church order is Scripture. We have also endeavoured to show how he interpreted this authority, and how much he was prepared to concede to tradition. The second reason is that such an examination reveals the kind of proof required by a Nonconformist of the seventeenth century to prove that the Scriptures are the Word of God, and also illustrates the difference between the attitude of a leading Nonconformist of that age and the attitude of present-day Nonconformist thinkers to a problem equally vital to both. We can compare these attitudes by a short examination of Professor C. H. Dodd's work, *The Authority of the Bible*, which deals with the same problem as that which we have been discussing in this chapter. His arguments are summarized in the last chapter of his book, in which he recapitulates his theory, and his solution to the problem of the authority of the Scriptures. Like Baxter, he starts with the axiom that authority in religion resides in the mind and the will of God, and that the authority of the Bible depends solely on whether it is the revelation of God's will. His contention is that the Bible does in fact mediate God's will, 'First through the "inspiration" of individual genius, conferring, not inerrancy, but a certain cogent persuasiveness; next through the appropriation of "inspired" ideas by a whole community, whose experience through many generations tests, confirms and revises them; and finally through the life of One in whom His followers found so decisive an answer to their needs that they hailed Him as the Wisdom of God incarnate.'[1]

In order to compare his approach with that of Baxter, there are certain presuppositions behind Professor Dodd's argument which we must bring out.

1. His argument is an 'idealistic' one, for what he is examining are the ideas of certain men, the thoughts that moved them

[1] C. H. Dodd, *Authority of the Bible* (Nisbet, 1938), p. 290.

to action, and he *assumes* without proof that these ideas have a basis in reality. The same assumption lies behind his argument in relation to our Lord. The disciples, he says, found that He answered their needs, and so they hailed Him as the Wisdom of God incarnate. But this, however, is no proof that He *was* the Wisdom of God incarnate, it is merely proof that some people *thought* that He was; it is still open to the unbeliever to use the argument, which lies at the basis of the Communist criticism of religion that, while the idea of God has certainly affected men's actions, that idea was as fallacious as the idea that the world was flat, though the actions to which it incited men may have been good. Nothing can demonstrate the authority of the Bible to men unless it can be shown that God has acted in history, the record of which is in the Bible. It is precisely here that Baxter's approach differs from that of Professor Dodd's, for he was looking for some argument which would demonstrate that it is *God's actions* that are recorded in the Scriptures, and that the Bible is not merely the record of what some people thought about a being who may or may not exist. Baxter thought that he had found the answer in miracles, for if they actually happened, then they must testify to the power of God for, by definition, it is only He who can do such things. It may be that there is nothing that can solve the 'idealist' impasse, but Baxter at least tries, and for that reason his approach is the more profound.

2. Professor Dodd is indeed conscious of this difficulty, for the question he poses, 'Granted that religious authority somehow resides in the Bible, how does it become authoritative for me?'[1] is really the same question as that which we have been discussing—namely, 'How can men come to see that the Scriptures are the record of God's actions, and not merely a record of men's thoughts about a being who may or may not exist?' Baxter solved it in the way we have described, and Professor Dodd answers it in the only way left open to him, a way we shall see Baxter rejected at the outset as unsound. Professor Dodd falls back upon what he calls the 'Subjective criterion', which he identifies as the 'Interior witness of the Holy Spirit' of Reformation theology. He recognizes too, what Baxter recognized, that his argument involves a *circulus in probando*, for 'We look to the Bible', he says, 'for guidance

[1] ibid., p. 290.

towards religious truth; we recognize this truth by reference to our own sincere religious standards', which standards have themselves been formed by the Bible.[1] Baxter's criticism of this solution is, that if it is offered as proof to all men, it assumes that all men have the testimony of the Holy Spirit to recognize it, which is obviously false. The argument may appeal to those who have that testimony, but then they don't need it, and it still leaves the others where they were, for there is no common meeting-ground. That is why Baxter relies on miracles chiefly for his proof, and not on the testimony of the Holy Spirit, for if miracles do happen, then they are demonstrable to both believers and unbelievers alike, for they are judged by the five senses and reason, which all men possess in some degree.

It is not in our province to decide whether Baxter proves his case or not, but only to show the kind of argument he uses to prove that the Scriptures are the authentic Word of God. In some respects it was more necessary for him to be certain on this point than it was for his opponents, for his whole position on the form of Church government was derived from the revelation of God in the Scriptures, whereas theirs was not. To him, of course, his own arguments were decisive, and admitted of no interpretation other than that the Scriptures were the revelation of God's will, but as we have seen he recognized that the human instruments which God used to convey His revelation were imperfect, so that the Word is hidden within the written word. Each Christian has a 'Judgement of discerning' in interpreting this Word which he must exercise under the guidance of the ministry of the Church, to whom is given the guardianship of the Scriptures. But he has no doubt that if a man uses his reason correctly and without prejudice, then he must come to see that the Scriptures are the Word of God, not only for him, but for the whole world.

[1] C. H. Dodd, *Authority of the Bible* (Nisbet, 1938), p. 297.

Chapter X

THE SACRAMENTS

NONCONFORMISTS have often been accused of underestimating the importance of the Sacraments, and sometimes of having no sacramental doctrine at all. This accusation may have arisen because of the emphasis that Nonconformity has always laid on 'conversion', and particularly in the later half of the nineteenth century and early years of the twentieth century. But whatever is the truth today, it has not always been so in Nonconformity. As we have seen in earlier chapters, one of the main causes of the dispute over Church discipline, which divided the Puritans and the Episcopal party, was the necessity of safeguarding the Sacraments. Both sides agreed that the Sacraments should not be given to certain types of people, but the crux of the discipline problem was: who had the right of judgement in the dispensing of the Sacraments—the bishops, the parish ministers, or the people, or was it the magistrate or a combination of these persons? Those who criticize the supposed Nonconformist attitude to the Sacraments usually do so because they think that Nonconformity is deficient in churchmanship, but our thesis has been that Nonconformity in its early manifestations arose out of a vigorous sense of churchmanship, and a particular view of Church government, and that this is equally true of Baxter. In this chapter we propose to examine whether Baxter had any views on the Sacraments, and if so, what was his doctrine of the Sacraments?

We have already noted certain incidents which give us an indication of his attitude to this question in the preceding chapters. We have seen in the summary of his life that he refused the Sacrament of Holy Communion to Sir Ralph Clare when the latter asked for it to be given to him on a certain day, and that he should receive it kneeling. We have observed that Baxter did not refuse it to him because of these requests, but because Sir Ralph would not accept it on Baxter's terms— namely, that he should live under discipline. It was Sir Ralph and not Baxter who was deficient in churchmanship, for he wanted to treat with the Christ in the Sacrament on his own, whereas Baxter insisted that he should treat with Christ in the fellowship of Christ's Body, and accept the discipline necessary to keep that Body clean and wholesome. This incident gives us our first clue to Baxter's attitude, for just as he was no Latitudinarian as regards the form of Church government, so he was no Latitudinarian as regards the Sacraments. The Sacraments were precious and not to be cast before the unregenerate or the unrepentant. This attitude of his is apparent, not only with regard to Holy Communion, but is equally apparent in his view of Baptism. He would not baptize indiscriminately even when he had the rubrics of the Church to support him, for, to his mind, to baptize all who came without due regard to the circumstances made a mock of a solemn and holy rite. Again, we have pointed out above that his reason for founding the Worcestershire Association was not merely to obtain discipline in the Church for the sake of discipline, but that the Sacraments might be rightly and duly administered, and the Sacraments could not be administered properly unless there was a Church discipline to distinguish between those who did strive to live holy lives and those who did not. We see also this 'firmness' of his toward the administration of the Sacraments in his analysis of the duties of congregations to their ministers. He points out that congregations must receive the Body and Blood of Christ from the hands of their regular pastors, and that not as an optional act, which might or might not be done according to the predilections of individual members, but as an obligation on all Christians, that they might, to use the old Puritan phrase, 'Improve their Baptism'. These examples are sufficient to point out to us that Baxter had very definite views on the importance and place of the Sacraments in the life of the Church.

HOW MANY SACRAMENTS ARE THERE?

We ought therefore to discover, first of all, how many Sacraments Baxter admitted before we go on to analyse his doctrine, and we can find his view fully explained in *Christian Ecclesiastics*, Part 3, Question 99. There he defines what he means by a Sacrament, and says that his use of the term is not as large as the Latin interpreter who translates it as 'Mystery'. A Sacrament is, he says, 'A solemn dedication of man to God by a vow expressed by some sacred ceremony signifying mutually our covenant to God, and God's reception of us, and his covenant with us'.[1] He points out that the name was brought into the Church from the Roman military oath, in which the soldier swears fidelity to Caesar, renouncing father and mother for his service, and he quotes as his authority for this Tertullian's work, *The Soldier's Crown*. The word itself is not a Scripture word, and therefore is not necessary for the faith or peace of the Church, but it is taken from the covenant sworn to, or from the sign, or ceremony of consent, or from both together. Any solemn renewal of a sacred vow or covenant is a 'Sacrament', so that civil, economical, and ecclesiastical offices, having their vows and covenants, have also their appropriate and distinct Sacraments. But the renewing of a vow without any instituted sign is to be distinguished from the renewing of a vow by such a sign as God Himself instituted.

Thus there are as many Sacraments as covenants, but as there is *in specie* but one covenant of Christianity, so there is only one Sacrament variously expressed, that is, if we take the word Sacrament to mean the nobler part of the covenant vow—namely, the covenant itself. This is, strictly speaking, an improper use of the term. If the term is taken properly from the covenant sworn to and the ceremony of consent, then there are two Christian Sacraments, the Sacrament of Baptism, or initiation, and the Sacrament of the Lord's Supper, or of confirmation, exercise, and progress. These signs or ceremonies are of divine institution. But if the word is taken less properly for the same covenant of grace renewed by any arbitrary sign of our own, then there are as many Sacraments as there are solemn renewals of our covenant with God. These later sacraments are observed—

1. When an infant-member of the Church proceeds to adult membership, in the ceremony called by Calvin and some Protestants, Confirmation.
2. When we solemnly own our Christian faith, as when we stand to say the Creed.
3. At solemn fasts, or days of humiliation.
4. Upon the public repentance of some particular sinner and his absolution.
5. When a man is going out of the world and commends his soul to God by Christ.

[1] Orme, vol. V, p. 449.

These Sacraments are improperly so called, being divine as to the covenant renewed, but human as to the expressing sign.

The basis of his sacramental doctrine is that there is one covenant of Grace, inaugurated by Christ and sealed by His sacrificial death. The lives of men are touched at various points by this grace, so that in a sense we can say that all life is sacramental when lived 'In Christ'. Two of these points are of supreme importance, the first when a person enters into Christ by baptism, and the second when his interior life is fed by Christ's sacramental Body and Blood. These ceremonies are of divine institution and obligatory on all Christians. There are other times when this covenant is consciously renewed, and these moments may be called sacramental, though the sign or ceremony is arbitrary. Other occasions too have their sacramental significance. Thus ordination is not improperly called a sacrament, for it is a solemnizing of a mutual covenant between God and man, setting the man aside for a special service. It is also of divine institution, though the laying on of hands is not so solemn a ceremony, by mere institution, as Baptism or the Lord's Supper, for these owe their origin to Christ Himself. Ordination therefore is not a Sacrament of the Christian covenant, but a sacrament of orders, or of a particular office. Marriage too is an economical Sacrament, which may be expressed arbitrarily by lawful signs or ceremonies. So the inauguration of a king is a civil sacrament in the same manner as when a judge enters into his office, when it is done solemnly by an obliging vow or covenant.

The foregoing may seem to suggest that Baxter comes very near to the Roman Catholic view as to the number of Sacraments he admits, but he is careful to guard against any misinterpretation of his position by giving his objections against the Papist view. The Roman Catholic Sacrament of Confirmation, where it is claimed that the Holy Ghost is conferred upon infants, he says is an unwarrantable imitation of the old miraculous operation by the Apostles, and is neither a Christian Sacrament nor a warrantable practice, but a presumption, and the same may be said of their Sacrament of Extreme Unction. Their Sacrament of marriage is no more a Sacrament than the inauguration of a king is, which is as much approved by God as marriage, and signifies also an honourable collation of power from the universal King. Their Sacrament of Penance, too, is only a Sacrament in the sense in which any renewing of our covenant vow is a Sacrament. So the Roman Catholic seven Sacraments are confused, partly redundant, partly defective, and unworthy to be made a part of their faith or religion.[1] On the other hand, he rebuked those people, particularly the Separatists' sects, who said that there were only two Sacraments, without distinguishing the nature of the Sacraments. They, he thought, were too concerned to justify their position in opposition to the Roman Catholics, rather than because they had examined the meaning of the Sacraments and found that there were only two strictly so called. Having seen what Baxter's definition of a Sacrament is, and how many he admits, we now propose to analyse his doctrine of the two which he considers the most important, the Sacraments of Baptism and the Lord's Supper.

THE SACRAMENT OF BAPTISM

To understand Baxter's doctrine of the Sacraments we must understand the importance he attaches to the conception of a covenant between God and man. God has promised in His infinite mercy to enter into covenant with man to save him from sin, death, and Hell. This covenant is revealed, ratified, sealed, and offered in Christ's life, death, and Resurrection. By this covenant God has promised to pardon, justify, adopt, and glorify them that believe in Christ. It is an agreement made between two persons: God in His condescending mercy, in that the Creator should so treat with His own creature, over whom He possesses the power of life and death, and man in his sinful, yet believing nature. It is not a covenant between two equal or even similar beings, but is expressive of that grace which manifested itself in Him who 'Laid His glory by, and wrapped Him in our clay'. The knowledge of this agreement freely offered by God results in two dispositions in the believing soul. The first is that evangelical piety which acknowledges its salvation through the Blood of Christ, and the second is the knowledge that sinful, impotent man has been raised to a position of responsibility, in that he too has a condition to perform by the aid of God's grace. To Baxter, Baptism is the outward seal of this covenant, and is the outward mark of the Christian. Therefore to baptize a human soul is to confer upon that soul

[1] Orme, vol. V, p. 452.

a legal right to the benefits of the covenant.[1] It is a rite instituted by Christ, recognized by God, and incorporates the soul into the universal Church which is the Body of Christ.

Baptism does not confer grace or infuse grace into the soul, *ex opere operato*, because it is what he calls a moral instrument, and not a physical one, by which we see that he did not believe in Baptismal Regeneration.[2] 'We must distinguish', he says, 'betwixt a Donation Physical which works the said Physical Effects (as when you put money into a man's hand), and a Donation Moral which gives not any Real Physical being immediately, directly of itself; but only so gives a Right to such a Being or Good, as you give away your house or Lands by a word, or by a written Deed of Gift, without moving the thing itself.'[3] Baptism therefore confers a status and not a state, a status in which the baptized is entitled to God's grace, and not a state of grace *per se*. After Baptism the person has to enter into possession of the grace to which Baptism has entitled him, or, to use the traditional Puritan phrase, he must 'Improve his Baptism'. He discusses the whole question in his criticism of a pamphlet written by Mr. T. H. Bedford on *Baptismal Regeneration*, from which we have quoted. Mr. Bedford held that Baptism conferred and effected the grace of regeneration of nature on the baptized person. The Sacrament gives a seed of grace out of which future acts of grace and holiness, 'watered by the Word and good education', may in time spring forth.

The Anabaptists, on the other hand, believed that Baptism presupposed faith on the part of the baptized, and so they refused to baptize until adult life, when the recipient could give proof of that faith. Baxter in his early years inclined to the Anabaptists' view, but, partly through the study of Scripture, and partly through his controversy with Mr. Tombes on Baptism, he came to believe in the practice of infant Baptism. We can see, therefore, that he was faced with the paradox of believing in infant Baptism, and yet feeling that Baptism presupposed faith. He recognized that infants at the time of their Baptism could not fulfil any condition whatsoever, whether the condition

---

[1] Richard Baxter, *Animadversions* (Appendix to *Plain Scripture Proof*, 1653 Edition), p. 298.

[2] Richard Baxter, *Certain Disputations of Right to Sacraments, etc.* (1658 Edition), p. 118.

[3] Richard Baxter, *Animadversions* (Appendix to *Plain Scripture Proof*, 1653 Edition), p. 295.

was that of faith, or whether it was a promise to improve their Baptism by the right use of the means of grace, and while it is no problem to those who believe that regeneration, and faith itself, are conferred in Baptism, it was a problem to Baxter. He falls back, therefore, on the doctrine that the seed of believers are in the same covenant as their parents, because the covenant in the Old Testament was given to Abraham and to his seed for ever. Infants are in covenant or agreement with their parents, because their parents' wills are theirs, to dispose of them for their own good, 'and therefore they consent by their parents who consent for them'.[1] We can see now why he could not baptize indiscriminately, but only the children of believers. There must be consent to the terms of the baptismal covenant, and since infants cannot consent, the only people who can do so on their behalf are their parents. To baptize indiscriminately is quite logical for those who believe in baptismal regeneration, and that logical Jesuit, St. Francis Xavier, did so in India, where he baptized all and sundry, even in masses altogether, and without any instruction. But whatever their doctrinal views, no Church does this today; the parents are expected to be present, though those Churches which have a 'Catholic' tradition insist on the presence of Godparents who in some sense take the place of parents. Nor does the actual doctrine of the operation of baptismal grace seem to matter a great deal, for even Mr. Bedford conceded that the efficacy of Baptism depended on the watering of the seed of grace by the 'Word and good Education'.[2] And since no one knows by any human means, nor is it revealed in Scripture, whether a seed of grace is given in Baptism, or whether, as Baxter believed, a legal right to the covenanted mercies, it would appear that the same results are obtained *in foro coeli* by the Sacrament of Baptism, though the theories do vary!

But there is one point which we must mention, in which Baxter did differ from most of his contemporaries, and from the general tradition of the Christian Church. He could not agree that Baptism by a layman was valid in cases of necessity, although most Churches admit it in theory, if not in practice. His argument against it was that God had made the Sacrament of Baptism a part of the work of the ministerial office; cf. Matthew xxviii. 19, 20. Nowhere, says Baxter, has God commanded or

[1] Orme, vol. V, p. 334.
[2] Richard Baxter, *Animadversions* (Appendix to *Plain Scripture Proof*, 1653 Edition), p. 294.

obliged anyone else to do it, or promised to bless their action if they did. On the contrary, He has often punished people who invaded the ministerial office without any right; therefore the usurpation of the work of that office by a person unqualified is a sin, and therefore there can be no question of necessity in a case that causes anyone to sin. Anyone who is in covenant by open profession needs nothing else for his salvation, where it cannot be had in a lawful manner. This applies not only to believers, but also to their children, who in his mind are the only children entitled to the Sacrament. He took the same attitude here as he took of ordination, both Sacraments are in their own way the outward seals of a covenant relation, and the relationship is still there even if it cannot be sealed in the outward form of the Sacrament, but as in ordination, Baxter thought it was a sin to refuse this 'badge of Christian Status' when it might lawfully be had.

However, he did go a little farther in his doctrine of the Sacrament of Baptism than has been outlined above, for he says: 'Baptism is both a Seal of the proper Conditional Covenant of Grace, *and a means of conveying the good therein promised, according to the capacity of the subject.*'[1] Or again: 'Baptism is a means of increasing inward Grace, and so making a Real Change upon the souls of those that have Faith and the use of Reason.' This is so because all believers and their children do, in Baptism, receive, through God's promise, a *jus relationis*, a right of peculiar relation to all three Persons in the Blessed Trinity: to God as their real, adopted father; to Jesus Christ as their Redeemer, and actual Head and Justifier; and to the Holy Ghost as their Regenerator and Sanctifier. This right and relation adheres to them, and is given them in order to factual, actual, operation and communion. Just as the marriage covenant gives the relation and right to one another, in order to the subsequent communion and duties of the married life, Baptism is an engagement between two persons which needs consummating, as it were, to make it efficacious. Now as these rights and relations are given immediately, so those benefits which are relative, and of which the infant is immediately capable, are given by way of communion. In this way infants (as well as adults) have pardon of original sin, by virtue of the sacrifice, merit, and intercession of Christ, they receive a state of adoption, a right

[1] *Animadversions*, p. 297. (Italics mine.)

THE SACRAMENTS

to divine protection and Church communion according to their natural capacity, and a right to everlasting life.[1] Thus we may say that Baxter held that Baptism essentially confers a right to the covenanted mercies of God on the recipient, but that as a means of grace, it conveys the grace of God to the soul in the capacity in which that soul can receive it.

THE SACRAMENT OF THE LORD'S SUPPER

As Baptism is the Sacrament of initiation into the Body of Christ, so the Lord's Supper is the Sacrament of confirmation and growth in grace. They are the same benefits that are conferred in the Lord's Supper as are conferred in Baptism, for 'Baptism uniteth to Christ and giveth us Himself first, and with Himself the pardon of all our past sins, etc. The Lord's Supper by confirmation giveth us the same things: it is the giving of Christ Himself, who saith by His minister, *take, eat, drink*; offering himself to us under the signs and commanding us to take himself by faith, as we take the signs by the outward parts: He giveth us the pardon of sin, sealed, as procured by his body broken and blood shed.'[2] The ends to which Christ instituted this Sacrament he sums up under five heads.

It was instituted to be:

1. A solemn commemoration of the death and Passion of Jesus Christ, to keep His death in the eye of the Church until He comes.
2. A renewing of the holy covenant which was entered in Baptism between Christ and the receiver.
3. A lively objective means by which the Spirit of Christ should work to stir up, exercise, and increase the repentance, faith, desire, love, hope, joy, thankfulness, and new obedience of believers.
4. A profession of believers in their faith and obedience to God, and a badge of the Church before the world.
5. A sign and means of unity, love and communion of saints, and their readiness to communicate to each other.

THE MEANING OF THE SACRAMENT

While the purposes of the Sacrament are those outlined above, the rite itself, he says, contains three parts.

[1] Orme, vol. V, p. 347.
[2] Richard Baxter, *Certain Disputations of Right to Sacraments* (1658 Edition), p. 119.

1. *The Consecration*

In the consecration the Church first offers the creatures of Bread and Wine to be accepted by God to this sacred use, and God signifies His acceptance of the elements and His blessing of them, in the words of His own institution, and by the action of His ministers and their blessing, for they are the agents of God to the people, and the agents of the people to God. In this consecration, the Church acknowledges God to be the Creator and Governor of all creatures, the righteous lawgiver who requires satisfaction, and has received the sacrifice and atonement of Christ, and, lastly, that He is our Father and Benefactor who has given us a Redeemer. As Christ was incarnate and true Christ before He was sacrificed to God, and was sacrificed before that sacrifice was communicated for the life and nourishment of souls, so in the Sacrament the consecration must first make the creatures to be the representative flesh and blood of Christ, then the sacrifice of that flesh and blood must be represented and commemorated and lastly the sacrificed flesh and blood communicated to the receivers for their spiritual nourishment.

2. *The Commemoration*

The commemoration chiefly respects God the Son as the consecration does God the Father, 'for Christ has ordained that these consecrated representations should in their manner and measure supply the room of His bodily presence while His body is in Heaven: and that as it were in effigy, in representation, he might still be crucified before the Church's eyes; and that they might be affected, as if they had seen Him on the Cross. And that by faith and prayer, they might as it were, offer Him up to God, that it might shew the Father that sacrifice, once made for sins, in which they trust.'[1]

3. *The Communication*

In the communication the Sacrament has special reference to the Holy Ghost, as being that Spirit given in the flesh and blood that quickens souls, and whose operations convey and apply Christ's saving mercies to us.

The thing signified in the Sacrament is the crucifying and sacrificing of Christ, who also gives Himself with His benefits to

[1] Orme, vol. IV, p. 316.

the believer. But here again we note that the grace of God given in this Sacrament is not given *ex opere operato*. Christ's benefits are given to the believer and only the believer can benefit from them. Thus the Sacrament is not a 'Converting ordinance',[1] for God did not command ministers to give it to infidels to convert them to Christianity. Indeed, He requires us to give it to none that profess not a true saving faith and repentance. But there is much in the nature of this Sacrament which might tend to the converting of hypocrites, Baxter thinks, for the minister must give the Sacrament to all who profess faith and repentance, even if he suspects that such a profession is only hypocrisy; in such a case, maybe, the Sacrament will convert, but if it does it is merely a secondary or accidental use of the rite. Baxter differs here from the view of John Wesley as he expounded it a century later, for Wesley held that the Sacrament is a converting ordinance. It was Wesley's experience that many of his converts had been converted at the Sacrament,[2] and although he knew that many held that the Sacrament was a confirming and not a converting ordinance, he taught that it could convey to men preventing, justifying, or sanctifying grace according to their several necessities. The only thing required at the time of communicating was not fitness, but a desire to receive whatever Christ pleased to give, and a sense of one's utter sinfulness and helplessness.[3] The distinction between Wesley and Baxter seems to be without much difference, for all that Baxter requires is faith and repentance, and anyone who comes with a desire to receive what Christ pleases to give surely must be in a state of repentance, and must have some faith; the very fact that such a person comes to the Sacrament at all implies that there is a predisposition to Christ on his part.

One more thing we may mention in connexion with Baxter's view of the Lord's Supper, and that is that he considered that it was meant to be a sign of the unity of the Church. This is the fifth head under which he sums up the uses of the Sacrament. As we have shown in the chapter on the Universal Church, Baxter was greatly concerned about the unity of the Church, and this Sacrament was to him peculiarly the Sacrament of its

[1] Orme, vol. V, p. 446.
[2] *Journal of John Wesley* (Standard Edition, Epworth Press), vol. II, p. 361, 27th June 1940.
[3] Letter to Dr. Gibson (Bishop of London), 11th June 1747; *Letters of John Wesley* (Standard Edition, Epworth Press), vol. II, p. 282.

unity, yet it was there more than anywhere else that the centre of controversy lay between the various parties. It was bound up in his day, as in ours, with different conceptions of Church order or government, but even so he felt that the differences about this Sacrament, which so divided and separated Christians, were to a large extent the result of prejudice and pride, not to mention ignorance. When answering the question whether a man could, with a good conscience, receive the Sacrament according to the Book of Common Prayer, he is moved 'to tell the people of God, in the bitter sorrow of my soul, that at last it is time for them to discern that temptation, that hath in all ages of the Church almost, made this Sacrament of our union, to be the grand instrument of our divisions'.[1] He feels that among Christians of all sides the manner of their worship is 'not so odious as prejudice and faction and partiality representeth it', and that God accepted what they rejected.[2] So wonderful a thing is prejudice, he says, that every party is brought by it to account that ridiculous and vile which the other party counts best. So one of the aims of the Worcestershire Association was to overcome these prejudices and evolve a system of Church discipline acceptable to Separatists, Presbyterians, and moderate Episcopalians alike, so that the Lord's Supper might be administered in the parishes and testify to the unity of the Church. This laudable aim perished with the death of Cromwell and the return of Charles II. Cromwell, who assumed dictatorial powers, despite his aversion to autocracy chiefly to preserve religious freedom, had he lived, might have contributed, by this very freedom, to a united Church of England, after the model which Baxter desired. And though Baxter disliked Cromwell personally, his admission that there was more freedom for religion under the Protectorate than was enjoyed either before or after emphasizes the thought that in later life he looked back upon the period of Cromwell's Protectorate as a time of opportunity for Church unity, which the turn of events seemed to have destroyed for ever.

BAXTER'S VIEW OF TRANSUBSTANTIATION

We cannot leave this discussion of Baxter's doctrine of the Sacraments without outlining, at least, his attitude to the Roman Catholic doctrine of Transubstantiation. As a convinced

[1] Orme, vol. IV, p. 332.   [2] ibid.

Protestant, though much more lenient to the Papists than most of his contemporaries, he rejected the Roman Catholic claim that at the consecration of the bread and wine in the Sacrament there was a physical change of the whole substance of the bread and wine into the natural Body and Blood of Christ. His main objection to the Roman Catholic position was that it was based on a philosophical contradiction, and that therefore it was impossible. He divides the controversy with them into two parts:

1. Whether after consecration there is no longer Bread or Wine?
2. Whether that which was bread and wine is turned into the real Flesh and Blood of Christ?

His contention is that if the Papists are right, then there should be no bread or wine after the consecration,[1] but only the Flesh and Blood of Christ. Why he maintains this will be explained later. However, our senses tell us that the elements are still bread and wine, and not only that, but Scripture also calls the elements bread and wine after the consecration. Now, he contends, we must trust our senses before we do anything else, for if we cannot trust our senses we can never get anywhere, we cannot believe that there is a Gospel, or that there were Apostles, or even that there is a Pope, or man, or anything. The Roman Catholics explain the fact that our senses testify to bread and wine after the consecration on the philosophical supposition that the 'Substance' of the bread and wine is changed into the human Body and Blood of our Lord, but that the 'Accidents' of the elements remain as before, the accidents being the colour, shape, taste, etc., of the elements, so that while our senses testify to the fact of bread and wine, they only really testify to the 'Accidents', the 'Substance' is hidden from them and can be changed without the senses recording the change. Baxter contends that this is a contradiction, and therefore impossible either for God or man to perform. It is impossible for God to contradict Himself, he maintains. He cannot hate goodness, love sin, or make any contradiction true,[2] and it is a contradiction to say that there can be accidents of no particular substance,[3] for though, if the substance remains the same, certain

[1] ibid., p. 313.
[2] Richard Baxter, *Roman Tradition Examined, etc.* (1676), p. 6.   [3] ibid., p. 8.

accidents belonging to it may vary, i.e. a round bit of wood may be cut into a square, the substance remaining the same, but the accident 'roundness' changed into the accident 'squareness', it is impossible to change the substance and yet keep the accidents the same. For every substance is capable of accidents appropriate to itself, it is not capable of accidents appropriate to another substance, though some of the accidents may be appropriate to both. Thus if a substance is changed, then the accidents appropriate to itself only must change with it. To separate substance and accidents means the destruction of the whole. Thus if the philosophy of substance and accidents has any relation to reality at all, which is doubtful, the foregoing conclusions are in the nature of axioms and unvariable. Even God cannot alter them, for by definition He cannot make contradictions true. Therefore if the substance of the bread and wine are changed into the real human Body and Blood of Christ, then the accidents must change also into those appropriate to the human Body and Blood of Christ. Baxter takes up the same position with regard to this problem as he took up when he denied that Christ's own righteousness could be imparted to the believer by faith. Christ's own righteousness was an 'accident' (in the philosophical sense) pertaining to Himself, and inseparable from Him, for to separate substance from any accident appropriate only to itself is to destroy the whole. We can now see why he makes the basis of his attack on this doctrine the question whether there is no longer bread and wine after the consecration, for after the consecration there is either the substance and accidents of bread and wine, or the substance and accidents of the Body and Blood of Christ. There cannot be both, nor a mixture of both, and since the fact that only bread and wine are patent to the senses after consecration is undeniable, this is sufficient proof that the change, as the Roman Catholics explained it, had not taken place. In other words, if Christ is present in the Sacrament under the forms of bread and wine, He cannot be present there in His natural human body.

This is further proved for Baxter by the fact that Christ has no natural human body now. The Scriptures testify that the Body of Christ is in Heaven. Nor is it His natural body which is in Heaven, but His natural body changed and glorified, for flesh and blood cannot inherit the Kingdom of God. When Roman Catholics teach the doctrine of Transubstantiation, he says that they thereby testify to their belief that Christ has two bodies, a glorified one in Heaven and a natural one into which the substance of the bread and wine is changed. This is not only contrary to the teaching of Scripture, but is absurd.[1] But if they say that the substance of the elements are changed into the substance of Christ's glorified Body, as apparently some did say in the controversy with Baxter, then, says Baxter, how can it be a sacrifice which is offered in the Mass? For Christ's glorified Body is impassable, immortal, and incorruptible, and can neither suffer nor be slain. Thus we can understand why it seemed obvious to Baxter that Christ spoke to His disciples of His representative Body and Blood, especially as His natural body had at that time neither been broken nor slain. Nor did it seem reasonable to him to suppose that the disciples believed at the Last Supper that they were eating Christ's real Flesh and Blood, when He Himself was there before them.

In order to answer such arguments as Baxter put forward, the Roman Catholics explained that the change in the elements was the result of a miracle, and they drew a parallel between this and the Incarnation of our Lord to justify its possibility. Baxter then claims that a miracle is not contradictory to well-qualified sense, though it is above sense and reason. There is nothing, he says, in Christ's birth which is contrary to sense, for it is as possible for God to impregnate a Virgin as it was for Him to make Eve. Nor is it contrary to sense for God to take a human nature into union with the divine nature. Nor is the doctrine of the Trinity contrary to reason, though it is beyond its scope to discover such a doctrine unaided by revelation. But to create one body which has all the accidents of another body, and none of its own appropriate accidents, is contrary to sense, unless the accidents themselves are not real, but only apparently so, in which case God would be deceiving our senses and telling a lie, a thing He is incapable of doing. He does not say that God could not do this, but questions whether He would do it. Is it consistent, he asks, with God's holy nature to represent a thing to be other than what it is? He reiterated that it is not consistent with God's goodness to do such a thing, for the objection he makes to the Roman Catholic claim is not, 'Why does not God show us this miracle to our sense?' but 'Whether God deceive all our Senses and Intellect, which there perceive Bread

[1] *R.T.E.*, p. 7.

and Wine when there is none'.[1] It is not whether Sense perceive Christ, but whether Sense perceive Bread and Wine? It is not whether 'Sense do *privately not perceive*; but whether it here do *positively erre*, and the first *Intellective* perception of the Sensate Object be an Errour'.

We have now concluded our analysis of Baxter's doctrine of the Church, and have seen what he understood to be the nature of the Church itself, the ministry, the Word, and the Sacraments. Sufficient has been said to show that Baxter had a profound and decided belief in the Church as the Body of Christ, and that his Nonconformity arose from his doctrine of the Church.

[1] *R.T.E.*, p. 65.

Chapter XI

BAXTER AND THE HIERARCHICAL CONCEPTION

THE HIERARCHICAL PRINCIPLE

MR. C. S. LEWIS, in his book, *A Preface to Paradise Lost*, has a very interesting chapter on the hierarchical conception which underlies Milton's poem. He emphasizes the fact that this idea is not peculiar to Milton, but belongs to the ancient orthodox tradition of European ethics from Aristotle to Johnson, and a failure to understand this principle, he says, entails a false criticism of nearly all Christian literature before the Revolutionary period, and to prove his point he draws illustrations from Donne and Shakespeare, and shows how this principle is consistent with Milton's aristocratic republicanism in politics.

The conception, he says, is derived from Aristotle, who maintains that to rule and to be ruled are things according to nature, for 'The soul is the natural ruler of the body, the male of the female, reason of passion'.[1] All things except God have their natural superiors, and all things except matter have their natural inferiors,[2] so that there is a gradation of power running through the creation, and those who possess the right to rule possess it, not by the will of man but by a natural right which is to be traced to the will of God. Now, this conception underlies Baxter's thought also. According to his view, in family life the man is the natural ruler of the woman, the parents of the children and servants; in civil life the king is the natural ruler of the people, who are bound to obey him as the chief magistrate, and his properly appointed officers, the magistrates of town and borough, whose power is not given to them by the people, but is derived from the king; while in ecclesiastical life all are bound to obey Christ the King and his officers, the ministers, in their proper sphere. A good deal of Baxter's casuistical writings are taken up with the examination and elucidation of particular examples of this relationship, such as the relation of husbands to wives, ministers to their congregations, magistrates to the people, and vice versa.

[1] C. S. Lewis, *A Preface to Paradise Lost* (Oxford University Press, 1942), pp. 72, 73.
[2] ibid.

When we recapitulate the matter of the chapters on the Church and ministry, we can see that this principle underlies Baxter's conception of Church order too, for the Church is the universality of all baptized, unexcommunicated Christians, headed by Jesus Christ, and localized in particular Churches headed by their pastors. In both these bodies, the whole and the part, there are those who rule and those who are ruled, or, as Baxter calls them, the *Pars Gubernans* and the *Pars Gubernata*, and as the universal Church is defined by the relative union between Christ and His flock, so particular Churches are defined by the relative union of the minister and his people, for where there is no minister there is no particular Church. An interesting parallel to this conception of hierarchy has been revealed by the recent death of the Speaker of the House of Commons while the House was still sitting. It was pointed out that without a properly appointed Speaker, Parliament was no longer Parliament, but merely a company of gentlemen. Without a Speaker, Parliament could not make laws, its function was destroyed, and to become a law-making body it had to have a Speaker. In fact, Parliament can be defined as the relative union of Speaker and Members. This conception is the exact analogy of Baxter's conception of the Church, whether in its universal or its particular aspect. The Church, he says, is not an amorphous company of Christians, but a 'Political Society', with its two sections: the ministry, who because of their office have the function of ruling and guiding the congregation, and the congregation, who must obey the ministers in things spiritual. We can say that Baxter was a convinced 'Clerical', even to the extent of confining to the ministry certain functions which the general orthodox tradition of the Church allowed in certain circumstances to be performed by the laity.

In Baxter's thought this hierarchical principle could be elaborated by the appointment of lay elders, who, though their office was not of divine institution, had an 'Ecclesiastical' function. They could help the ministry in its rule over and guidance of the congregation, by representing the people on the one hand, and on the other hand by giving a greater weight of authority to the decisions of the ministry. To Baxter, lay elders were not of the *Esse* of the Church, but might be of the *Bene Esse* in certain circumstances. He organized his own church in Kidderminster along these lines, and provision for the appointment of lay elders was made in the constitution of the Worcestershire Association, though their exact status was not defined.

The instrument by which the hierarchical conception functions is 'Discipline', for there can be no order, which is the essence of hierarchy, without discipline, and the corollary to discipline is obedience, for there can be no discipline without obedience. Therefore Baxter is insistent that in family matters the wife should obey her husband, the children their parents, and servants their masters; in political matters, the people must obey their properly appointed magistrates; and in Church matters the people must obey their pastors. This obedience is not, however, servile, but rational, as, for instance, he explains when discussing the duties of congregations to the pastors, and it will be rational only when this conception of hierarchy is recognized as essential for the welfare of families, communities, and the salvation of souls. Where it is not recognized, then there is either revolt or servility, neither of which is good. It is for this reason that Baxter was disconcerted at the outbreak of civil war; he could not blame Parliament altogether for the war, for much of his sympathies lay with them, nor could he altogether blame the King, for he believed in kingship; finally, he threw the blame upon those who divided the King and Parliament,[1] upon those, in other words, who destroyed the smooth working of the principle of hierarchy. Again, without discipline there could be no order in the Church, for without order the hierarchical principle is destroyed, and without the hierarchical principle there could be no 'Political Society'—in other words, no Churches. Therefore he opposed anything which seemed to him to destroy or impair the working of true discipline.

The spiritual outcome of true discipline in the Church is holiness, for holiness is itself a kind of order in the spiritual sphere, because it is the right ordering of men's lives in relation to God and to their fellow men. The Church is in its essence holy, and that holiness should be visible and apparent to the world. The right exercise of discipline is to separate the holy from the unholy, so that those who are holy can receive the benefits of churchmanship, and those who are unholy can be brought, if possible, to repentance and restoration. Baxter, in common with all orthodox Christian thought, held that the Church was both visible and invisible, the invisible Church

[1] *Autobiography* (Everyman, 1931), p. 37.

being made up of sincere heart-covenanters, as he calls them, and the visible Church being made up of the universality of baptized, unexcommunicated Christians. So far he was in agreement with Augustine, who held that the invisible Church was known only to God, as it was God alone who knew the number of the elect. Strictly speaking, Augustine, believing in predestination, has no logical place for the Church, as a soteriological community at all, and Holl says that he never succeeded in relating the visible and invisible Churches. One of the chief reasons for his conversion was the majesty and catholicity of the Church, but afterwards he took the Church for granted, and the paradox of believing in the Church, outside of which there was no salvation, when salvation did not depend on churchmanship, but on the fiat of God, does not seem to have crossed his mind. At any rate, Baxter was not confronted with this difficulty, for while he believed that God elected some to salvation as an extra grace as it were, he also believed that salvation was open to all that believed in Christ. So that while there seems to be no logical place for the Church in Augustine's thought, except perhaps as a worshipping community, and a place for the preservation of Christian morals, Baxter leaves the door open to those who would be saved. Thus there is a real place for the visible Church in his thought, and it is the exercise of discipline which serves, as far as it is possible in a human sinful world, to preserve the purity of that Church.

BAXTER AND LUTHERANISM

Baxter owed very little to Luther directly. He rarely quotes him, and when he does it is only as a general example of one of the Reformers. In so far as Luther's ideas had penetrated into the thought of the Church of England, then Baxter inherited some of this thought. However, Luther's ideas were not very active in England, for most of the Reformers, at least from Elizabeth's day, were under the influence of Calvin, and looked for their inspiration to Geneva, though Cranmer, in his doctrine of the Sacraments and in his work enshrined in the Prayer Book, owed a great deal to Luther. Calvinism also was the predominant spiritual atmosphere of the Church of England until the ascendancy of the Laudian divines, who tended to follow Arminius, but as the Lutheran Church was a Reformed Church and the Church of England was a Reformed Church, anyone brought up in the Church of England, and faithful to its principles (as Baxter always claimed to be), must owe something to the great Reformer.

Baxter would have agreed with Luther that it is the Word of God which creates the Church, and when Luther says that it is the Word of God which divides mankind into those who hear and obey and those who hear and do not obey, and that those who hear and obey belong to the Church, again Baxter would have agreed with him. Luther and Baxter saw a distinction between the indifferent masses and genuine Christians, but whereas Luther confined the Lord's Supper to genuine Christians, but allowed Baptism to every child in the community,[1] we know that Baxter confined both Sacraments to true Christians and their children. According to McGiffert, Luther thought that the Church existed for the sake of the world, and not for the sake of its own members, and its mission was to preach the Gospel to the world.[2] Baxter would have said that the Church existed for the sake of God, and that while one of its main duties was to preach the Word to unbelievers, its chief purpose was to fit itself for the presence of God. Baxter, although he was a Puritan, is in a sense more 'Catholic' than Luther; his emphasis is on the other world rather than on this world.

It is often said that Luther was not a great ecclesiastical statesman, and it is true that the arrangements he made for the Church seem rather haphazard; possibly this is due to the fact that Luther was not consistent in his thinking, for while he believed thoroughly in the hierarchical principle in civil life, his theory of the priesthood of all believers strictly precludes hierarchy in the Church. Luther found that his Church theory did not work, and more and more he was driven to rely on the State to support him. Starting from the priesthood of all believers, the logical expression of his Church theory should have been a form of Quakerism, or at least Congregationalism— that is to say, the formation of a series of autonomous 'Fellowships'. But he also wanted a Church that embraced all, and in the conflict between these two ideas he was forced to rely finally on the civil authorities to get the reformation he wanted.

Of course, his problems were very different from Baxter's. He was confronted with the need of defining the Church which

[1] McGiffert, *Martin Luther* (Fisher Unwin, 1911), p. 313.   [2] ibid.

had become corporealized by the preaching of the Word, into an actual fellowship, so that it could satisfy people who had been brought up in the Catholic obedience, while Baxter was concerned to defend what he thought was the true form of the Church of England against the encroachments of Prelacy. Consequently, Luther enumerates the signs of recognition of a Church which would be helpful to people in a state of transition from Catholicism to Protestantism, while Baxter never does so. Before Luther came to write, *Von dem Concilien und Kirchen*, he enumerated three signs of a true Church, i.e. Baptism, Sacrament, and Gospel, but afterwards he enlarged these signs to seven—namely:

1. The Word of God rightly preached.
2. The Sacrament of Baptism rightly administered.
3. The Sacrament of the Altar rightly administered.
4. The Power of the Keys rightly exercised.
5. Pastors and Preachers rightly called.
6. Public Prayer and Praise.
7. Christians suffering according to the example of Christ.

The last sign was necessitated partly by the changing nature of the times, and partly to support the morale of those of his followers who lived in Catholic states. It would also apply to those who were restive under their secular rulers.[1] While Baxter would have agreed with these definitions, he would have interpreted some of them differently from Luther, particularly the fourth and fifth. Luther held that any Christian had the right to do all those things usually associated with priesthood, although he qualified this by saying that Christians may not exercise that right save by the agreement of the community or by the call of one greater, i.e. the *Landesherr*. The right also to appoint specially qualified people to preach or teach belonged to the ordinary Christian congregation, though this right was ideal rather than actual, for in normal times Luther held that the spiritual power should appoint the clergy; if they failed, then the secular authority should do so, and if they failed, and only in the last resort, each fellowship of Christians should do so, for they held the ideal right.[2]

If we examine these two points and compare them with Baxter's views, we shall see where they differ. Let us take the second point first. Baxter categorically denies the people's right

---

[1] cf. E. Evans, *Erastianism* (Epworth Press, 1933), p. 63. [2] cf. ibid., p. 62.

to call, or consent to, the ordination of a minister.[1] They have no such power given to them in the Word of God, and they are generally unqualified to do the work. In other functions that are exercised by skill, such as that of a lawyer or a physician, the people do not make a man a lawyer or a physician, but choose who shall be their practitioner from those who have already been approved by their equals. There is some reason, he says, why this congregation or that should choose their own pastors, or at least consent to the appointment of a particular man, but purely because their consent is necessary if he is to do his work with success. This attitude of his does not follow logically from his theory of ordination, for if, as he says, all the ordainers do is to call or choose and invest the person who receives his authority from God directly, there does not seem to be any reason why the congregation should not do the choosing just as efficiently as a bishop or a presbytery, for none of them convey any special grace to the ordinand. His attitude seems to be taken up from the point of view that the ministry is a work of skill, and that the proper persons to choose someone to do such a work would naturally be those who know most about it.

His position is consistent, however, with his belief that laymen were not entitled to do the work of a minister of which ordination was a part. He gives his view of the question when discussing whether Church assemblies may be held where there is no minister, or what public worship may be so performed by laymen.[2] He takes his stand on his oft-repeated conviction that an assembly of Christians who have no pastor is not a Church. But despite this, they should meet on the Lord's Day for mutual help and the public worship of God. He then defines what they may do in such worship in the way of mutual edification, but the sting comes in the tail, for he then says what they may not do. None of them, for instance, may do these things as a pastor, ruler, office-bearer, or priest of the Church, nor may they baptize nor absolve ministerially, nor administer the Lord's Supper, nor exercise the power of the keys—that is, of government—and, finally, they must do their best to get a minister as soon as they can. It would seem from this that Baxter did not hold the doctrine of the priesthood of all believers which figures so largely in Luther's thought, and this is confirmed when we see how he explains his interpretation of the word 'priest', when applied to

[1] Orme, vol. V, p. 291.   [2] ibid., p. 539.

all Christians, in the New Testament. He is discussing whether the words 'priest', 'sacrifice', and 'altar' may lawfully be used instead of 'Christ's ministers' and 'holy table'.[1] He points out that the New Testament uses the word 'sacrifice' (when applied to other things than Christ's death) about our thanksgivings, praises, and works of mercy, rather than of the Lord's Supper, and the word 'priest' of all men who offer these aforesaid sacrifices to God. Thus he thinks that the word 'priest', when used in the New Testament of all Christians, does not mean that all Christians are entitled to do the works usually associated with priesthood, but refers specifically to these sacrifices of praise and thanksgiving which all Christians are bound to offer. Presumably, if these works were not called 'sacrifices', then Christians would not be called 'priests'. We see therefore that in the realm of Church government the specific difference between Baxter and Luther lies in the views they respectively held of the place and function of the laity in the Church.

BAXTER AND CALVIN

When we come to consider Baxter's indebtedness to Calvin, we find ourselves in a very different atmosphere. The very persistence with which Baxter reiterates the word 'discipline' is a pointer in the direction of Calvin. We know that theologically Baxter was a moderate Calvinist, for although he was independent enough to preserve a line of his own, his bias was in the direction of Calvinism rather than Arminianism. The same is true of his theory of Church government. The Calvinist theory and organization of the Church, especially as it was exemplified in Presbyterianism, is the nearest approach of all Church government theories to that of Baxter. Like Calvin, he believed that the Church was both visible and invisible, but, unlike Calvin, he believed that salvation was possible to all men. The same paradox applies to Calvin as applies to Augustine—namely, what is the purpose of the Church, or preaching, if man's future is determined by the secret election of God? Calvin did feel this difficulty, and, like Augustine, he did not carry the logical issues of his doctrine of election to their ultimate conclusion. In his *Institutes of the Christian Religion* he explains his belief in the Church by saying, 'God, who could have made His elect

---
[1] *Christian Ecclesiastics*, p. 493.

perfect from the start, chooses not to bring them to manhood in any other way than by the education of the Church',[1] and again, 'So long as we remain in the bosom of the Church we are sure that the truth will remain with us'. So that the Church is necessary, but only for the perfecting of the elect, and in actual practice all those who clung to the bosom of the Church did so because they thought that they were the elect. Again, he realized that the founding of the Church is specifically mentioned in the New Testament, and therefore it must have been founded for some purpose. One of these purposes, he explains, was the value of Christian fellowship, to which he often refers, and another was that Christ had chosen to dispense His forgiveness through the medium of the Church. At any rate, he thinks that those who were elect would be in no danger of falling away if they remained in the Church, and being, through the Church, in communion with Christ, they would, by this communion, have sufficient evidence of their election. The Church, of course, contained both tares and wheat, for Calvin never thought of the Church as a company of saints, but because there were sinners and hypocrites in the Church, discipline was needed to keep the Church as pure as possible. By the exercise of discipline against sinners, the dishonouring of Christ's name was prevented, the righteous were safeguarded from contamination, and sinners could be made ashamed and brought, if possible, to repentance. Discipline, therefore, was not merely a condition of the Church for the sake of order, but one of the means by which Christ's name was honoured, and was a part of the very fabric of the Church in the same way as preaching, baptism, and the Sacrament of the Lord's Supper.

Now, the very fact that discipline is the essence of Calvinist theories of Church government implies a conception of hierarchy in Calvinism which is logically absent in Lutheranism, for where every man is a priest and entitled to do all the works of the priesthood, there can be no order. When there is no king in Israel then every man does that which is right in his own eyes, though Luther in his later years did give the pastor the right to excommunicate. The local *Gemeinde* meet for fellowship and the means of grace, but these things are not necessary, though they are useful. Indeed, where all are priests no Church is necessary, for each man is priest and Church in himself, and religion then

[1] Calvini Opera, Berlin (1900), Book IV, ch. 1, sect. 5.

really can be defined as what a man does with his loneliness. This is why Lutheranism degenerated into a pietistic Erastianism, and had to rely on the State to supply the discipline lacking in his conception of the Church. It is also the reason why Calvinism was stronger and much more virile than Lutheranism. Wherever Calvinism appeared it defied the State, and either made advantageous terms with it, as in Scotland, or withdrew from its influence, as in England.[1] Discipline made hierarchy necessary because it implied the existence of those who discipline and those who are disciplined. It also made it possible. This Calvinist hierarchy was carefully graded into orders of ministers, doctors, deacons, and elders of the consistory. 'By combing the relevant passages in *Ephesians* and *Romans*, Calvin arrived at his four classes of office bearers. *Pastors*, who must preach, administer the Sacraments, and exercise discipline; *teachers*, who are charged with the interpretation of Scripture so that right doctrine may prevail amongst the flock; *elders*, who share in the work of government by pronouncing censures and also exercising discipline; and *deacons*, who look after the sick and minister to the poor.'[2] One Church court rose out of and supervised the other. It was a system capable of almost indefinite expansion, and, as Bernard Manning says, 'The full authority of the Divine Society, necessary for salvation, could be exercised as circumstance demanded, by a tiny congregation alone in a hostile world, or by a national assembly or by an ecumenical council'.[3]

But while Baxter's conception of the organization of particular Churches is very near to Calvin's, his view differs from the Genevan Reformer's in one aspect: he did not give as much importance to the congregation as Calvin. Keller points out that the basic cell of the Calvinist Church organization is the congregation. 'The congregation becomes more important than the Church',[4] he says, and if this judgement is slightly exaggerated, what is true in it is that all the faithful had a voice in the government of the Church. All voices had not an equal influence, but each had a suitable influence, for the authority of the Church is the whole company of the faithful elect. What happened in actual practice in the Genevan Church, when ministers were chosen, was that the ministers were first of all

[1] Bernard Manning, *Making of Modern English Religion*, p. 98.
[2] A. Dakin, *Calvinism* (Duckworth), p. 131.
[3] Bernard Manning, *Making of Modern English Religion*, p. 99.
[4] A. Keller, *Church and State on the European Continent* (Epworth Press), p. 168.

chosen by the ministers themselves, then they were presented to the Council, then approved (after a trial sermon) by the people, then ordained by the laying-on of hands. The doctors, elders, and deacons went through much the same process, except that they were not tested by the people. Calvin's chief objection to the Roman priesthood was that the people were not consulted at any stage, although in the Roman service of ordination there is a section called the 'Interrogation', which is now garbled off in Latin, but is obviously reminiscent of a testing by the people. Baxter, on the other hand, concedes nothing to the congregation in the ordination of the minister, though, as we have pointed out, in the appointment of a minister to a particular flock the consent of the congregation is advisable. But this difference is a very minor one in comparison with the large agreement that there is between Calvin and Baxter. To both these men the question of the Church's government is a matter of doctrine and not of expediency, and to both of them the ministry is as important as it is to the Roman Catholic. The ministry is essential to the life of the Church, and therefore to salvation.[1]

BAXTER AND THE SEPARATISTS

Having discussed Baxter's view of Church government in comparison with that of Luther and Calvin, we now propose to compare his view with that of the Separatist sects and we find that we cannot read Baxter for long without realizing that he heartily disliked all Separatists, though he conceded that some of them, especially the Independents, were godly, serious men. His decision to join the Parliamentary Army was taken when, during a visit to the Army after Naseby, he realized that the Sectaries were gaining control of the Army, and that it was necessary that someone should join them to attempt their conversion to more orthodox Christianity. It was through their influence that Cromwell came to power, usurped the authority of the monarch, and finally killed him. This did not endear them to Baxter, although he recognized that the work of Cromwell and his followers was in many ways for the good of the Church. He says that one good thing that they did was to

[1] For the sections on Calvin and Luther, I am indebted to the Rev. R. E. Davies, who allowed me to read the relevant portions of his thesis on '*The Problem of Authority in the Continental Reformers*', which he successfully presented for the B.D. degree in the University of Cambridge.

institute Triers in the Church, whose chief work was the purging of the ministry. By their work they saved many a congregation from ignorant, ungodly, or drunken teachers, and despite all that has been said to deride this institution, Baxter confesses that many 'thousands of souls blessed God for the faithful ministers whom they let in, and grieved when the Prelatists afterwards cast them out again'.[1] But his objection to Separatism was more fundamental than merely a personal dislike, and even more fundamental than his sorrow that they divided the Church. He really disliked them because they were democratic, because they claimed that the local congregation was the supreme authority in Church government. This applied to Independents and Anabaptists, for while the latter's objection to infant Baptism was a mistake, it was not a very culpable one; their real error was their democratic form of Church government, and their claim to govern themselves. In other words, the absence of the hierarchical conception in their organization.

About the year 1669 he heard that Dr. Owen, the leading Independent, was talking of a concord between the Independents and the Presbyterians, so Baxter resolved to try once more for this concord by seeing Dr. Owen. He was encouraged to attempt this reconciliation because of a book which Dr. Owen had written called *A Catechism for Independency*. In this book, says Baxter, 'He there giveth up two of the worst of the principles of popularity, acknowledging:

1. That the people have not the power of the keys.
2. That they give not the power of the keys, or their office-power to the pastors.[2]

It was this claim to authority by the local congregation to which Baxter objected, and it was this claim for the most part that produced their other errors, such as their complete objection to any kind of bishop, and their complete separation from the parish churches. To these errors was added their objection to the Book of Common Prayer, for they refused to acknowledge that a man *could* worship God by using that book. Baxter refused to give his assent and consent that there was nothing in the book contrary to the Word of God, but did join in the worship prescribed there for want of a better, but the Separatists considered that to join in the worship set out in the book was

[1] *Autobiography* (Everyman, 1931), p. 71.   [2] ibid., p. 212.

a grave sin. Baxter answered their arguments against a stated liturgy, and worshipping in parish churches, in his pamphlet called *An Account of the Reasons why the Twelve Arguments said to be Dr. Owen's, change not my Judgement about Communion with Parish Churches*. But although his arguments seemed cogent to him, they had no effect on the intransigent Separatists.

His objection to the Separatists had much in common with his objection to Prelacy, for the Prelatical party claimed that ministerial authority was transmitted by the bishop to the candidate on ordination, while the Separatists claimed that ministerial authority was conferred by the congregation to the pastors. The principle was the same in both cases: they each claimed to give something which was not in their power to give. God gives the authority, says Baxter; the ordainers merely choose who should receive it. Of course, this attitude of the Prelatists is quite in accordance with a conception of hierarchy, but the same cannot be said of the Independents, because their attitude to the authority of the ministry is a direct result of the absence of the hierarchical conception in their view of the Church government, for the minister has no authority independent of his congregation.

Another point that Baxter emphasizes in his opposition to Independency is that they had departed from the practice of the Separatists of an earlier day, who did not disdain to communicate and worship in parish churches, nor renounce the use of the liturgy. He quotes the *Confession and Protestation of Faith* of the Brownists to prove his contention. They confessed that parish churches were true, visible churches, and that the use of the liturgy was not unlawful, though they thought that to force it upon the congregation so that they had to pray always in the same words was not 'so profitable'.[1] Nor did they object to Churches that had many pastors, and one of them having the precedence and priority over the others during life, but they would not agree that this particular pastor had power over the others. In fact, says Baxter, they did not differ greatly from the old Nonconformists, for these used to begin their reasons for not subscribing in the following words: 'We protest before Almighty God, that we acknowledge the Churches of England, as they are established by Publick Authority, to be true visible Churches of Christ: That we desire the continuance of our

[1] Richard Baxter, *Unnecessary Separating Disowned* (1684), p. 19.

Ministry to them above all Earthly things, as that without which our Lives will be bitter and wearisome to us; That we dislike not a set form of Prayer to be used in the Churches and finally that whatsoever followeth here, is not set down of any evil mind, or of purpose to deprave the Book of Common Prayer, or Ordination, or Homilies; but only to show some reasons why we cannot Subscribe to all things in the same contained.'[1] When the Separatists complained of him that, although a Nonconformist, he still attended the parish church, he answered them by saying that he would not be more of a Separatist than the Separatists themselves.

BAXTER AND THE STATE

There is one other feature in Baxter's conception of the Church about which we must say a word, as it has a bearing, even if only an indirect one, upon his Nonconformity, and that is his view of the relationship between the Church and the State. In the first chapter of this thesis, we drew attention to the conflict between the Presbyterian Puritans of the sixteenth century and the Queen and the bishops. This conflict arose partly because each side had different conceptions of the relationship between the Church and State, conceptions which proved to be mutually incompatible. The Elizabethan Church was settled on the principle that the monarch was the supreme governor over causes civil and ecclesiastical, so that in the monarch, the Church and State were united, and the Church was the State in its religious aspect. The monarch was not therefore merely a secular official, but was both priest and king. This conception is to be found in Hooker's *Ecclesiastical Polity*, where he points out that the Church and State are the same society, the State dealing with all things related to public affairs, and the Church dealing with all things relating to religion.[2] This same theory is contained in the writings of a divine of a later day, Archbishop Laud, who says: 'Both Commonwealth and Church are collective bodies, made up of many into one, and both so near allied that the one, the Church, can never subsist but in the other the Commonwealth; nay, so near, that the same men, which in a temporal respect make the Commonwealth do in a spiritual make the Church.'[3]

[1] *Unnecessary Separating Disowned*, p. 19.
[2] Hooker, *Ecclesiastical Polity*, Book 8, ch. 1, par. 5.
[3] F. J. Powicke, *A Life of the Reverend Richard Baxter, 1615–91* (1924), vol. II, p. 226.

Opposed to this conception was that of the Presbyterian Puritans, whose views were derived from Calvin. In their view the Church and State were two separate societies, which were, in an ideal State, necessary to each other, but not dependent on each other. All things pertaining to religion were the sole province of the Church, whose ministers were the guardians of the Word of God. For our purpose, the cardinal difference between these views, which superficially might appear similar, may be summed up in the question: Is the Supreme Magistrate subject to the Church or not? Puritans, following Travers and Cartwright, said, though with a reluctance understandable in the circumstances, that the supreme magistrate was subject to the Church, and a corollary to their view was that monarchy was not necessarily the only form of a civil society, but that an aristocratic, or even a democratic, form might serve equally well. In Hooker's view, of course, the monarch could not possibly be subject to the Church, because he was the supreme governor of the Church.

The question we have to discuss is: Which of these two conceptions do we find in Baxter? The tradition of Nonconformity, particularly in the last century, has been the Presbyterian-Puritan one. They have conceded the monarch no authority in matters of Church order, worship, or morals. They have thought of the Church as outside the control of the State in these matters, and have claimed a right to decide these matters in the councils of the Church. But whereas some may consider that this is a *sine qua non* of Nonconformity, it is not necessarily so, for of the two views, Baxter, the leader of seventeenth-century Nonconformity, inclined decisively to the Elizabethan Church view. Dr. Powicke, in the second volume of his very scholarly life of Baxter, draws attention to the fact that Baxter's views on this question seem to be in substantial agreement with Hooker, Laud, and even Hobbes, though as regards the two latter he would have been horrified to learn that some thought that he approved of their views, while as regards Hooker, Dr. Powicke notices that Baxter takes him to task because his views are too democratic. Dr. Powicke thinks that this was an unfair judgement on Hooker, whose sole concern, he says, was to show that kingly power is derived originally from the people. But we suggest that this is precisely why Baxter took Hooker to task, for he is never tired of pointing out that power or authority is never derived from the people,[1] whether it be in Church government or in secular government. The authority of a minister is derived from God, and the authority of a magistrate is derived from the King, who in his turn derives it from God, the most that the people could do is to choose who is to exercise that power, but once the person is settled in his office he is to be obeyed, not because it is the will of the people that he should be obeyed, but because he has received a collation of power from God. To Baxter power is a spiritual quality, and is a gift of God directly to minister or magistrate.[2] Kingship, too, is not a convenience of State, but an order inherent in Nature, for there must be those who rule and those who are ruled. It is interesting to note, as Dr. Powicke has noted, that Baxter was prepared to recognize a Cromwellian dynasty if Providence so willed it.[3] Remembering Baxter's dislike of Cromwell, it is impossible to reconcile his willingness to recognize a Cromwellian dynasty if kingship is merely a convenience of State, but quite understandable if we see that to him kingship is an order inherent in Nature, and not derived from the will of the people. For if it was derived from the will of the people he would have objected strongly to Cromwell's government, as being derived, not from the will of the people, but from the power of the Army, who were certainly in a minority. The main point to him was that the office of king stood, though Cromwell held the power, and if God allowed him to hold the power, then he occupied the office. It was the office that mattered, and its attendant power was derived from God. Baxter had nothing in common with the sentimental attachment of Cavaliers and bishops to the dynasty of Charles. He believed in kingship, and what the Restoration party, in the person of the Earl of Lauderdale, had to do to win him to their side was to convince him that Charles's son was the right person to occupy the throne.

To Baxter the kingly office was divine, and carried with it the headship of both Church and State. He believed that there must be a national Church, and that it was the monarch who in his person made it national. He is, as he says, the *Forma informans, specifica et unifica*, at the same time both Church and State. His views may be seen set out in his book, *Of National Churches*, or

---

[1] Richard Baxter, *Second Part of The Nonconformists Plea for Peace* (1680) ('Judgement of Things Indifferent'), p. 37.

[2] ibid.

[3] F. J. Powicke, *A Life of the Reverend Richard Baxter, 1615–91* (1924), vol. II, p. 227, note 2.

the portions relevant for an understanding of his position may be read as summarized in the second volume of Dr. Powicke's life of Baxter, to which we have previously referred.[1] As the king is not a purely secular official, neither is the magistrate, for he holds his authority from the king, and as we have shown in an earlier chapter, Baxter thinks of the magistrate as one of the guardians of the Church, with power to legislate for its life. The magistrate even has power to appoint the ministry under certain circumstances, for if the bishop or ordainers command the people to receive one minister, and the magistrate another, the people must obey the magistrate, provided that both candidates are worthy. The people may disobey the magistrate only when his candidate is obviously unworthy.[2] Seeing that both the king and the magistrates are not simply secular officials, it is their duty to study the Scriptures, and make themselves proficient in ecclesiastical affairs, and it is a great error of the clergy to tempt these officers to think that they are only civil officials, and to leave the study of Scripture to the bishops and priests. Similarly, it is a great error of the Separatists to decry national Churches, even while some of them wait for a national Church under the Fifth Monarch in the Millennium. So he concludes that the orthodox Protestant Nonconformists are as truly members of the Church of England as any Diocesans or Conformists, and if they are not better confuted than they have been they may truly be said to be the soundest, most judicious, and most peaceable members of this Church. To deny such Nonconformists to be true and honourable parts of the Church of England implies some dishonourable definition of the said Church. In a truly national Church, ruled by a Christian king, administered by sober, Godly clergy, and based on the simple essentials of doctrine, the problem of Dissenters would not arise, for there would be few Dissenters to tolerate.[3]

[1] ibid., p. 228.   [2] Orme, vol. V, p. 275.
[3] F. J. Powicke, *A Life of the Reverend Richard Baxter, 1615–91* (1924), vol. II, p. 231.

Chapter XII

THINGS INDIFFERENT

BEFORE we attempt to estimate the cause and extent of Baxter's Nonconformity, we must discuss his attitude to certain things usually associated with Nonconformity and the Puritan temper, such things as the use of the surplice and the use of the sign of the Cross in baptism, etc. We have already outlined in the first chapter of this thesis the attitude of the Elizabethan Puritans to these things. We know that all the early Puritans had strong objections to certain rites and ceremonies extant in the Elizabethan Church. Among these rites and ceremonies to which they objected were the use of the surplice, the use of the sign of the Cross in baptism, kneeling at the Communion, the use of the ring in marriage, and the use of images in churches. Their objection to these things was because in their minds they were associated with Popery. But we also distinguished two different reactions to these things in the party itself. Some Puritans objected so strongly that they refused to use these ceremonies, and were ejected from their livings for that reason, whilst others, following Cartwright and Travers, used them where necessary and refused to make them a matter of conscience. These latter considered such ceremonies as we have mentioned above as 'things indifferent', and thought that they were justified in compromising with the Church authorities over these things in order that they might pursue their larger aim of working for the conversion of the national Church into a Presbyterian organization without disturbance, and from within the framework of the Church itself. Once this was done, then lesser objectives, such as the abolition of the surplice, would follow naturally. They thought that nothing could be gained by jeopardizing their positions in the Church by constantly objecting to things which in themselves were of little importance. In view of this attitude of the majority of Elizabethan Puritans, we cannot define Elizabethan Puritanism as the refusal to use certain ceremonies in the Church to which they objected, but must define it with reference to the main object of the party—namely, the conversion of the Church into a Presbyterian organization after the model of the Scottish Church. The question we have to answer in

Baxter's case is whether his Nonconformity arose from his known objection to 'Popish' ceremonies, or whether its origin is to be looked for elsewhere.

BAXTER AND 'THINGS INDIFFERENT'

We cannot do better than to repeat at the outset one of his favourite aphorisms, 'Unity in things necessary, liberty in things unnecessary, and charity in all things', which can be our guide in discussing his attitude to such ceremonies as we have mentioned above. It is seldom that human actions can have as clear a distinction as to their rightness or wrongness as is to be seen, say, in the distinction between black and white. For there is a great deal of grey in this world, and the majority of human actions take place in that pale and indistinct sphere between black and white, where it is not always easy to weigh up the pros and cons, and where, in the sphere of faith and morals, simple minds too often erect prejudices into principles. But there are occasions when greyness merges into blackness, and where the distinction between right and wrong is obvious, and it is at such moments as these that a man becomes a Nonconformist, if to conform is to violate his conscience. Now, to say that Baxter was a Nonconformist is not to say that he saw everything in terms of black and white, because, indeed, for him there was a good deal of grey. But whereas for many of his contemporaries life was all grey and any attitude of compliance could be taken to the oaths and 'assents and consents' with which they were faced, to Baxter greyness was an intermediate colour between black and white, and to conform in certain things would have landed him in blackness and violated a conscience always 'tender'. Nor must we assume that it was always easy for him to follow his own conscience, for he was a sociable man, and did not dislike the geniality of friendship, which was often jeopardized by his intractability. He was not of that perverted brood who enjoy being always 'agin the government', for he had too much respect for authority lightly to disobey it. Nor was he a man framed to be carried away by one idea, and to stand by that idea when reason, religion, and friendship seemed to be against it. His mind was not in the least simple, nor his character unanalysed; but in a very real sense he 'swung the world a trinket at his wrist', and was free from the cloying pleasantness of sensuous contacts. That is why his language is often vigorous and sometimes even rude, for it never occurred to him that when he was telling the truth that he could be rude. Nor did he bridle at strong language from his opponents. He had no vanity or pride to be injured, and if his anger was sometimes sudden and hot, it was always short, and had the Scriptural commendation that it was 'righteous'. It will be our contention in this chapter that the actual signs and ceremonies to which he and the Puritans objected were for him 'Things indifferent', and that they were a part of that greyness in which liberty of conscience could be and should be allowed. Or if we follow the aphorism quoted above, they were not among those things in which unity was necessary, but among those things about which liberty could be exercised.

THE USE OF THE SURPLICE

We can take as our first example for examination the vexed question of whether a minister should wear a surplice or not in public worship. Since the Reformation this had been a bone of contention in England, and after the death of Mary, the returned exiles inclined more to wearing a black gown—the famous 'Turkey gowns' of the Hampton Court Conference—than to wearing a surplice. Having lived under the influence of the Reformed Churches of the Continent, the exiles under Mary naturally tended to follow the example of the Lutheran and the Calvinist Churches, who had discarded the surplice in favour of black gowns. All the Elizabethan Puritans objected to the surplice because it was the distinctive priestly garment of the pre-Reformation Church, and seems to have been regarded with special awe because of its holiness; at least one of the canons of the national Church emphasized that no holiness was to be attributed to priestly garments. Cartwright, however, had specifically stated that if it was a question of being forbidden to exercise one's ministry unless the surplice was worn, then it was better to wear the surplice, for the exercise of one's ministry was a direct command of Christ, whereas the refusal to wear a surplice was not. It was this attitude of Cartwright which Baxter followed. To him a distinctive garment for the ministry was as right for them as distinctive garments for lawyers or judges, and 'Some of us', he says, 'hold a surplice rather to be used than the ministry forsaken: and those that think otherwise, think not the matter of so much weight as to eliminate their love and communion with those that use it'. Obviously, therefore, he was not going to make the use of a distinctive garment by the ministry, not even the surplice, a matter of conscience. It was one of those things in which liberty should be given to every minister to decide for himself. To him the attitude of those who said that all should wear a surplice was just as wrong as the attitude of those who said that none should wear it, for it was to elevate into a matter of principle a thing which was not necessary for salvation. All that was wanted was that there should be decency and reverence in worship, and within those limits liberty of expression should be allowed.

THE USE OF THE SIGN OF THE CROSS IN BAPTISM

We can take as another example the question of the use of the sign of the Cross in Baptism, which always had been a difficulty with the Puritans because of its Popish significance. Baxter examines the use of the sign and its place in the ceremony of Baptism in the *Nonconformists Plea for Peace*,[1] in order to explain the attitude that many Nonconformists took towards it. He points out that the liturgy commands its use in Baptism, not as a part of the Baptism, but as an extra thing added to our covenanting with God. Now, the essential part of the Sacrament of Baptism is that part instituted by Christ. This makes it a Sacrament of God's making, which is in a different category from a Sacrament instituted by man, a difference we have pointed out in the chapter on Baxter's view of the Sacraments. Because of this, says Baxter, 'the great fear of the Nonconformists is, lest this be a second Sacrament of the Covenant of Grace made by man added to Baptism, or at least have most of the nature and uses of it; and lest Christ will take it as an invasion of his prerogative so to use it; and make a *new badge or symbol* of our Christianity; As the King would take it ill of one that would without him make a badge or symbol for his subjects as subjects, or of the Order of the Knights of the Garter as such. And the rather because it is the *use of an Image* (though transient,) in *God's worship* and to such a high end.'[2] The objection of the Nonconformists to the use of the sign of the Cross was that:

[1] Richard Baxter, *Second Part of The Nonconformists Plea for Peace* (1680) ('Judgement of Noncon'), p. 104.
[2] Richard Baxter, *The Nonconformists Plea for Peace* (1679), p. 180.

1. It was made compulsory on all.
2. There was a danger that a man-made 'Sacrament' would take the honour, as it were, from the Sacrament instituted by Christ.

Their objection was of the same order as the objection of the Reformers to the 'Sacramentals' of the medieval Church. The multiplication of such signs lowered the significance, and finally made contemptible the two Sacraments instituted by Christ. Baxter's own attitude to the use of this sign is very interesting as explaining his general position: 'Though we are not satisfied', he says, 'of the lawfulness of using the transient Image of the Cross, as a *Dedicatory Sign* and *Symbol of Christianity*, so much Sacramental (much less refuse from Baptism and Christendom all Christian Infants unless they will have them so crossed, no more than if a Crucifix were so imposed and used:) yet we do not condemn *all use* of either Cross or Crucifix.'[1] His own attitude is therefore that:

1. Though he was not certain of the lawfulness of using the sign of the Cross, he was prepared to use it.
2. But he objected to having to refuse Baptism to those who scrupled at it.

This once more illustrates his position; what was obligatory on all in Baptism was the bare command of Christ, what should be left to the personal decision of the minister were those signs and ceremonies invented by man. Though in this case he was prepared to sink his own feelings for the sake of peace and use the sign.

KNEELING AT THE COMMUNION

Another vexed question which disturbed the Nonconformists was whether the Communion should be received kneeling or sitting. They were not all of one mind on the issue themselves. Some thought it lawful to receive it kneeling, but not necessary or eligible were they allowed to choose their own method of receiving; some thought it not necessary, but eligible, while others thought it definitely unlawful to receive it kneeling. Those who considered it unlawful to receive it kneeling did so for the following reasons:

[1] Richard Baxter, *Second Part of The Nonconformists Plea for Peace* (1680), p. 103.

1. Because our Lord and His disciples *sat* at meat in the Upper Room. At least, that is what they thought happened. Today's opinion is that our Lord and His disciples *reclined* on cushions, as was the custom in the East when eating. Whether these Nonconformists would have insisted on receiving the Communion reclining in imitation of Christ had they known what was the custom, we don't know; but their point was that the manner of receiving the Communion was a doubtful case, and in such cases our duty lies in following the surest side, and to them the surest side was to receive it as they thought the disciples received it.

2. The second reason was that kneeling at the Communion violated the Second Commandment, being used by the Papists and many Anglicans to signify the adoration of the Host, which the Nonconformists called 'Bread-worship'. They supposed that the Second Commandment forbade the use of images, as being 'External, corporal Idolatry', even though the mind intended the worship of the true God.

3. The third reason was that they thought that the canons of the greatest General Councils (not repealed by any other Council) and the tradition of the Church were of stronger obligation than the canons of the Anglican Church. These canons and the tradition of the Church forbade adoration by genuflection on any Lord's Day and on week-days between Easter and Whitsuntide. These were generally operative for about 1,000 years, and were never actually repealed, but changed gradually by contrary practice until it became customary to adore God in the Sacrament by kneeling at the appropriate places. Baxter, in presenting their position, says that the *Apostolic Constitutions* seem to command all people to receive the Sacrament standing. Whether this is a correct interpretation of the Constitutions, which only says that the Sacrifice should be made, all people standing and praying silently, is a moot point, but to this type of Nonconformist it was sufficient to support their point that the Sacrament should not be received kneeling. But whatever the opinions of different sorts of Nonconformists on this question, they all held that it was wrong to forbid the Sacrament to those who would not receive it kneeling. And this was Baxter's position. The manner of receiving the Sacrament was quite secondary to the command to receive it, and consequently liberty should be allowed to all to receive it as they thought fit. He himself was

quite prepared to give the Sacrament to Sir Ralph Clare, who wanted it kneeling, if only Sir Ralph would live under 'Discipline'. To him the method of receiving was a 'thing indifferent', and varied in conforming churches. He quotes an occasion when he attended Sacrament at a conforming church,[1] where one half of the congregation received it kneeling and the other half sitting, and, as he says, without any violation of love or concord between the people and without any mischievous effects. His attitude to this question may be summed up by saying that the manner of receiving the Sacrament should not be made obligatory. The divine command was that all should take and eat of Christ's Body and Blood, and not that they should take them in a certain way. To make a law of the Church to exclude all those who wished to receive the Sacrament sitting was to promote schism.

THE USE OF IMAGES

We have seen from above that some of the Nonconformists who objected to kneeling at the Sacrament did so on the ground that the Second Commandment forbade the use of images in the worship of God. We know also that Cromwell's Army, which contained a majority of extreme Puritans, took every opportunity to break and destroy the images and pictures which filled the pre-Reformation Church and which still remained in many churches. Dr. Powicke has pointed out, however, that Baxter did not hold that all use of images was unlawful, and he quotes a paragraph from the *Second Part of The Nonconformists Plea for Peace* in support of his statement.[2] Baxter was far from being a Quaker and forbidding all use of image or picture in the worship of God. What he did was to distinguish the end to which the image or picture was put. In his *Christian Ecclesiastics* he analyses the use of images at great length when answering the question, 'What images and what use of images is lawful or unlawful?'[3] He finds that images or pictures may be used as 'objects of our consideration, exciting our minds to worship God', but not as 'a worshipped medium, or the terminus, or the thing that we worship mediately on pretence of representing God, and that we worship Him in it ultimately'. This, he thinks, is what is forbidden directly in the Second Commandment. So that it is lawful at the sight of a crucifix to be provoked to worship

[1] Richard Baxter, *Second Part of The Nonconformists Plea for Peace* (1680), p. 160.
[2] ibid. ('What Meer Nonconformity is not'), p. 104. [3] Orme, vol. V, p. 472.

God, but it is unlawful to offer Him that worship by offering it to the crucifix first, as the sign, way, or means of our sending it to God. The question which interests us in relation to Baxter is whether it is lawful for a man to separate or become a Nonconformist from a Church which allows the use or abuse of images. Baxter says that it is not lawful to separate on such a pretext, nor indeed is such abuse idolatry. His view is that when a Church, or our rulers, set up images in churches, a man may lawfully worship there, if the images are not symbols of idol-worship, or of a religion so sinful in the substance that God will not accept it, and if we make no sinful use of such images ourselves. Even though others abuse them, that is not sufficient reason for us to forsake such a Church. But he still thinks that such a man, when he has a convenient opportunity, must express his dissent from the sort of worship which includes the abuse of images. His own conscience must be clear, not only to himself internally, but also externally, so that others may know that he does not approve of abuses. But he must not make the abuse of images in the Church a cause of Nonconformity.

The use of the ring in marriage is treated by Baxter under the use of symbols or images. It is difficult to know why the Puritans objected to the use of a ring. Two possible reasons suggest themselves to us. Firstly, they rejected it for the same reason that they rejected the sign of the Cross in Baptism, because it was associated with the Popish marriage ceremony, superfluous to the ceremony itself, and not commanded in Scripture. Or, secondly, their objection might have arisen from the Puritan attitude to divorce. We know that they were the first people in England, in any numbers at least, to advocate divorce, and they may have objected to the use of the ring because it is the symbol of perpetuity, and therefore unsuitable to symbolize an alliance which could be broken up. Baxter himself, when he wrote his *Reformed Liturgy* and marriage ceremony, does not mention the use of a ring. But it is doubtful whether he considered its omission important, for elsewhere he concedes that it is lawful to use an arbitrary professing sign about holy things, 'Which signify no more than words, and have by nature or custom an aptitude to such use', and instances the use of a ring in marriage as such a lawful sign, saying that it is a symbol of perpetuity and so of constancy.[1]

[1] ibid., p. 478.

THE USE OF A LITURGY OR FORM OF PRAYER

We have already discussed in a former chapter Baxter's attitude to the use of a liturgy, when pointing out where he differed from the Separatists, so that we need say little on this point. He confessed that Nonconformists used a stinted liturgy themselves, and that forms of prayer were inevitable in public worship, on the ground that those prayers which were used by all must be set forms. The desire of the Nonconformists of his generation, and of such men as Cartwright, Travers, Hildersham, and Dod of a previous generation, was for the reform of the liturgy and not for the abolishing of it. He himself joined with Mr. Ball and others in thanking God that England had a more reformed liturgy than most Churches in the world. But that did not alter the fact that he considered that the liturgy used in the national Church was defective and unsound in parts. He mentions that certain parts of the liturgy were definitely untrue, such as the rule for defining when movable feasts and holy days begin. The rule defined Easter Day by saying that 'Easter Day (on which the rest depend) is alwaies the first Sunday after the first full moon which happens after the one and twentieth day of March'. This rule is false, he says, as any calendar will show, as the table for finding Easter Day for ever will show, and as the practice of the Church shows, which keeps Easter on another day. He also quotes instances of false translations of Scripture, some of which directly altered the sense, such as the translation of Psalm cv. 28. The words of the liturgy were, 'They were not obedient to His word', but the correct translation was, 'They rebelled not against His word'. But, despite these defects, he was prepared to use the liturgy prescribed for the want of a better.

We have now given enough examples to show that Baxter's Nonconformity did not arise from his objections to certain signs or ceremonies in the Church, but that his objections to these things arose from his desire to put first things first. To him unity was only necessary where there was certainty of divine commandment, but where there was no certainty then there should be liberty. That certainty he looked for in Holy Scripture, and particularly where in Scripture there was a direct command of Christ. His Nonconformity did not consist either in making Scripture the particular rule of all circumstances of Church government and worship, but where there was Scripture precedent then such a system must be the basis of all Church government and worship, and should be obligatory on all. For the rest, Nature and Scripture supplied sufficient general rules for guidance, so that 'things, Be done in unity, charity, to edification, decently, and orderly, etc'.[1] Where there was not direct command of Scripture approving or forbidding, then it was sinful to make a rule on the matter obligatory on all.

THE NATURE OF UNITY IN THE CHURCH

So far we have been concerned in this chapter to analyse Baxter's attitude to those things about which he thought liberty should be allowed, but before we leave this question we intend to examine what he meant when he said that there should be unity in things necessary. In a previous chapter (p. 101) we have shown that he considered that, despite their differences, there was a certain underlying unity in the various branches of the Church. Unfortunately, that underlying unity was not obvious to all, and for actual Church communion he felt that there must be terms of union on which all are agreed. He lays his first stress on holiness, for the best way to universal peace is to make men holy and the best men more holy. In the meantime, while trying to accomplish this end, the best terms of unity must be discovered, for 'it is Just Terms that must heal the Church on earth'.[2] These terms must be such as do not oppose holiness, but subserve it. For peace and holiness must not be separated. They must be such terms as would take into the Church all that Christ would take in—that is, all who are fit for Church communion, and terms which all Christians would have agreed to, if they had been imposed, in all ages of the Church until now. They should also be such terms as the Church has actually been united in, in some age if not in all ages, for why should we think that the Church now would unite on such terms as it was never united in before? There would be a chance for Church unity if terms were produced which fulfil the conditions which have been outlined above. However, Baxter thought that the terms offered then in England were impossible, and certainly

[1] Richard Baxter, *Second Part of The Nonconformists Plea for Peace* (1680) ('What Meer Nonconformity is not'), p. 89.
[2] ibid., p. 152.

would not reconcile in one Church Episcopalians and Separatists, so he set himself to find possible terms of union which might be agreeable to all.

Before he set out the terms he thought would reconcile the opposing parties, he discusses the nature of unity, and how far it has to be qualified. Unity, he says, may be had with uniformity or without it, but unity with uniformity can never be had, except by placing uniformity in the Scriptures, or primitive simplicity of the Church—that is to say, uniformity must be placed in a few things so needful, and so lawful that no sensible Christian could question them. On the other hand, unity without uniformity can only be had by toleration in the points of uniformity which are disputed, leaving each Church to its proper liberty, but making those things necessary to all which are necessary to the unity of all—that is, the essentials or great points of Christianity. The plan which he has in his mind as the best way to achieve the unity in the Church which all men in their hearts desire is then outlined under three heads:

1. To unite in things necessary to all by imposition on such as are capable of understanding them.

2. To unite in things of unquestionable convenience, by prudently reducing them to their primitive simplicity, and this not by imposing severe laws for their acceptance, but by persuasion and gentle correction.

3. If any will go farther (as to ornaments, crossings, etc.) to let them do it as a matter of liberty, just as cathedrals and parish churches vary, without a breach of charity.

For, he says, he that would unite mankind must unite them in those things in which they are agreed; he that would unite Christians must do it in those things in which they are agreed; and those who would unite Protestants must unite them in those things in which they are agreed. For the things in which they do not agree cannot possibly be the terms of their agreement.

He then enumerates the things in which all Protestants are agreed, and finds them to be the Baptismal Covenant, the Faith or Creed therein professed, the Lord's Prayer and Decalogue as the summary of things to be willed and practised, and in the Scriptures generally. In these things, not only are the Protestants agreed, but also the Greeks and Papists as well. No one can unite all Christians on narrower terms than these. In addition,

Protestants are agreed also in the sufficiency of Scripture as containing all things necessary for Salvation, and also in the fact that magistrates and pastors are appointed to govern the Church, the one by the sword and the other by the Word and Keys. It is impossible to unite the Church on any terms over and above these. For just as the attempt to unite all mankind by uniformity of language, habit, and temperament would set all mankind by the ears, so the attempt to unite the Church by an oath of obedience to the Pope, or in any superadded doctrine or tradition would set the Churches in a greater flame than they are already. As regards the Papists, Baxter thought that before the Council of Trent there was some hope of restoring unity between the Papists and the Reformed Churches, but now, until the Papists renounce their doctrine of Papal infallibility, there is no hope of more unity than would come about if they confessed the truth (though not the sufficiency) of Protestantism, so that all could live together without uncharitableness or cruelty. The same thing applies to those Protestants in England who make canons that all Protestants shall agree in subscriptions, oaths, forms, and ceremonies, which they are not all agreed in. Their attitude serves not to heal the Church but only to promote schism.

'TRUE AND EASIE TERMS OF UNITY AND CONCORD'

We can conclude Baxter's views on unity in things necessary with a summary of what he calls 'The true and Easie terms of Unity and Concord', which he sets out in twelve articles. He suggests that all should assent to:

1. The Sacramental Covenant, the Creed, the Lord's Prayer, the Decalogue, and to the infallible truth of Scripture.
2. That every Church have its faithful pastors set over them and related to them by the joint consent of the ordainers and the flock.
3. That the magistrate should be the only one to govern by the sword, and that the bishops and flocks be subject to them.
4. Let every pastor before his ordination be examined in a written catalogue of all the great and clear points of religion. Such a catalogue not to be contradicted or preached against. The catalogue should contain no uncertain points. 'We can', he says, 'conscionably forbear preaching against many points

which we cannot conscionably subscribe Assent or consent to in themselves.'[1]

5. Let men be punished who preach against the civil or spiritual government. After two warnings, let the heretical and turbulent be avoided by the Church, and the magistrate distrain them at his discretion.

6. Impose no homilies, forms of preaching, liturgies, or forms of prayer on any save those who because of ignorance need them, but let the pastors have liberty sometimes to use more or less of them according to times and occasions.

7. Let the variable circumstances, such as what chapter, psalm, tune, method, or subject of preaching, be left to the discretion of the pastors.

8. Let the work of every pastor be to baptize, preach, pray, administer the Lord's Supper, etc., refuse the ignorant and heretical until they repent, and all this subject to the magistrate or ecclesiastic if he abuse his power.

9. Let neighbouring Churches keep such correspondence as is necessary to their unity, so that any cast out of one Church may not be admitted to others without consultation.

10. If Christian rulers think that these neighbour Churches should hold regular synods, let them be used only for the sake of unity, and for the edification of younger and weaker ministers.

11. If it seem good to the magistrate that any one pastor should have chief oversight of that Church, or any one pastor be the regular moderator over the synod, or any one in a diocese or province have a general inspection over all ministers and Churches, let none be forced to swear him obedience, nor profess or subscribe to the lawfulness of his place, but only actually to obey him. And if this prelate claim only the spiritual power, et him not exercise it as a prince without the council of pastors, and let him go no farther than the spiritual power goes, that is only to conscience and consenters. Nor let the magistrate be his executioner with the sword, nor put any forcing power into the clergyman's hand. But if the king will make any clergymen magistrates, let it be declared that they and their courts use civil power in ecclesiastical matters only as the king's officers. And let no lay chancellors or other laymen exercise the power of the keys.

---

[1] Richard Baxter, *Second Part of The Nonconformists Plea for Peace* (1680) ('What Meer Nonconformity is not'), p. 89.

12. Let all ministers and people alike swear obedience to the king and take the oaths of allegiance and supremacy to that end.

If this plan, which is a practical expression of his belief that there should be unity in things necessary, liberty in things indifferent, and charity in all things, were accepted, then, he thought, there would be real peace and unity in the Church.

Chapter XIII

A MERE NONCONFORMIST

WE are now in a position to attempt an estimate of the cause and extent of Baxter's Nonconformity, and it will be convenient at this point to summarize the conclusions we have reached in the preceding chapters. Tracing the causes of Nonconformity back to Elizabethan days, we have shown:

1. That the main purpose of the Elizabethan Puritans was to reform the national life of England into the form of a Church organized along Presbyterian lines.

2. In conjunction with this, we have tried to show the steady growth of Episcopalian ideas in the work of Whitgift, Hooker, and Bancroft, developing into a doctrine of Episcopacy under the influence of Andrewes and Laud, which is called 'Prelacy'.

3. Into this background of history we have attempted to fit the life and influence of Baxter, showing the importance of his work for Church unity both at Kidderminster and in the national life.

4. In analysing the causes of his Nonconformity, we have started from the conviction that it arose from his doctrine of the Church, and have therefore analysed his conception of the Church under the headings of the Universal Church, Particular Churches, the Ministry, the Word of God, and the Sacraments.

5. To understand his conception of Church order, and the relationship between the Church and State, we have analysed his view of the principle of hierarchy, and compared it with that of Luther, Calvin, and the Separatists.

6. Lastly, we have examined his attitude to forms and ceremonies, under the title of 'Things Indifferent', and outlined his scheme for unity in the Church.

BAXTER'S USE OF THE WORD 'NONCONFORMIST'

Following on the summary we have given above, we must note the use which Baxter makes of the term Nonconformist as applied to himself. In the month of March of the year 1672–3, two events occurred by which the King pushed his defiance of Parliament to a climax. He declared war on the Dutch, and issued an indulgence to all Dissenters from the national Church. Both these events troubled Baxter. The first because it was a breach of the Triple Alliance, and a blow to a small Protestant Power, whose Catholic neighbour, France, was waiting for the opportunity to overpower it, and the second because he felt that it was merely a cover to allow the King to rely more on the support of the Catholics for his policy of independence from Parliamentary control. This Indulgence granted preaching licences to Nonconformists on condition that they were approved by the King, and provided that they were applied for in the name of some sect such as the Presbyterians or Independents. For some time Baxter refrained from approaching the King. His reasons were: that in the first place he did not approve of an Indulgence to Catholics, and, secondly, he objected to applying for a preaching licence in the name of some sect, for he considered that he still belonged to the national Church. Eventually he was persuaded to apply for a licence to preach, and did so as a 'Mere Nonconformist'. Through the efforts of Sir Thomas Player, Chamberlain of London, such a licence was granted. It is the words 'Mere Nonconformist' which are interesting in this application, for they sum up Baxter's feeling about his Nonconformity, and assert what he meant them to assert, that he was as little of a Nonconformist as it was possible for him to be, for he loved the Church in which he was brought up, and clung to it for years after he had been cast out of its ministry.

That he was as little of a Nonconformist as he could be is shown by his very conciliatory attitude whenever there was any suggestion of an agreement between the leaders of the national Church and the Nonconformists. But there was a hard core of conviction under his apparent pliableness which nothing could break, and almost everything from curses to bribes was tried to get him to renounce his position, though he was fundamentally opposed to unnecessary separating from the Church and hated schism. In his pamphlet on *Unnecessary Separating Disowned*, he lists the things that the Nonconformists objected to, but were prepared to agree to in 1660 and 1661 if only agreement could be obtained with the bishops. 'We never said a word', he says, 'against a *Form of Prayer*, nor most of the *Liturgy*, nor *Holy Days* nor

Kneeling at the Sacrament, (but only against excommunicating the faithful that scruple it), nor the *Surplice*, nor the *Ring in Marriage*, nor *laying* the *Hand on a Book* in *Swearing*, and other such, because at least much may be said for them, and if we laid our stress on doubtful things, many would think the rest were no other.'[1] Most of the things to which the earlier Puritans objected are in this catalogue, and if the Nonconformists of 1660 were prepared to waive their objections to them in order to get agreement with the bishops, then only a very little grace on the bishops' part was needed to heal the wounds of the Church.

BAXTER AND THE OLD NONCONFORMISTS

Nor did Baxter's Nonconformity coincide exactly with the Nonconformity of the Elizabethan Puritans, for he knew that the difference between them and the Conformists was to be found fundamentally in their different attitudes to Scripture. The root difference between them, he says, was that the Nonconformists thought that they should stick to Scripture in the doctrine, worship, and government of the Church, while the Conformists thought that it was allowable to retain customs and practices from the pre-Reformation Church, 1, if they were not forbidden in Scripture, or, 2, if they were introduced into the Church before the Papacy had attained dictatorial powers, or, 3, if they were common to the Roman Church and the Greek. The difference was the difference between Cartwright and Hooker, and Baxter is in many respects more like Hooker than he is like Cartwright, particularly in the place he gives to tradition in the Church. On the other hand, he goes back to the Elizabethan Puritans in the emphasis he lays on the revelation of Scripture, not only for the doctrine of the Church, but also for the government of the Church. He draws a much sharper distinction between divine revelation in Scripture and human contrivance, in Church government, than did his Episcopalian opponents (a result probably of his Calvinist outlook), but, in opposition to the extreme Puritans, he held that a human polity, over and above divine revelation, was acceptable to God in Church worship and discipline. We have explained this mental attitude of his with respect to many issues in previous chapters, such issues as the use of the sign of the Cross in Baptism, his particular doctrine of Church government,

[1] Richard Baxter, *Unnecessary Separating Disowned*, p. 21.

his peculiar explanation of the doctrine of predestination, etc., and can summarize it by saying that, when facing any issue, he first of all determined what was the command of Scripture, and when he had found it he laid that down as obligatory on all. Then he examined the tradition of the Church on the subject, and lastly exercised his common sense as to whether liberty should be allowed to individuals on that which was not specified in Scripture on any particular issue. In almost every sphere of faith or morals there was a Divine Command, which bound all men to the same view, and to the same action, but there was also a divine liberty, if we may call it that, which allowed the good sense and honest effort of men free play in ordering their lives, government, and worship in any thing over and above the direct commands of Scripture.

Another thing we must understand to appreciate the difference between Baxter's Nonconformity and that of the Elizabethan Puritans is the different type of opposition they both faced. Baxter often complained that the things he opposed in the national Church were new things, and summed them up in the phrase, 'The new Prelatical way'. He thought of himself and the Nonconformists of his type as the true successors, in doctrine and Church government theories at least, of the bishops and clergy of the Elizabethan Church, and, as we will see, his Nonconformity largely arises from his opposition to the Prelacy of Laud and his successors in the Church after the Restoration. The Puritans at the commencement of Elizabeth's reign were faced with a largely unorganized opposition among the bishops and clergy of the Church; their chief opponent was the Queen. We have shown how that opposition gradually hardened and became more organized through the work of men like Whitgift, Bancroft, and Hooker, particularly in respect to a doctrine of Episcopacy. But even so, at the end of Elizabeth's reign there was no Nonconformity proper in the Church, but two opposing parties, one Episcopal and the other Presbyterian, struggling for the control of the Church. With the advent of Laud, the Episcopal party took a new turn, for Episcopacy came to be considered a necessity for true Church order, and with it the attendant doctrines of the necessity of Episcopal ordination and Episcopal rule over the inferior clergy. It was the influence of this party, which Dr. Powicke calls the 'Anglo-Catholic party', which Baxter opposed, and it was in opposition to this party's control of the Church that we shall find his Nonconformity develop. It is not too much to say that had Baxter lived in Elizabethan times he would not have been a Nonconformist.

BAXTER'S TERMS FOR CONFORMING

We cannot emphasize too much the fact that Baxter was eager to conform if he could do it without violating his conscience. In his pamphlet on *Unnecessary Separating Disowned* he gives three terms on which he would, as he says, joyfully conform, and as they form a convenient summary of his reasons for not conforming, we propose to analyse them under the headings which he gives.

'I will joyfully conform', he says:

'1. If they (the Church authorities,) will impose on us no *Sinful Oaths, Covenants, Promises, Subscriptions, Declarations* or *Practices*.

'2. I would rejoice in the Reformation, if while some essentiate a Church by a Bishop, they would restore the Parishes to be *Churches*, which they make but *Parts* of the lowest Churches as chappels are, and make the Parish-Ministers Pastors again, whom they have degraded to be Half-Pastors or Curates to the lowest Pastors.

'3. I would hope that we would escape back-sliding into Popery, if that part of the Clergy never govern the Ship, who are not content with a National Government, but make it our necessary duty as against Schism that all come under a *Foreign Jurisdiction:* And if the true Protestant Clergy will joyn in the renunciation of that Jurisdiction, (but not of Communion with Foreign Churches).'[1]

The first two reasons are definite proposals which, if they are carried out, would solve the difficulties of Nonconforming clergy. The third is only a pious hope about the policy of the rulers of the Church, but a hope which would have some substance if the first two proposals were accepted. We will deal first of all with his first condition.

THE IMPOSITION OF OATHS AND SUBSCRIPTIONS

There had been from the early days of Elizabeth attempts to bring some sort of unity into the worship of the Church, by the

[1] Richard Baxter, *Unnecessary Separating Disowned*, p. 26.

imposition of regulations and subscriptions upon the clergy after the manner of Archbishop Parker's *Advertisements*. But in those days the bishops had not been powerful enough to see that these rules were obeyed, for the Queen tacitly refused to place effective power in their hands. It was Bancroft who first saw the way in which these regulations might be enforced, by using the Court of High Commission to supplement the authority of the bishops in their own dioceses. In the hands of Laud this became a potent weapon for the unification of Church worship and discipline. Laud, too, from his own point of view was fortunate that he did not have to trouble about Parliament, but, in conjunction with Strafford, and receiving authority from the King, he could put his theories into practice without much open opposition. Until his day these oaths and subscriptions had been mostly concerned with the worship of the Church, the wearing of ecclesiastical garments, the *Book of Common Prayer*, etc., and Laud had used his power to restore to the Reformed Church something of its old 'Catholic' appearance. But he had also at the height of his power attempted to use his power to settle once and for all the government of the Church as under archbishops, bishops, deans, etc., in the famous *Et cetera* Oath which was passed by Convocation when Baxter was at Bridgnorth. The purpose of this oath was to establish throughout the Church the conviction of the Laudian party that diocesan Episcopacy was not merely a convenience of Church government, as many earlier divines had said it was, but that it was of divine right, so that no one could alter it. It was a move in Laud's policy to restore the independence of the Church, and in its way was just as subversive of the Elizabethan settlement of the Church as Presbyterianism was. Baxter's first objection to an imposed oath was his refusal to take the *Et cetera* Oath.

For Baxter to remain in the ministry of the Anglican Church it was necessary for him to subscribe to the Act of Uniformity and the oaths contained in the Act and the subsequent oaths, such as the Oxford Oath, imposed on the clergy. In his refusal we can discern three underlying reasons which impelled him to his action. These three reasons were:

1. Plain honesty.
2. His desire for liberty in things indifferent.
3. His desire that the government of the Church should be settled on more Scriptural lines.

1. Plain Honesty

In the Act of Uniformity he was asked to give his assent and consent to the use of the *Book of Common Prayer*, the *Book of Ordination*, and the *Homilies*, and to give his approbation that there was nothing in them contrary to the Word of God. We know that his attitude to the *Book of Common Prayer* was that it was defective and needed revising in the light of surer knowledge. Some things in it were obviously false, and some translations in it were not only wrong, but gave a sense diametrically opposed to what was intended by Scripture. But he was prepared to use the Book if he was allowed to recognize that it was defective; what he was not prepared to do was to take a solemn oath in the name of God that there was nothing defective in it! In reality what he was asked to do by the Church authorities was to tell a lie, and even if this had been the only controversial thing between him and the authorities of the Church it would have been enough for him to have refused to conform. But there was more in it than this, for the Act brought to an issue his desire for:

2. Liberty in 'Things Indifferent'

While we know Baxter's desire for such liberty, it is important to notice that what he claimed was liberty, not necessarily for himself, but for others. As we have pointed out, he was prepared to follow the rubrics in these matters in his own ministry, but he was not prepared to turn away those who had a more tender conscience—such people as had a real scruple against using these forms in the entirety. Yet to take the oath would mean that he would have to deny salvation, as the Church understood it and as he believed, by refusing Baptism to those who, while willing to accept Baptism for themselves or their children, yet objected to the use of the sign of the Cross. This was to make salvation depend, not on an act of grace by our Lord, but on a transient, human ordinance. Thus he felt that he dared not damn children and adults because of some scruple, which, though indifferent in itself, was yet real to them. This leads us on to the third underlying reason, namely:

3. His desire for a Church Order based on Scripture

A part of the oath presented to him in the Act of Uniformity was that there was nothing in the government of the Church repugnant to the Word of God. Coupled with this, later on, was the Oxford Oath, which stipulated that there should not be any endeavour to alter such a government. Baxter could not take these oaths with a good conscience because he thought that there was a good deal in the government of the Church which was repugnant to the Word of God. The point of his objection has been explained before in this thesis, and can easily be seen when we realize that, in Baxter's view, the government of the Church by bishops, archbishops, etc., would not be repugnant to the Word of God only when the offices themselves were defined by the Word of God. To him the only Governor of the universal Church was Christ, and in particular Churches the governor was the pastor, who had the power of the keys. Where Churches were organized nationally, as Baxter thought they should be, then the governor was the king. He did not object to the name 'bishop' or 'archbishop', provided that the offices were defined by Scripture. He was willing to conform if he had liberty to reform, but these oaths were an attempt to take away that liberty, and to clamp on the Church a form of government which was unscriptural and therefore without divine sanction. Any form of government in the Church over and above what was specified in Scripture was a human contrivance, which might or might not be good—at any rate, it was no proper subject for a solemn oath. This too was the root of his objection to the oath of canonical obedience, for as the Church was then governed it achieved the same object as the Oxford Oath and made parish ministers subject to the bishops, and consequently curtailed their true authority.

We have gone into detail in explaining his objection to these oaths, but in reality these reasons are fundamentally derivatives of his main reason for not conforming—namely, the necessity for:

THE RESTORATION OF PARISH CHURCHES AND MINISTERS TO THEIR TRUE POSITION

This is the second condition which he lays down if he is to conform, and it is the crux of his position. For if this obtained in the Church, then the reasons for Nonconformity as far as he was concerned would be obviated. The government of the Church to Baxter was not a matter of expediency, but a matter of doctrine, and therefore its form should be modelled on the prime revelation of God, namely, the Scriptures. With Cartwright and the other early Puritan leaders, he contended that bishop and presbyter were the same office,[1] and that, as far as particular Churches were concerned, the minister was 'Episcopus', and inherited Christ's priestly, prophetic, and kingly functions. This is the *fons et origo* of his Nonconformity and of his objection to Prelacy. All clergy were partakers of the same kind of office, and whereas it might be expedient that one should have the preeminence over the others for the sake of order, he was still only the 'first among equals'. This explains his objection to the *Et cetera* and Oxford Oaths; it explains his objection to re-ordination; it explains his objection to the Act of Uniformity and the various oaths associated with it—because if parish ministers were recognized as true bishops and their churches as true churches and not sub-chapels of diocesan cathedrals, the right of exercising the full ministerial office would lie with the parish minister and with no one else. It would be he who would decide, and not the diocesan, whether to baptize with or without the sign of the Cross; it would be he who would decide to give the Sacrament of the Lord's Supper to the recipients whether they knelt or sat; it would be he who would decide whether to wear a surplice or not; it would be he who would decide whether to give Christian burial or not; and it would be he who would decide whether to excommunicate or not. He was prepared to bow to the judgement of his peers if he misused his office, but he was not prepared to bow to the judgement of those who arrogated certain parts of his office to themselves and turned him into a sub-presbyter, a bishop's curate, a utensil of the diocesan. This desire of Baxter's for 'Parish Bishops' laid him open to the accusation that what he wanted was that each parish minister should be a little pope, answerable to no one but God. This he strongly refuted and showed in the Worcestershire Association how such a conception could work in the absence of diocesan Episcopacy, for redress could be had at the hands of the Association of Ministers by anyone who was unjustly treated. There was also the possibility of expanding the close framework of minister and people by the appointment of 'Lay-Elders' who would not only help the minister, but also represent the people. The thing which appealed to Baxter in this system was that it was the person

---

[1] Richard Baxter, *The nonconformists plea for peace* (1679), sect. 16, p. 27.

on the spot who would exercise discipline, and not someone who knew little about the people and in many cases lived far from them.

PARISH BISHOPS AND THE HIERARCHICAL CONCEPTION

This view of Church government also fits in with his conception of hierarchy, although at first sight his opposition to diocesan Episcopacy might lead us to think otherwise. Given his first premises, the equality of bishop and presbyter, his position is closer to a true conception of hierarchy than that of the diocesan framework, for the diocesan framework, as expounded by the Prelatical divines (and it was this view of Episcopacy that Baxter opposed) was subversive of true hierarchy, simply because it made the diocesan bishop a 'Tyrant'. That is why Baxter accuses the Prelatical divines of tyranny, and even though the system might be worked by the mildest of men it was still tyranny for one to lord it over equals. Mr. C. S. Lewis, when explaining the conception of hierarchy, says that Hierarchy can be destroyed in two ways. '1. By ruling or obeying natural equals, that is by Tyranny or Servitude. 2. By failing to obey a natural superior or to rule a natural inferior, that is by Rebellion or Remissness.'[1] With regard to Baxter, the point at issue was whether bishop and presbyter were the same office—that is, equals as regard their ministerial orders. His claim was that they were equals, and that the idea that they were not was something new in the post-Reformation Church in England. Even considering the pre-Reformation Church in England, he says that his view, the Scriptural view, obtained, in theory at least, and quotes the Canons of Alfrick in support of his contention. He draws evidence from the writings of that great scholar, Dr. Stillingfleet, to show that Cranmer and other Reformers considered bishop and presbyter to be the same office,[2] and he even points out that the Roman Church has never defined as *de fide* the doctrine that bishops and presbyters are distinct offices *in specie*, but allowed its doctors to hold the contrary view. Taking his stand on what he considered the old view of the Church of England, and opposing the new view of the Laudian divines, we can see why this new idea was to him tyrannical, for it was

---

[1] C. S. Lewis, *A Preface to Paradise Lost* (1942), p. 75.
[2] Richard Baxter, *The nonconformists plea for peace* (1679), p. 196.

the usurpation of authority by one man over his equals. Those who exercised such authority were guilty of tyranny and those who obeyed it were guilty of servility, both of which were monstrosities.

One of the results of Prelatical government according to Baxter was an increased

DANGER OF BACKSLIDING INTO POPERY

It is because of this danger that Baxter includes as his third condition, if he is to conform, the hope that the government of the Church would not remain in the hands of the Prelatical party. He was convinced that there was a danger of the Church of England slipping back into Roman Catholicism through the influence of the High Church party, and though some think that Baxter greatly exaggerated the danger, there were many others who thought as he did. Parliament was certainly concerned with the danger to the Church and State from Roman Catholicism, and a number of bishops and inferior clergy thought the same. That there was a powerful group of people who trifled with Popery, particularly among the Laudian clergy, is without doubt, and the Roman Catholics themselves were a powerful minority, particularly among the aristocracy, and they had their affinities with the Court. James I was a Calvinist, and Charles I is claimed to have suffered as a martyr for the Church of England. But Charles I's wife was a Roman Catholic, and her house became a centre of Roman Catholic intrigue. The marriage upset the balance of power as between Protestant and Catholic in the State, and this became more obvious as Charles came to rely more and more upon his wife's advice. After the restoration of the monarchy, the Roman Catholic interests at Court were centred around the Duke of York, who was a Roman Catholic himself. But it was not with the Roman Catholics proper that Baxter was concerned in this issue, but with that party in the Church of England who, while they were in many ways opponents of Rome, used 'Catholic' arguments to justify the Church. We can illustrate what we mean by considering the case of Dr. Richard Montagu, the Rector of Stamford-Rivers in Essex. One day he discovered a man in his parish reading a book entitled *The Gag for a New Gospel*, written by a Roman Catholic to show that the Church of England was Calvinist. He read the book, and in 1624 wrote a pamphlet called *A Gag for the New Gospel? No: A New Gag for an Old Goose*, rebutting the charge. His arguments today would be called 'High Church', and were called 'Romanist' by the Puritan section of the Church. Pym, in the last Parliament of James I, declared that the book was full of the dangerous opinions of Arminius, and contrary to the established articles of the Church of England in at least five points. James, however, was pleased with the book, and said that 'If that is to be a Papist, so am I a Papist', and permitted Montagu to write another book called *Appello ad Caesarem*, but died before it was published. It eventually appeared with a dedication to Charles I. The book was discussed in Parliament and declared to be seditious, but Charles made Dr. Montagu his chaplain! Later on, the Parliamentary Committee on Religion discussed Montagu's book again, and Pym, reporting the findings of the committee, elaborated under five articles the contention that Montagu's book conformed to the Church of Rome rather than to the Church of England. Charles further aggravated the matter by raising Dr. Montagu to the bishopric of Chichester. The point of this quarrel between Charles and Parliament which interests us here is that it reveals that there were powerful people in the country who thought as Baxter did about the danger of the national Church backsliding into Popery through the activities of the Laudian party. The Pope himself apparently suffered from the same delusion, if delusion it was, for he offered Laud a cardinal's hat.[1] To those who stood by what they thought were the old Protestant standards of the Church of England, it looked as if Laud and his party were leading the Church of England straight back to Rome.

At any rate, Baxter thought so, and it was one more argument for modelling the Church on Scripture, and making the parish clergy more independent of the diocesan bishops. This fear of Baxter's that there was a design among the Laudian clergy to link up the Church of England with the Church of Rome naturally died down during the Protectorate, but flamed up again when the Restoration bishops were seen to be of the Prelatical type, and it was this conviction that inspired Baxter to write his book, *Against a Revolt to a Foreign Jurisdiction*, in which he collected together his evidence that there was such

[1] *Diary of Archbishop Laud*, Entries for 7th and 14th August 1663, p. 7.

a move on the part of the Prelatical clergy. Dr. Powicke thinks that Baxter was largely the victim of a delusion in this matter,[1] but if he was there were others who shared that delusion. The actual danger that Baxter feared was that the English Church and the Gallican Church would unite on the basis of acknowledging the authority of a General Council of the whole Church under the presidency of the Pope. The Gallican Church was in communion with Rome, but did not accept wholeheartedly the findings of the Council of Trent, and was opposed to the theory of the absolute authority of the Pope, a theory popular in Spain and Italy. It was because the French feared to lose the liberties of their Church that they supported the view that Popes had no authority over kings in temporal affairs, could not depose kings, and that General Councils of the whole Church were above Popes and had the right of reforming the Papacy. They also held the view that the Pope was not infallible except in conjunction with the Church or Councils. Baxter felt that the attitude of the French Church was a more insidious danger to Protestantism, just because it seemed more reasonable, than the attitude of the 'Italian' party in the Roman Church. The difference, as regards England, between these two parties was that the French Church was prepared to form an agreement with the English Church to strengthen their hand in their conflict with Rome, while the 'Italian' party, since they could not get the government of the English Church, wanted a toleration for Catholics in England. The 'Italian' party, represented by the Jesuits in England, supported the full absoluteness of the Papacy, as against Councils and kings, and would have no truck with Gallicanism. Baxter felt that if the Church had to be Papist, it was better to be of the Gallican variety, but he feared this variety more than the 'Italian' variety, because it was more acceptable, and yet would ultimately destroy the form of the Protestant Church by bringing it under one universal human sovereignty, however that sovereignty was defined. It would, he thought, depose Christ from His position as the only universal Sovereign and Lawgiver of the Church, which is one of the fundamental articles of Protestantism. And it was because he feared Gallicanism that he attacked its supporters in the Church of England so vehemently.

That there were some grounds for his fears in the days of Laud

[1] F. J. Powicke, *A Life of the Reverend Richard Baxter, 1615–91* (1924), vol. II, p. 179.

is obvious, for if Laud's design for an independent Church had succeeded, then it is quite conceivable that it would have led to some link with Rome. But the position of the Restoration bishops was very different from that of the Laudian clergy. Laud had real power, so long as the King supported him and Parliament was kept out of the Government, but the Civil War ended that situation, and real power after the Restoration lay not with the King, nor with the bishops, but with Parliament. Any move towards Rome would have had to have the approval of Parliament, and Parliament showed, in the days of James II, what it thought of any Romanizing policy. But Baxter was getting an old man toward the end of Charles II's reign, and perhaps cannot be blamed if he interpreted the language of the Restoration divines to be as effective as that of Laud, and failed to see that the balance of power in the nation had changed so that what might have been a danger under Laud and Charles I was not under Sheldon and Charles II. Whether Baxter was right or wrong in his estimate of the danger to Protestantism in Prelacy does not alter the fact that what danger there was partly arose from the excessive power of the bishops, particularly when that power was in the hands of Prelatical bishops. He was a firm believer in the adage that 'Power corrupts, and absolute power corrupts absolutely', and, as we have seen in an earlier chapter, he traced a good deal of the sin and error of the Church to the increase of power and authority of the diocesan bishops. When he came to the conclusion, after his study of the rise and growth of Episcopacy, that even the spiritual authority of diocesan bishops had been usurped from the lesser clergy, he became more and more convinced that the only cure by human means for the disunity of the Church was to restore to presbyters the authority he believed to be inherent in their office. Until this was done, he felt that he must remain a 'Mere Nonconformist'.

Chapter XIV

SOME ASPECTS OF REUNION RECONSIDERED

On one occasion, when the philosophical Tony Weller was discussing his recent marriage with his son Sam, he wondered whether it was worth while going through so much to learn so little! The gentle reader may have the same feeling after reading the preceding chapters, and in his mind there may be the thought that while the passions and beliefs of men which once rocked whole nations may make an interesting academic study for those who like such things, they can have little bearing on the problems of the Christian Church of today, and, that being so, it would be better to let these 'Old, unhappy, far-off things, and battles long ago'[1] rest undisturbed in the graveyard of history. Yet there is a sense in which the Preacher was right when he said 'There is nothing new under the sun', at least it seems to be true of ecclesiastical history, for the old controversies, like King Charles's head, keep cropping up in every discussion on Christian reunion. The issues over which men fought and died in the seventeenth century are still alive to-day, not quite so lusty as they were, and confined to a smaller circle of people, but within the Christian Church the beliefs which divided our forefathers still divide us.

The *milieu* in which these ideas operate has changed with the increase of secularism and materialism, and therefore the circle of their influence has narrowed. The relative strengths of the various protagonists have altered too, and other movements have arisen which put forth those ideas in different forms, and clamour themselves to enter the ecclesiastical ring with the older contestants. Yet, while all Christians lament the change in the balance of power between the Church and the world, one thing it has done: it has forced the Christian Churches to draw closer together in spirit, if not in practice, and has dispelled a great deal of the enmity that existed between the various branches of the Church. Movements like the 'Faith and Order' movement, the 'Life and Work' movement, the South India Scheme, and many other signs, testify to a greater sense of the

---

[1] W. Wordsworth, *The Solitary Reaper*.

tragedy of the broken Body of Christ among Christian people, as well as to the growing conviction that, in face of the mounting enmity to Christian ideas in the world, a 'house divided against itself cannot stand'. Even the Roman Catholics, despite their excessively parochial outlook, are much more friendly with Protestants, and in the 'Sword of the Spirit' movement have an instrument by which they can co-operate with Protestants in moral and social questions.

Yet it is not only because of the general interest in the question of Christian reunion that we venture into the field of ecclesiastical controversy, but also because Christian unity was the main purpose of Baxter's activities, and, since all things must come to an end, we feel that no end could be more fitting to a work on Richard Baxter than one which touches the cause which he had so much at heart. To Baxter's passionate soul, Christian unity was the crying need of the times in which he lived. To this end, he dedicated, not only his ministry at Kidderminster, but also his life when in exile from the Church he so much loved. Yet he was not prepared to sacrifice everything even to such a cause. Time, money, and mental effort he could give, and he gave them without stint, but those convictions which inhabited the secret places of his heart, and without which life was not worth living, he could not surrender. So he clung pitifully to the fringes of the Anglican Church, bearing with patience the indignities which were put upon him; in it when he could attend its worship, but not of it by reason of the integrity of his own convictions. In our remarks on the thorny subject of Christian reunion, we propose to touch on four points which have a bearing on the matter; they are:

1. The problem of 'Clericalism'.
2. The Episcopal Office.
3. The Sacraments.
4. The relation between the Church and the State.

1. THE PROBLEM OF 'CLERICALISM'

A Frenchman who visited this country in the nineteenth century is said to have remarked that the difference between this country and his own which seemed most striking to him was that, whereas in his own country there was one Church and a multitude of sauces, in England there was only one sauce and a multitude of different Churches. Being a Frenchman, we may pardon his interest in these gastronomical details, but his remark might almost be taken as an epigram on the difference between the Catholic and Protestant worlds, for while in Catholic countries only one Church form is allowed, but innumerable political parties flourish above and 'underground', Protestant countries seem to be more politically stable, though there are numerous Church forms in existence. A comparison of the histories of such Catholic countries as Spain, Austria, the South American states, Poland, and even France, with Protestant countries such as Britain, America, and the Scandinavian countries will show how difficult it seems to be to get real, stable governments in Catholic states as compared with Protestant states. The Catholic solution to the perpetual problem of revolutions in Catholic states seems usually to be a repressive dictatorship, such as we see in Spain, and many South American countries, and did see in pre-war Austria, Italy, Hungary, Poland, etc. It is not without significance that Fascism flourished in these states, and that Nazism was born in Catholic Bavaria, and had an unexcommunicated Catholic as its chief. At the same time, in these Catholic states there is usually a large atheistic Communist Party, and even the Socialist parties there are usually atheistic and anti-clerical. To an onlooker it seems as if the legitimate child of Catholicism in civil government is Fascism, while its bastard child is atheistic Communism!

The late Bernard Manning suggests that the reason for this apparent instability in the civil and economic life of Catholic countries, and their tendency to produce large atheistic minorities, is due to the absence of evangelical religion in those countries.[1] The choice before a man in a Catholic state, as regards the Christian faith, is usually a 'clerical' religion or nothing, and those who cannot accept a 'clerical' Church drift into atheism and anarchy. The result of this is the growth of a vicious anti-clerical spirit and an open hostility to the Church. In Protestant countries the anti-clerical feeling is negligible, and though there may be indifference to the claims of the Churches, there is little hostility to them. It may be argued that this is because the Protestant Churches are so supine that they do not engender enmity, but it may also be argued that the use which Evangelical Churches make of laymen in all their work and councils has

[1] Bernard Manning, *Essays in Orthodox Dissent* (Independent Press, 1939), p. 131.

produced in the laity a consciousness that the work of the Church is as much their concern as it is of the ordained ministry. Even those who are indifferent to the Churches have friends or relatives who are 'Church people' and have a real 'say' in the control and organization of their Church. This is a state of affairs which cannot obtain in Churches which have a 'Catholic' tradition, for the proper office of the laity there is to learn, and the proper office of the priesthood is to teach, while the control of the Church is vested in the priesthood alone. This difference between the 'Catholic' tradition and the 'Evangelical' tradition in Church government is a vital one for Nonconformists in any discussion on Church reunion, and in any such reunion Nonconformists must ask the question whether the proposed reunited Church is to be a 'clerical' Church or not?

We propose, therefore, to define more closely what we mean by a 'clerical' Church. A 'clerical' Church, as we understand it, is a Church which is defined by its ministry, and not a Church which, under God, defines its own ministry. As a rider to this definition, we may say that in a 'clerical' Church it is the ministry alone who have the control of the Church, and all ministerial acts, whether of preaching the Gospel or the administration of the Sacraments, are the sole prerogative of the ministry. In a non-clerical Church, laymen are admitted to the control of the Church, and have the right of performing ministerial acts, although those rights are not always exercised. Obviously, we have here two different theories of the Church and ministry: in the one the Church is divided into two sections —those who have the right to ministerial authority and those who have not; in the other, the whole Church has the right to the ministerial authority, though for the sake of order in the Church those rights are only exercised by those who are chosen by the Church. We can perhaps emphasize our point by an illustration from the civil government of our country. We have had for many years a force of men who maintain order in the State—namely, the police force. But the duty of maintaining order, and even the power of arrest, is not the sole prerogative of the police; it is the duty and right of every member of the State to preserve order, and even to arrest a felon if he is seen committing a crime. The police are a separated body of men who do this work as a full-time job, and the work is done better than it would be if there were not this force, but the theory behind it is that all have the right and obligation of preserving order, but for efficiency and convenience a body of men are charged directly with the task. This is an accurate analogy to the Evangelical or non-clerical view of the Church, where the ministerial rights belong to all, but the exercise of those rights is normally confined to the few.

In both 'clerical' and non-clerical Churches, the source of ministerial authority is believed to come from God, but they differ in their conception of the means by which that authority is conveyed to the minister. In a non-clerical Church, ministerial authority is believed to be given *direct* by God, and is first displayed by the consciousness of an inward call, by one of the members, to exercise those rights which are the property of all. The office of the Church in ordination is to test that call, under the guidance of the Holy Spirit, and to seal the ordinand as a proper and fit person to do the work that the call implies. The Church has the right to test a man's call and commission him to work in its own sphere. In a clerical Church, on the other hand, ministerial authority is believed to be conveyed to a suitable person by the ordination of a bishop, who himself derives his power through a succession of such ordinations back to the Apostles. Only those who have such a succession are conceived to be true ministers, and only they have the right to ministerial authority. It follows, therefore, that only a Church which has such a ministry is a true Church, and the Church is defined by the ministry. In technical language, that is a true Church which has the Apostolic Succession.

Even so, it is not the possession of the Apostolic Succession in itself which is the cause of 'clericalism', but a particular belief about the Apostolic Succession. Indeed, the possession of such a historic continuity can have a valuable psychological effect for good, particularly in an age such as this, in which the nostalgia for 'historic' things is so pronounced. But it is true to say that the possession of the Apostolic Succession makes it much easier for 'clericalism' to gain a hold on a Church, simply because the doctrine provides a vehicle by which a particular view of ordination is given a sensible framework. The particular view of ordination to which we refer is that which Baxter called the 'Prelatic' view. That is the view that the bishop gives the 'grace' of ministerial power in ordination to the candidate, first because only he possesses it, and second, because God willed that it should be so. It is this view of ordination, coupled with the Apostolic Succession, which makes a possible framework and justification for confining ministerial authority and power, by right, to a particular body of men, to the exclusion of all others, and thus tends to the creation of 'clericalism' in the Church.

On the other hand, there is a form of 'clericalism' operative in Nonconformist Churches, and that is the form that is exemplified in Baxter. Baxter did not believe in the Apostolic Succession, nor in the Prelatic view of ordination, but he did believe that once a man was commissioned to the Christian ministry he entered into an engagement for life, and had the right of exercising Christ's priestly, prophetic, and kingly ministry, to the extent to which it is possible for a fallible human being to exercise it. A layman invaded the ministerial office at his own peril. Baxter even went so far as to confine valid Baptism to the ministry alone, a conception directly contrary to the whole tradition of the Church. But Baxter's 'clericalism' was tempered by the fact that he recognized that quasi-ministerial functions, at least in the government of the Church, could be exercised by laymen, in conjunction with the ministry, and organized his church at Kidderminster on those lines. In the Worcestershire Association, he provided for the appointment of lay elders, but was not prepared to give them the right to administer the Sacraments. The point with him was that outside the conception laid down in Scripture of one universal Church with one Leader, Christ, subdivided into particular Churches each with their bishop or minister, the Church could organize its polity in any way it chose, under the guidance of the Holy Spirit. Those so chosen to help the ministry in the government of the Church received their authority from God also, and it is a moot point whether they should be called ministers or laymen. It was this freedom, anchored to Holy Scripture, which preserved Baxter's system from the worst features of 'clericalism'.

It is obvious to anyone who knows Nonconformity at all that they will never consent to a united Church which is 'clerical' in practice; they feel that the doctrine of the priesthood of all believers must be admitted, whatever safeguards are put around the ministry. Not to do this, they believe, is to define the Church by the ministry, and make a particular ministerial polity necessary for salvation. This also means that the idea of the Apostolic Succession must be freed from any prelatic view of ordination.

To Nonconformists, those who claim salvation because they have St. Peter or the Apostles to their fathers are in no better case than the Jews, who claimed the same thing because they had Abraham to their father.

THE EPISCOPAL OFFICE

This leads us on naturally to our second point—namely, the question of Episcopal government in the Church. Now, it is an assured thing, which Nonconformists must recognize, that there will be no united Church without some form of Episcopacy. Those Churches which possess a ministry under the name of 'bishops' value it so highly that they are never likely to surrender it. Despite the old adage, 'What's in a name?' Nonconformists can admit that there is something in a name, especially when that name has such a long tradition in the Church, and is hallowed with so many holy memories; and, indeed, for the comfort of those Nonconformists who are really concerned with the possibility of Church reunion, it is not Episcopacy as such that their fathers in the Faith disliked, but Prelacy—that is, that conception of Episcopacy which arrogated to the office of diocesan bishop powers and rights which they thought were the property of every ordained minister. Therefore Nonconformists, when they are asked to accept Episcopacy, want to know what is meant by the term.

It is only the study of Church history which can supply the answer, and yet Church history gives many answers—as many answers almost as the preconceived ideas of Church historians attach to it. This is the real trouble, for it is extremely difficult for a historian to approach the subject detached, as it were, from his own tradition and his own predilections. We are so apt to find in history what we look for. Let us look at one example of this. *The Didache*, in Chapter 15, exhorts the people in these words: 'Now appoint for yourselves bishops and deacons worthy of the Lord, men meek and not avaricious and upright and proved'; nothing is said of their ordination, and it looks as if they received their commission from the congregation. Now let us see how this is treated by one historian pleading a particular kind of Episcopacy: 'As to the presbyter-bishops and deacons', he says, 'we may justifiably believe that they needed Ordination before they could minister. The *Teaching*, being addressed to the laity, naturally only deals with the manner of choosing them: they are to be "appointed" by the lay people. It can hardly be doubted that they would afterwards be ordained by one of the wandering "Apostles".[1] Now, we may ask, are the assumptions lurking behind this comment fair assumptions? We submit that they are only fair if the threefold ministry of bishops, priests, and deacons is the one which history teaches is normal in the Church from earliest days, and if the manner and necessity of their ordination is such as the comment assumes. But this is precisely what we are trying to discover. Now, if this sort of special pleading, with its 'We can justifiably believe', and its 'It can hardly be doubted', is a right method of discovering historical truth, then a good case can be made out for the 'Catholic' theory of Episcopacy in the early Church, but an equally good case can be made out against it! Now, the same thing applies to the study of any other branch of the Church, and to the study of any other controversial problem in Church history. If we take the history of the Church of England from the Elizabethan settlement, we can find a good case for the 'Catholic' theory of Episcopacy in Mason's *The Church of England and Episcopacy*, but, on the other hand, if we read Hunkin's *The Call to Christian Unity*, we can find an equally good case made out that the Church of England has not always maintained an unbroken succession, and has never approved as a whole the theory of the Apostolic Succession as a necessity for true Church order. We suggest that all that can be truthfully said about Episcopacy is that in the past able theologians believed in the 'Catholic' theory, and that other equally able men did not believe in it, and that at least two views of Episcopacy are tenable in the Church of England, as, indeed, we understand they are in the Roman Church. Therefore, we say, all that should be asked of Nonconformists in any scheme of Church reunion is that they should tolerate those views of Episcopacy with which they do not agree, but that the validity of their own 'orders' should be recognized, and that some scheme should be worked out which will unite the practice of both opinions. But the first thing to be recognized is that none of these views of Church government are proved by history to be the only form of Church government God intended, but are only opinions, and therefore equally entitled to their place in any united Church.

[1] K. D. Mackenzie, *The Case for Episcopacy* (S.P.C.K.), p. 31.

The same thing may be said of the relationship between Episcopacy and ordination. The Church of England has recognized that those Nonconformists who go under the name of the Free Churches have a valid ministry, but they qualify it by saying that their ministries, though 'valid', are 'irregular'. To Nonconformists this attempt by the Anglican Church to have its cake and eat it is an illustration of a comment on that Church by one of its own prominent theologians, that the Anglican Church is like an animal with a brain in its head and in its tail, so that when it moves it moves sideways! Though Dr. Henson wonders whether it has even moved sideways, for in a letter to *The Times* dated 22nd January 1944, on the Archbishop of Canterbury's speech in Convocation, he says that his Grace appears to identify the 'tradition of the Church of England and of the Anglican Communion' with the Tractarian doctrine of Apostolic Succession, and begs to dissent from such a view which appears to him to be inconsistent with the history and formularies of the Church of England, and destructive of any reasonable hope for reunion with non-Episcopal Churches.

The point at issue is what is meant by 'validity' and 'regularity'. If by 'validity', as applied to Free Church ministries, the Anglicans mean that the mercies of God, covenanted in Christ, are secured (the ancient meaning of the term 'valid') to those Churches by their ministry, then it is difficult to see what can be meant by calling them 'irregular'. Unless, of course, 'regularity' refers merely to the *historical* fact that Nonconformist ministers are not ordained in the manner which has been the normal 'rule' of the Church, i.e. by diocesan bishops, and has no reference to any theory of the transference of grace. In this case, we cannot see why it was mentioned, for, from the nature of the case, it must be obvious to all that Nonconformist ministries must be 'irregular'. But we suspect, in the absence of any clearer definition of the terms, that this is not what is meant by the Anglicans. Therefore Nonconformists may be pardoned if they ask how God can bless a 'valid' ministry in everything that the term implies and yet act 'irregularly', whose very acts are the standard by which we measure what is regular and what is not? If God acts at all, He must act 'regularly'.

Another point we must mention in this discussion of the relationship between the Episcopate and ordination is the question of 'delegated' authority. It was an important point to

Baxter and the early Nonconformists, and Baxter was quite unequivocal in insisting that ordinary parish priests were not full ministers. He calls them sub-presbyters, or bishops' curates, and one of his demands in any solution of the question of Church unity was that the presbyter should be restored to his primitive authority. This issue obviously troubles Mackenzie, who takes the view that in the primitive Church the presbyter received such authority as was convenient for his ministry from the true occupant of the pastoral office—namely, the bishop. The presbyter did not act as a minister in his own right, but merely as doing such of the bishop's work as he was allowed to do. But, says Mackenzie, 'It cannot be argued that because the presbyter was at one time merely the bishop's delegate, therefore he has no rights of his own. The whole parochial system depends on the idea of a permanent delegation of authority which cannot be resumed by the bishop at his own will.' Baxter's comment on this would have been that the bishop has no ability or right to give away any of his authority; it is God who gives ministerial authority, and what He gives to the presbyter is the same as He gives to the bishop. The fact that the bishop cannot take back what he has once delegated is immaterial; the point is that the bishop cannot delegate authority. Or, to put it in the way that Baxter usually puts it, the bishop has arrogated some of the authority to which the presbyter is entitled to himself, so that the presbyter in any Episcopal Church is not a full minister. Baxter's objection to what he thought the growth of the Episcopal office had done to the office of presbyter is somewhat the same as Mackenzie's own complaint about what the growth of the Papacy had done to the office of bishop in the Roman Church. 'Most of the Papalist theologians', he says, 'would indeed allow that bishops exercise jurisdiction by "Divine right" the voice of the episcopate is the infallible voice of the Church; it would be difficult to exaggerate the authority which is assigned to the episcopal office in theory. But in actual practice the Roman bishop is little more than a delegate of the Apostolic See. He is usually appointed by the Pope and in all cases his election must be confirmed by him. The bishop only exercises his jurisdiction on sufferance. . . . We are here faced with a real corruption and a degradation of the proper liberties of the episcopal office.'[1] If 'presbyter' is substituted for 'bishop', and

[1] K. D. Mackenzie, *The Case for Episcopacy* (S.P.C.K., 1929), p. 107.

'bishop' for 'Pope', Baxter might have written it, for with these substitutions it sums up exactly his own complaint about the degradation of the office of presbyter. What is sauce for the goose apparently cannot be sauce for the gander!

Seeing, therefore, that Nonconformist ministries are claimed to be not only valid ministries, but to be of the same order as that of bishops in the Episcopal Churches (for any bishop or president in Nonconformist Churches is only *primus inter pares*, or, as Baxter would say, of the same ministerial office as others *in specie*, if not *in gradu*), it hardly seems feasible to expect them to surrender their proper liberty for the doubtful privilege of calling one of their brethren 'My lord'.

Yet this is not the whole of the matter, for nearly all Nonconformists recognize the value, and even the necessity, of different spheres of authority in the Church, unless they are intransigently Independent. In any matter of discipline in the Church, there must be a final court whose decisions are binding on the members if discipline is to be exercised with justice. And many Nonconformists are coming to see also the value of such a territorial and pastoral office as a chairman or president of the ministers in an area, who shall have the oversight of the district. This in its practice is analogous to diocesan Episcopacy. The chairman of a Methodist district or the moderator of a Presbyterian synod probably has much the same sort of work to do as an Anglican or Roman bishop, though the theory behind their appointments differ. The things which are common to these various offices indicate the fact that the task of organizing the Church gives rise to the same type of problem in every denomination; and indeed, it would be strange if it were not so, for behind our differences is the same purpose: the conversion of the world to the righteousness which is in Christ, and the preparation of human souls for Heaven. Not only is the end the same, but fundamentally the means are the same. It is not by accident that the Roman Catholics carve over the door of Westminster Cathedral, 'Jesus Christ, King and Redeemer, save us by Thy Blood', and that the Methodist, Charles Wesley, sings of the same fount of redeeming grace in: 'And can it be, that I should gain an interest in the Saviour's blood?' Because, therefore, the Faith we severally hold is one, it may not be too much to hope that some day our order may be one, for hope, after all, was never a pagan, but a Christian virtue.

THE SACRAMENTS

Arising out of the different views of the place, function, and authority of the ministry in the Church comes the question of the Sacraments. Nonconformist ministries are ministries of the Word and Sacraments, and both functions are equally important; the one cannot take precedence over the other. But in the discussions which arise from the consideration of Church reunion the Sacraments stand out as one of the chief causes of division. In common with all Protestants, the Nonconformists recognize two Sacraments as being of divine institution, the Sacrament of Baptism and the Eucharist, or Sacrament of the Lord's Supper. But the cause of our division is not to be found in the necessity of the rites themselves, but in the interpretation put upon those rites. The Sacrament of Baptism, again, is not such a powerful cause of division as the Lord's Supper, because of the tradition of the Church, which is observed in theory if not always in practice, that Baptism by heretics is valid, if the proper form is used. It is the Sacrament of the Lord's Supper, pre-eminently the sign of unity, which is universally the sign of Christian disunity. It is here, above all places, where prejudice and passion, ignorance and conviction find a happy hunting ground for exploitation, particularly—and we say it in love— among those who abuse the word 'Catholic' and confine it to a sect. To Nonconformists the 'matter' of the Sacrament of Holy Communion consists of the representative of Christ (usually the ordained minister), the Elements, and the faithful people; added to which are the verbal and manual acts of Christ, as they have come down to us in Scripture. And this in its essence is the 'matter' of the same Sacrament in any Church. Now, where we differ is not in the 'matter' of the Sacrament, but in the interpretation put upon the sacramental act itself. The interpretation, however, is not 'revelation', but 'tradition', and our plea is that no interpretation should be allowed to separate Christian people. What happens in the Sacrament has not been revealed to us, except that we know that it is a means of grace of our Lord's instituting; therefore, Nonconformists cannot see why a particular interpretation of the Sacraments should be made a *sine qua non* of salvation any more than a particular view of the Episcopal office should. We are not saved by tradition, though, with many other helps, it may be a good guide to the source of saving grace.

We may offer as an example of the type of thought which sees the necessity of agreement on 'interpretations' before Church reunion is feasible a comment by Mr. T. S. Eliot in *Thoughts after Lambeth*, on the Lambeth Conference (1930). On the phrase in the report, 'A bishop might authorize and encourage baptized communicant members of Churches not in communion with our own to communicate in his diocese with Anglicans, when the ministrations of their own Church are not available', Mr. Eliot remarks: 'But what does the suggestion imply? Surely *if* Dissenters should never communicate in Anglican churches, or *if* in certain circumstances they should be encouraged to do so, two very different theories of the Sacrament of the Altar are implied. . . . What is required is some theory of degrees of reception of the Blessed Sacrament, as well as the validity of the ministration of a celebrant not episcopally ordained.'[1] The key-word for our purpose is 'theory'. Now, a theory, to be of any value, must fit the known facts of the case, and where facts arise which contradict that theory it must be disregarded, and a new theory which does fit the facts must take its place. We have already touched on Mr. Eliot's second point—namely, the question of the validity of non-Episcopal ministries—and we should like to say something about the 'theory of degrees of reception of the Blessed Sacrament'. If any theory on this issue is required for any reunited Church, the question arises as to where the facts are to be obtained which will form the basis of this theory. Generally, the facts which form the basis of any theory on the reception of the Sacrament are taken from the opinions of those who study Church history, and form a corollary to their view of the validity of non-Episcopal ministries. Those who receive the Sacraments from such ministries are said by those of the 'Catholic' tradition to receive 'The uncovenanted mercies of God', and are therefore excluded from the covenant of grace revealed to us in Christ. No Nonconformist can accept this view, and it is difficult for them to see how it would be possible to produce a theory of the degrees of reception of the Blessed Sacrament which would do justice to all the facts. For the main facts are to be found not in the study of Church history, nor in the decrees of Church

[1] T. S. Eliot, *Thoughts after Lambeth* (Faber and Faber).

counsels, but in the experience of those who receive the Sacrament, and in the holiness of life which their attendance at the means of grace produces.

Those who insist on the necessity of some theory of the reception of the Sacrament will find themselves in the predicament of the late Cardinal Manning. The Cardinal, faced with the obvious holiness of life of many Protestants he knew, and particularly of some of those he admitted to the Church of Rome, was prepared to argue that the Holy Communion was a dispensable means of grace, and that a Christian could advance to great holiness without it.[1] He was driven to this view by the rigidity of the ministerial theories of his Church, which compelled him to say that Protestant Sacraments were invalid. He could not say that Protestant Sacraments were true Sacraments, and so was forced to think that Christian holiness could be attained without the Sacrament of Holy Communion, and he concluded that these people were in the grace of their Baptism, though, since the grace of Baptism is given, whoever the ministrant, according to the 'Catholic' and traditional view of the Church, it would seem that the Cardinal was 'spiking his own guns'. There are therefore only two logical attitudes to be taken with regard to this Sacrament, and they are, (1) that only our own Sacrament is valid and everyone else is excluded from the covenanted mercies of Christ, or (2) all Sacraments are valid where the intention of the Church is to receive the covenanted mercies of Christ. This latter is the Nonconformist attitude, and, we believe, the traditional attitude of the Anglican Church, as found in the words of Whitgift, Bancroft, and Hooker. To say that some theory is needed to define how much sacramental grace each communicant can receive is absurd, and to Nonconformists takes its place among all those irreverent theories of the Sacraments, which try to limit what Christ may do with His own.

Nor does this attitude to the Sacraments on the part of Nonconformists mean that they are neglected, for Nonconformists as a whole are at least as regular at Holy Communion as Roman Catholics or Anglicans, and, although they do not demand a particular theory of the Sacrament of Holy Communion from the recipient, their hymns, which are their liturgy, testify to the fact that the Sacred Feast has always been to them more than

[1] See Archdeacon Gregg, *The Church and Non-conformity* (Arnold, 1912), pp. 139-41.

a commemorative meal, that it does, in fact, 'set forth the Lord's death until He come'. When Methodists sing with Charles Wesley:

> Victim divine, Thy grace we claim,
>   While this Thy precious death we show:
> Once offered up, a spotless Lamb,
>   In Thy great temple here below,
> Thou didst for all mankind atone,
> And standest now before the throne.
>
> We need not now go up to heaven,
>   To bring the long-sought Saviour down;
> Thou art to all already given,
>   Thou dost even now Thy banquet crown:
> To every faithful soul appear,
> And show Thy real presence here.

they praise in language that is not only Scriptural, but also traditional, the One whose Body was broken and whose Blood was shed, that men may eat and drink to life eternal. The word 'victim' which is used in the sacramental hymns of Wesley and of Doddridge is a word representing the Sacrificial element in the Sacrament, stronger than any to be found in the Anglican rite, and takes us back beyond the Elizabethan settlement to the tradition of the Medieval Church; while the presence in the Sacramental Section of the *Methodist Hymn-book* of hymns invoking the blessing and action of the Holy Spirit brings into promimence an older tradition still: that of the 'Epiclesis' of the early Christian Church, such as we find in Justin, Irenaeus, and in Serapion's *Sacramentary*.

We have already seen that Baxter thought that the differences between the various Protestant Churches with regard to the Sacraments were the result, not so much of theory, but of prejudice and ignorance. Whether Baxter narrows down the problem too much or not, we need not inquire, but it is certain that prejudice and ignorance play a great part in our differences. So great, in fact, that the common view among Christians is that intercommunion should be the last thing attempted in any efforts after a more formal unity. We should like to suggest, however, that intercommunion should be the first thing attempted, for it is the touchstone of the integrity of our desires and motives in reunion. If we cannot unite at what is by common consent the holiest place in any Church, we really cannot unite anywhere. If holiness be our desire for individuals and the Church, then that Sacrament, which is the Sacrament of confirmation and progress in the Faith, should be the centre of our union. Without this our discussions on Episcopacy and orders are so much beating the air, for our differences are a Gordian knot which will not yield to unravelling; what is wanted is a bold stroke which will cut the entail of the past, and open up a plain way to future unity.

THE RELATION BETWEEN THE CHURCH AND STATE

Another thing we may touch on which has a bearing on the question of Church reunion is the future relationship between the Church and State if and when Church reunion is consummated. We have already seen that Baxter, the leader of Nonconformity in the seventeenth century, was a firm believer in the Royal Supremacy. To him the ideal Church was a national Church, under a Christian king as supreme governor. Apparently, also, those Nonconformists who were expelled by the Act of Uniformity agreed to the same Elizabethan idea, since it was never an issue with them. Nor did these object to the endowment of Church livings. They were neither believers in a 'voluntary Church' nor believers in the separation of Church and State. They did not take the view of their contemporary, Helwys, the Baptist preacher, who repudiated the authority of the king in matters ecclesiastical, and pleaded for religious liberty for all.[1] We mention this to point out that disendowment and disestablishment are not *necessarily* a part of the Nonconformist case against Anglicanism. It was the price that Nonconformists of Baxter's type had to pay for the sake of their consciences. In Scotland, where the Nonconformists gained power, a different theory of the relation between the Church and the State was worked out. A theory which recognized the spiritual independence of the Church, but also recognized that these two organs of the community must work together. They were engaged in a common spiritual task, and therefore they owed mutual duties to each other. Had the Presbyterian party succeeded to the same extent in dominating English life, no doubt some similar

[1] Thomas Helwys, *The Ministry of Iniquity* (1612).

theory would have obtained here. Baxter would have served in the Church so established, though to him it would not have been the ideal Church.

Today the case is somewhat different. The Nonconformists have a long tradition of independent Church life, an independence forced on many of them, but an independence highly valued now by all. Yet many of them would not be opposed to some form of establishment in any united Church. What is fairly certain is that they would not agree to the present form of such an establishment. Even the Anglicans themselves feel restive under it, as the 'Archbishops' Commission on the Relationship between Church and State' shows.[1] The 1928 Prayer Book controversy brought home to many Anglicans their subservience, in matters of ritual and doctrine, to many who hotly disagree with them. It emphasized in a very painful way the fact that they were not masters in their own house. Yet this is the wrong phrase, for it is not their own house that they inhabit; it is a house which belongs to the nation. They are not even tenants of the house, allowed to decorate it as they please—in fact, they are more in the nature of caretakers, and must run the house according to the will of the owners. This arrangement worked admirably when the majority of the nation was Anglican, but now that a large minority of the nation is not even Christian, the position for the Anglicans becomes more and more difficult. Yet while we have a national Church, every member of the State has the right to a 'say' concerning the conduct of its worship, if only on the ground that he who pays the piper has a right to call the tune.

The Archbishops' Commission has its own suggested solution of the difficulty. Their solution is that after the Church in its own courts has decided its doctrine and worship, the Royal Assent should be obtained, and the Measure would then have the effect of an Act of Parliament. The review by the House of Commons would thus be avoided, and the Anglicans would be able to have their spiritual independence, while retaining their State connexion. If we may use a slang phrase, they would have their penny and the bun! It is hard to believe that this is offered as a serious solution to the difficulty, for if it is, then it means that the Anglicans, like the Bourbons, have learnt nothing and forgotten nothing. Their proposal is the old attempt

[1] *Press and Publications Board of the Church of England*, 1935, vol. I, p. 12.

to separate the King and Parliament, which was one of the chief causes of the Civil War. If Archbishop Laud, with all his power and the living tradition of Royal Supremacy behind him, could not do it, then the present emasculated Anglicanism won't be able to do it, and they must look for some other way out of what many of them think is an impossible situation. Even disestablishment is not a feasible way out, for it would probably result in an undignified, if not unchristian, struggle by the various denominations (not forgetting the Roman Catholics) to gain some use for themselves of the ecclesiastical buildings so vacated. There is indeed no solution in the present state of affairs. As we have made our beds, so must we lie on them, until we can find some ecclesiastical bed of Ware which can accommodate us all. If we can find such a bed, then the question of the relationship between the Church and State might be solved by some such arrangement as exists in Scotland, and so enable us to preserve what is valuable for the life of the nation in the present recognition of the Christian religion by the State.

THE KEY OF TOLERATION

We end with one thought of Baxter's which seems to us to be of value in any attempt to get beyond the present impasse between the Churches, and that is his conception of toleration. Baxter was not a tolerant man, but he came to see its value, not only within the State, but perhaps more so within the Church. We recall that he thought that unity in Church matters might be had in two ways. It could be had with uniformity of doctrine, worship, and government, or without it. Unity with uniformity was possible, but most improbable; therefore he thought that unity might be possible without it, and the key to the matter was tolerance. Of course, he set a limit to tolerance, for this tolerance was to be exercised within the limits of the Christian Church, defined first of all by the Sacrament of Baptism. This would naturally exclude deists, Socinians, Unitarians, and all who disputed the Faith of the Church as defined by the Scriptures and the historic Creeds. But there were large areas within the Church where there was no generally accepted definition, and where often no definition was needed, and it was here that toleration, as between sect and sect, could be exercised. This applied particularly to questions of Church government, where an amicable solution embracing all traditions could be worked out; to forms and ceremonies, and their use by those who felt a need for them; and it could be applied to matters of interpretation, given goodwill on both sides. Take the simple question of the presence of godparents at the Baptism of a child, which was a stone of stumbling to some Nonconformists. Baxter would not have objected to the presence of godparents, if it was also recognized that the presence of the parents, if they were believers, was necessary too. It was the framing of the rule almost to exclude the parents to which he objected. Here was a case where toleration would have solved the difficulty, and any number of similar cases could be cited. A present-day instance, perhaps, would be the custom of reserving the Sacrament in many Anglican churches. Nonconformists are inclined to think that this is superstitious, or possibly even tending to idolatry, while Anglicans, or at least some of them, point out that there is a very ancient tradition in the Church in support of the custom. The real difficulty occurs when those Anglicans who practise this custom say that those who do not practise it have a wrong theory of the Sacrament, and when Nonconformists say that it is these Anglicans who have the wrong theory. We are not arguing that the custom is right or even good, but we are arguing that neither side has the right to make their own view of the Sacrament the touchstone of the piety or devotion of the whole Church. It is this mania for definition, an inheritance from the Scholastic age, which is the curse of Church life, and until we realize that the purpose of a 'definition' is to divide, and that the fewer we have of them the better, a reunited Church is out of the question. A few definitions we must have, but they should be confined to the smallest possible number. This is not to say that we must not have dogmas—the more we have of them in any united Church the better—but we must remember that a dogma is that which we have agreed upon as being true, and not that which our own particular tradition, or inclination, tells us is true. One last thing we should like to see coupled with this conception of tolerance in working out a method of reunion is the application of some form of the doctrine of 'Intention'. This doctrine goes back to the early days of the Church, and is used by Athanasius in defending his view that Baptism by Arians and other heretics is useless, even though they use the correct words, because they have not a right intention. That is to say, those who use the Trinitarian formula, without holding the orthodox Trinitarian belief, cannot intend to baptize into the true faith, and their Baptism is therefore unprofitable.[1] Baxter knew of the doctrine and used it to criticize the Roman doctrine of succession of orders. 'The intention of the ordainer or consecrater is with them of necessity to the thing', he says, 'and no man can be certain of the intention of the ordainers.'[2] Therefore no man can be certain that he who gives him the Sacraments is a true priest. Baxter does not use the doctrine himself, because it is not necessary to his view of ordination. But if we use the idea of 'Intention' in the general sense of discovering what lies behind ecclesiastical acts and forms, then we can say that Baxter uses it persistently. His whole purpose was to discover what was the intention of our Lord in founding His Church, and then to frame a polity, and use such traditional forms as were convenient, to give the best effect to that intention. It is in this general sense that we feel that the doctrine could be used in approaching the question of Church reunion. Instead of examining the history of our own particular form of Church government, beliefs, and ceremonies, and making them the criterion of reunion, let us ask the question, 'What is the intention in the life and worship of the various separated branches of the Church?' If their intention is to receive and proclaim the covenanted mercies of Christ, let us make this our standard of reunion; then the forms by which those mercies are received and proclaimed could be treated as quite secondary, and capable of alteration and adaptation. By this means we should be going a long way to lift the discussion of Church reunion from the realm of particular traditions and interpretations, however valuable these things are, and to centre it, where such discussions should be centred, on that which is our only concern, the Work of Christ.

[1] J. F. Bethune-Baker, *An Introduction to the Early History of Christian Doctrine* (Methuen, 1929), p. 388.
[2] Richard Baxter, *Key for Catholics* (edited by J. Allport, 1839), p. 236.

Appendix

PURITAN PROPAGANDA

PURITAN DIFFERENCES

WE have seen in Chapter I that 'the object of the Puritan reformers was the organization of English society in the form of a Church governed according to Presbyterian principles'.[1] We have also seen how this purpose, besides having a natural enemy in the Episcopal party, engendered the enmity of the Crown because of the political implications contained in thoroughgoing Presbyterianism. We can now examine how the Puritans faced these two challenges, which in reality are one challenge, for the bishops took their orders from the Queen.

First of all, we must distinguish between two kinds of Puritans, those of the Separatist variety, and those who remained in the national Church. In matters of faith, the two sections were more alike than they were different; it was in matters of Church organization and policy towards the national Church that they differed. We can trace the seeds of Dissent to the Protestant congregations of Mary's reign who resisted her efforts to Romanize the Church. This Dissent tended to develop with the rise of the Puritan reform movement, and it seems that, at first, these Dissenters did not think of themselves as separated from the national Church, but that they were merely purer forms of organization and worship from which the national Church had temporarily departed. But gradually their conception of what was a true Church became clarified, and their view of the possibility of reforming the national Church from within became more pessimistic, until they came to advocate complete and instant separation. They differed from other Puritans in that they identified the true Church, not with the Society or nation, but with the godly congregation of believers—what Baxter and others were to call 'Gathered Churches'. Consequently, they did not consider parish churches as true established Churches.[2] They were also the pioneers of voluntaryism, believing that the Church and ministry should be supported, not by the State, but by the voluntary gifts of the faithful. The main body of the Puritans, on the other hand, were not opposed to parish organization, provided that the Church was Presbyterian, nor did they object to the retention of the endowments. Their attitude to the national Church was that it was only partially established, and would become

[1] William Haller, *Rise of Puritanism* (1938), p. 173.
[2] A. F. Scott Pearson, *Church and State* (1928), p. 118, note 1.

completely so when it was Presbyterianized. We have already seen that Baxter thought that parish churches were true Churches if they had true ministers, but that only the godly who accepted the discipline should be admitted to Communion; the others were treated as Catechumens, to be preached to and instructed. It was a form of compromise which he hoped would reconcile the Separatists and the Episcopal party in one national Church.

That the Separatists came to the conclusion that it was impossible to reform the national Church from within is illustrated by the career of Robert Browne, the founder of the Brownists. A kinsman of Burghley and educated at Cambridge, he lived for a time in the house of Richard Greenham, one of the Puritan leaders. However, he broke away from the main Puritan movement, rejected ordination, spoke openly against bishops, forsook any hope of reforming the Church from within, and retired to Norwich, where he gathered a Church on Separatist lines. Other little Churches were formed on the same lines, and received their lot of hardship and persecution. But until the Westminster Assembly in 1644 the Separatists contributed little to the main Puritan movement, and the leadership first of all was in the hands of those who remained in the national Church.

The attitude, of those Puritans who remained in the national Church, to the Church is important, because that attitude not only dominated Puritan strategy for two generations, but also comes up again after the Commonwealth period in the attitude of Baxter and other Nonconformist divines to the Church of their day. It also illustrates the point that Nonconformists were not Separatists; they did not walk out of the Church, but were thrown out.

We have noticed that in Cartwright's six points, which he submitted to the Vice-Chancellor of Cambridge as the marrow of his teaching, there was this clause: 'All should promote this reformation . . . the magistrate by his authority, the minister by preaching, and all by their prayers.' Now the implications of this clause are that both realms, the Church and State, have their place in the reformation proposed, the minister can foster it by his preaching, but it is the business of the magistrate to put the reformed system into practice—that is to say, the chief magistrates, the Crown and Parliament, must reform the Church on the advice of the ministry, who are the guardians of the Word of God. That being the case, then the ministers must remain in the Church and 'Tarry for the Magistrate'. Indeed, the fact that the chief magistrate did not reform the Church as far as she might have done was the shock from which the Puritan movement may be said to have sprung.[1]

[1] William Haller, *Rise of Puritanism* (1938), p. 8.

The question that faced the main Puritan reformers was not whether they should remain in the national Church, but whether, being in the Church, they should accept or reject the apparel and ceremonies which all Puritans considered obnoxious. There were two schools of thought over this. Some, such as John Field, Wilcocks, Penry, Standen, etc., refused to conform and were deprived of their livings; others, such as Cartwright, Greenham, and Travers, tended to consider such things as indifferent, as compared with the opportunity of ministering to the flock. Cartwright's view was that 'This charge being an absolute commandement of the lord, owght not to be laid aside for a simple inconvenience of uncomeliness of a thing, which in the (*sic*) own nature is indifferent'.[1] But both these sections thought of themselves as ministers of the national Church, those who refused to conform were suspended and imprisoned, only, on release, to take up the struggle again. The difference between them was superficial; they clashed over a matter of tactics in carrying out the general strategy of 'Tarrying for the Magistrate'.

This desire to enlist the magistrate's co-operation was not merely the policy of the Puritan ministers, but was also the policy of Puritan councillors high in the service of the Queen. 'As Conyers Read points out in his *Sir Francis Walsingham*, Elizabeth's secretary believed that the Queen's co-operation was necessary to the fulfilment of his Puritan designs, namely the creation of a Pan-Protestant league with England as its champion, and the reformation of the Church on Presbyterian lines, and feared that the cause might be spoiled if ardent individuals in the Puritan party alienated the Queen by excessive demands and headlong action.'[2] Walsingham's policy fitted in with that of Cartwright and Travers, who disliked 'Separated Churches' and wished to carry the Government with them as the instrument of reform. The Puritans firmly believed that they should give obedience to the magistrate 'in the Lord', and Cartwright himself states that the Puritans will submit themselves to punishment at the magistrate's hand rather than actively resist him or violate their conscience.[3] It is not within our province to inquire when a Puritan is justified in disobeying the magistrate, but to note that in the strategy of reformation the godly magistrate has his just task to do, and his position is necessary to the settled peace of the Church. Baxter's views are substantially the views outlined above, both in his attitude to 'Separatism'[4] and to the place of a magistrate in a Christian society.

---

[1] A. F. Scott Pearson, *Thomas Cartwright and Elizabethan Puritanism* (1925), p. 149.
[2] A. F. Scott Pearson, *Church and State* (1928), p. 73.
[3] ibid., p. 67.
[4] *Autobiography* (Everyman, 1931), p. 80.

PURITAN STRATEGY

1. *Preaching*

But the policy of tarrying for the magistrate was a failure, because whenever the Puritans succeeded in getting a Bill into Parliament, the Queen succeeded in stopping it; consequently, the Puritans set about organizing the party along different lines. Before the Parliament of 1586 was finished, the leaders, realizing that their Bill had failed, met in London to reorganize the party. By this time they had in hand a book which set out their view of Church government and defined their objectives. This book was the famous *Book of Discipline*, known in the English translation as *A Directory of Church Government*. It set out the Presbyterian view of Church government and services, as the Puritans thought they were to be deduced from Scripture, and, as Soames says, 'This became henceforth the Palladium of Presbytery'.[1] It certainly acted as a focal point for the Puritans, who discussed it and sought for subscriptions to it among the meetings of ministers known as 'classes'. However, not all subscribed to all of the book, although had the movement had time to gather strength it might have become as authoritative for the party as Marx's *Das Kapital* is for present-day Communists.

But besides accepting the book as a manifesto of the party's aims, Soames states that the Puritans began to form congregations 'upon the Presbyterian scheme of elective aristocracy. These were affiliated into regional classes, and the latter, again, were under the direction of a national assembly.'[2] A superficial reading of this passage gives the impression that the Puritans had organized a full-blooded Presbyterian system, but the facts do not seem to bear this view out. Congregations were formed, and classes were organized—indeed, there is extant the minute book of the Dedham classes recording the doings and discussions of the Puritan ministers of that district over some years—but although such classes were in contact with other similar classes, their main interest was local and advisory, and hardly attained to national significance.[3] In fact, before the movement had gathered weight enough to make such organizations really effective nationally, the conferences were suppressed, and the party had to subside into silence, waiting for a better day to dawn.

In following out their strategy there were four main ways by which the Puritans sought to propagate their ideas for Church reform. They were by preaching, by writing, by the use of the exercises, and by the use of the conferences, which were themselves modifications of the exercises. We have noticed that the Puritans believed the magistrate must aid this reform by his authority, but the minister

---

[1] Soames, *Elizabethan Religious History* (1839), p. 382. [2] ibid., p. 383.
[3] cf. M. M. Knappen, *Tudor Puritanism* (1939), p. 288.

had his duty to do also: he must aid the reform of the Church by his preaching. On the accession of Elizabeth, 'Not above a third of the clergy were entrusted with licences to preach'.[1] The reason for this was not merely the inability of many of the clergy, but also because many of them, who had conformed in Edward's day, still had a hankering after the system in which they were bred, and so the pulpit was largely silenced because the Government feared the possible Romanizing tendency of these men. But the preachers of the reforming party were encouraged to preach. As Heylin says: 'Nothing was more considered in them than their zeal against Popery, and their abilities in divine and human studies to make good that zeal.'[2] But after the Vestment controversy had made it plain that there was going to be a limit to the reformation of the Church, those Puritan preachers who violently objected to this half-reform were, at one time or another, silenced. Acts were passed by Convocation revoking the preaching licences, and where preachers refused to conform they were deprived of their livings.

However, the Puritans continued to preach; if they were deprived of their livings, then they preached in private houses, or in the 'Exercises', which gave such an excellent opportunity for airing grievances. The Queen was not enamoured with preaching; in fact, there is a story which says that she stated that three or four preachers in the country were sufficient, but although she had issued a proclamation silencing all preachers, her opportunism forbade her to suppress them altogether.[3] She only acted when a minister became too critical, or when groups were formed which in her view might lead to subversive activities. The main Puritan party were, in fact, in a cleft stick simply because they would not be constitutional. It was the Queen that they had to convert, and she would not be converted, because to do so was to make a rod for her own back, and give up some of her precious authority. But although she kept a watchful eye on them, the 'Puritan preachers were not effectively prevented from spreading their beliefs, from seeking proselytes, or from assuming the leadership of such bands of disciples as they were able to convert and hold together. Thus English Puritanism, denied opportunity to reform the established Church, wreaked its energy during half a century upon preaching and, under the impetus of the pulpit, upon unchecked experiment in religious expression and social behaviour.'[4]

Avoiding direct clashes with the Government, and allowed a certain toleration, the Puritan preachers turned more and more to setting

---

[1] Soames, *Elizabethan Religious History* (1839), p. 32.
[2] Soames, ibid., 1672 (2nd Ed.), p. 33.
[3] M. M. Knappen, *Tudor Puritanism* (1939), p. 182.
[4] William Haller, *Rise of Puritanism* (1938), p. 15.

out the Puritan way of life in pulpit and Press, rather than to erecting separate Churches in defiance of the law. As the years passed, this preaching not only increased the numbers of Separatists outside the Church, but also increased the number of Nonconformists within the Church. The failure of Cartwright and Travers, who had led the Puritan party into paths of political action in their efforts to reform the Church, led to the emphasizing of that form of Puritanism which is best known today—that is, the spiritual discipline and way of life based on their answer to the question, 'What must I do to be saved?' The preachers stirred popular imagination as they pictured man, the eternal warrior and pilgrim, striding towards the promised land, the kind of imagery of which Bunyan's *Pilgrim's Progress* is the classic example.

Many men who sympathized with Cartwright at Cambridge and approved of his scheme of Church government did not follow him into the paths of public controversy, but proceeded to orders and the cure of souls. Two such men were John Dod and Arthur Hildersham, who lived far into the seventeenth century. Men of this outlook 'proposed, that is, within the Church and under the conditions of the society around them, to try the experiment of living according to a self-imposed discipline which they derived from Paul, Augustine, and John Calvin'.[1] It was these men who made the pulpit famous, and there grew up around them a school of preachers and writers devoted to their example. Richard Greenham is a typical example of this type of Puritan, and one of the acknowledged leaders. He was once cited for Nonconformity, but soon gave up the way of controversy and set himself to edifying the hearts and consciences of his hearers, and to encouraging them to embrace true godliness. The pulpit became a power in the land, and crowds flocked to hear the preachers, both Puritan and Episcopal, and not until Laud determined to silence the 'Spiritual' preachers by law did they in any numbers refuse to conform. As Haller says, 'They could afford to wait. They had their pulpits and the increasing support of men of wealth and importance. From that vantage-ground they could work at the erection of a popular morale which would in the end prove to be of more effect than any premature departure from the existing frame of things.'[2] It is due to these men mainly that Puritanism, which at first was largely a clerical movement, became a popular movement strong enough to dethrone and destroy a king.

2. *Writing*

As an adjunct to the preaching there grew up a literature which supplemented the preaching. Controversial tracts setting out and debating the question of Church government were particularly prolific during the first phase of Puritan propaganda, and though they never

[1] ibid., p. 25.   [2] ibid., p. 20.

completely disappeared the emphasis came more to be laid on those writers whom Baxter, much later on, called 'affectionate practical English writers'. They were called affectionate because they appealed to men's emotions, and practical because they taught men how to believe and act. Baxter himself in an effort to keep alive the old godliness, drew up a list which he says ought to be found 'in the poorest or smallest library which is tolerable'. This list may be found in his *Christian Directory*. Of course, the Bible, with a commentary and catechisms, are mentioned first, then books which open up the doctrine of grace; then he recommends a list of fifty-eight 'Affectionate practical English writers', from the closing years of the sixteenth century to his own time. These writers were mainly preachers who published popular sermons and tracts, aimed at stirring up the souls of men to salvation by an analysis of sin in its various manifestations in the human soul, coupling with it the cure as the Puritans saw it. Besides these, there were writings such as the Marprelate tracts aimed specifically at the bishops, and warranted to be popular, not only for their humour, but also because of the scandals they exposed. Such tracts as these were not generally approved by leaders like Cartwright and Travers, nor by the spiritual preachers like Greenham, who is said to have disliked the tracts, because they made sin ridiculous rather than, as it should be, odious. Of course, there were plenty of Episcopal writers too, but an examination of the lists of printed books from the end of the sixteenth century to the Civil War shows that it was the Puritan writers, more than any others, who kept the public supplied with reading matter.[1]

The propaganda by preaching was given opportunity in various other ways. There was the institution of lecturers in different parishes, the appointment of the preachers as chaplains to great houses, or as tutors in such houses, and even the securing of benefices from Puritan patrons. In these last there would be some agreement with Presbyterian principles by part at least of the parish. But of all these means the most commonly used, and perhaps the most effective, was the institution of lecturers. This was the system whereby the ordinary services were performed by the incumbent, and the lectureship was paid for by the offerings of the congregation, or by a rich patron, or by a group of members from the congregation. The lecturer's duty was to preach or lecture on the Bible at times other than those of the usual services. The lecturer was also supposed to be licensed by the bishop. The first of a long series of such lecturers was Lever, an exile under Mary, who accepted no appointment under Elizabeth and, leaving the Court, became a lecturer at Coventry.[2] Many other

[1] cf. L. B. Wright, *Middle-class Culture in Elizabethan England* (Oxford University Press, 1935).

[2] M. M. Knappen, *Tudor Puritanism* (1939), p. 180.

APPENDIX—PURITAN PROPAGANDA 251

Puritan preachers held such lecturerships at one time or another. Travers held the lecturership at the Temple, and when his great Episcopal opponent was preferred for the Mastership, the congregation had the pleasant diversion of hearing Hooker preach Canterbury in the morning and Travers answer with Geneva in the afternoon. Baxter himself was in the tradition of the long line of lecturers, and in many ways preferred the freedom of a lecturer to the tied duties of an incumbent. For to the Puritans there were considerable advantages to this system, for those who scrupled at the vestments and the ceremonies were able to avoid the question of conforming as they had no regular living except that which was supplied them by the generosity of their patrons. No doubt, too, this system trained families in the systematic giving necessary to support a minister, a habit much appreciated by the ministers when they were deprived of their livings. It must also have helped considerably in the eventual establishment of Dissenting Churches.

Sometimes it happened that with the death of the incumbent the parishioners would petition the authorities to give the living to the lecturer, as was the case with Smith of St. Clement's and Baxter in Kidderminster. But usually the ecclesiastical authorities intervened and gave the living to someone more amenable to the desires of the bishops. An extension of this system was attempted by the Puritans after the failure of the Hampton Court Conference at the commencement of the reign of James I. Several clergymen, led by Gouge and Sibbes, in company with some lawyers, and others who had plenty of money, formed a society for buying up impropriations of tithes and glebe land which were in the hands of laymen. There were twelve such 'Feoffees' who in the course of seven years raised some five or six thousand pounds and bought thirteen impropriations. The income thus obtained was not returned to the various parishes, but used to set up Puritan preachers in places, especially large and growing towns, where there was a lack of preaching. The authorities, aroused by Laud, became alarmed at the success of this venture, and estimated that in fifty years, if they were allowed to continue, they would have bought up all the impropriations possible, and controlled a large part of the income of the Church.[1] Although the leaders protested that only preachers licensed by the bishop were appointed, Laud saw a danger to Episcopacy in this move, and the committee was adjudged an illicit corporation and was suppressed. It is Haller's opinion that, had this movement not been crushed, the reformation of

[1] Patrons of Benefices in 1603 in the Diocese of Winchester and the Archdeaconries of Suffolk, Sudbury and Norwich: (1) The King, 153; (2) laymen, 158; (3) impropriations, 390; (4) bishops, colleges, clergy, etc., 159; cf. W. Usher, *Reconstruction of English Church* (1910), vol. I, p. 112.

the Church from the inside would ultimately have been accomplished, whether the bishops liked it or not.

3. *The Exercises or Conferences*

Another means by which preaching could be used for the reforming of the Church was in the exercises or conferences, which we have mentioned before. These conferences originated in the practice of the Continental Reformed Churches, and were attended by the exiled English ministers in the days of Mary. On the change in the fortunes of the English Church many progressive bishops used them as a means of instructing both clergy and laity, and as a means of circumventing Elizabeth's known dislike of an educated and preaching ministry. Before Elizabeth's day, this system had been used by Bishop Hooper in the quarterly gatherings in his diocese. In Elizabeth's State papers there are references to such gatherings at Norwich as early as 1564, but more is known of the working of the institution at Northampton. M. M. Knappen, in his *Tudor Puritanism*, gives a description of the system as it was practised at Northampton.

Virtually it was a form of Presbyterianism grafted on to the Anglican system, with special emphasis on discipline. This is especially illustrated in the preparation for the quarterly Communion. 'Two weeks before that event the minister and wardens of each parish made a house-to-house canvass, taking the names of communicants and examining the state of their lives. If discords were found, the parties were brought before a joint session of the town council, some of the local justices of the peace, and the minister, where reconciliations were effected or punishment and excommunication administered, as the case might be. After the Communion a similar visitation was made to check on absentees, who might also be dealt with by a disciplinary tribunal.'[1] (Such a system as this was practised in Scottish parishes within living memory.) But the centre of the whole system was the 'prophesying', a combination of public forum and literary society, to use Knappen's words. Each of the clergy was assigned a passage of Scripture to study, which, when his turn came, he had to expound at the weekly exercise. He was followed by other clergy, who perhaps criticized his exposition or added new knowledge to the interpretation. Presidents checked any tendency to contentiousness, and the more learned clergy passed a final judgement on the performance. The actual disputation was confined to the ministers, but the laity were allowed to listen, and sometimes provision was made for questions from the floor of the house. Such discussions were a powerful stimulus to the clergy to perfect themselves in the art of preaching, and a considerable aid to the habit of study. And who knows what effect these

[1] M. M. Knappen, *Tudor Puritanism* (1939), p. 254.

exercises had in forming in our national life the practice of government by debate both in Parliament and in the local boroughs? At least it is significant that the Parliamentary side in the Civil War was the Puritan side, in opposition to government by autocracy and ukase.

But the Queen did not like the exercises; they were too useful a platform for the Presbyterian reformers, and so she endeavoured to suppress them. And as the bishops became more and more subservient to the Queen and withdrew their patronage, the 'exercises' came more and more under the control of the Puritans. Even Grindal, who had considerable sympathy for the exercises, noted that the ministers deprived of their benefices had obtruded themselves into the 'exercises' in some places and spread their opinions. In Northampton, for instance, Wade, Paget, Mosely, Gildred, and Dawson, who had all been deprived in 1574, spoke at the exercises, and three of them were actually moderators. After their suppression by the Queen, it was always the Puritans who proposed their revival, and when they could not get official sanction they met in private. The difference being that, having to meet in private, they consisted only of ministers, save that occasionally one or two schoolmasters, desirous of training for the ministry, were allowed to join them. Also, the fact that all who attended them by this time were Puritans meant that the discussions were not merely educative in a general religious sense, but were pointed towards the reformation of Church government. The dispositions taken from the Puritan prisoners examined before the Star Chamber show that the chief object of the Conferences was to discuss and prepare for a national Presbyterian Church. The conferences, however, were not revolutionary groups, for their avowed intention was to bring about this reformation by constitutional means, i.e. through the authority of the magistrates. The minutes of such a conference held at Dedham, covering a period from 1582–9, shows how a Presbyterian system could have gradually come into being from the ministerial arrangements practised there.

Although the conferences were officially suppressed by Elizabeth, they never actually died out until the energies of the Puritan Christians were absorbed in the organizing of the Dissenting Churches in the late seventeenth century, but meanwhile, with the failure of Cartwright and Travers's attempt to reform the Church by political agitation, they returned more to their original purpose—that is, the edification of souls. Samuel Clarke gives a picture of his own activities in Cheshire before the Revolution, where he was maintained by the contributions of the godly as a kind of itinerant preacher, there being few 'constant preachers' in the neighbourhood. He describes how people would gather from six or seven miles round for the preaching, spending the whole day there conferring upon the Word of God, catechizing the children, and discussing the sermon. Every three weeks these people would meet in the richer men's houses for the same purpose. Questions on the Scripture, which had been specified at the preceding conference, would be discussed, special meetings arranged for the children and young people, and provision made for food by the master of the family.[1] In fact, these conferences remind us rather of the present-day conferences at Swanwick and other centres, and no doubt filled the same purpose. Such meetings not only increased personal holiness, but served to maintain the Puritan frame of mind outside, almost, the national Church. At least when the break did come, it made the establishment of Dissenting Churches on a large scale much easier, for such conferences, drawing people from several parishes, made it easier to centre the religious life of a number of people in some other organization than the parish church, which was again helped by the fact that many people had got used to the idea of supporting a minister by voluntary offerings.

PURITAN SUCCESS

That the Puritans were not altogether unsuccessful in their efforts to Presbyterianize a part, at least, of the national Church is evidenced by the reorganization of the Churches of the Channel Isles and the English Churches in the Low Countries. The farther away the place was from the central government, the easier it was to adopt the new system. There were also political and economic reasons which helped this reformation. The Channel Isles were a place of refuge for the persecuted French Huguenots, whose presence helped to influence men's minds towards the form of Church government practised by the Continental Reformed Churches, while the English merchants in the Low Countries were staunch Protestants of the more radical variety, for it was in the Low Countries that the conflict between Protestant and Romanist went on with unabated and sometimes bloody fury. With the Stuart settlement, and the discrediting of Presbyterianism, these Churches tended to slip into Independency and look rather to the new lands of America, where Churches might be set up free from persecution.

Puritanism, therefore, was something more than a movement for the reform of personal life, closely confined to personal salvation, and without concern for society save in the realm of morals. It was a movement which aimed at the reform of the whole of society into the form of a Presbyterian Church, and that, though the movement failed in its object under Elizabeth, that aim was not forgotten. It was an internationalist movement which drew its inspiration from the Continental reformers, for the leaders in England were in constant

[1] William Haller, *Rise of Puritanism* (1939), p. 63.

touch with the leaders of the Reformed Churches on the Continent, and often took refuge among them. Although the movement was internationalist, it was also very loyalist, refusing to step beyond the bounds of passive resistance, and continually asserting its loyalty to the Queen. This was possibly its weakness; a show of force, if it was possible under the circumstances, might have accomplished more for them, as it did in Scotland under John Knox's leadership. Nor was Puritanism a strictly democratic movement, although the rights of congregations were to be respected, and their opinions asked for. In fact, there was no agreement among the Puritans on the question of pure democratic government; if anything, they were, as a whole, opposed to it.[1] Nor were they liberal in the modern sense—in fact, they approved of the use of the secular arm against those who differed from themselves, the modern idea of liberty of conscience would certainly not have been tolerated among them. 'We have seen', says Knappen, 'the Puritans in time of stress toy with the idea of religious toleration, without, however, intending it for any but themselves. We have watched them gingerly test the ideas of the social compact and democracy, but never apply them with any degree of boldness. Rather, the Puritans were always willing to accept the theory of divine-right monarchy if help should be forthcoming from the Crown, or of divine-right nobility if the Hastings, Russells, and Riches seemed to offer greater support.'[2] In fact, the only thing they were really consistent about was their desire to reform the Church according to their interpretation of the New Testament. In this they would not vary, whatever their views of the relation between Church and State, or the authority of the Monarch, or the value or otherwise of pure democratic government; they desired that the authority of the Church should be grounded in the Word of God, and this meant to them the establishment of a Presbyterian Church system, such as was established in the Continental Reformed Churches and in the Church of Scotland.

[1] M. M. Knappen, *Tudor Puritanism* (1939), p. 334, note 25, and p. 334.
[2] ibid.

BIBLIOGRAPHY

Church and State. A. F. SCOTT PEARSON.
Thomas Cartwright and Elizabethan Puritanism. A. F. SCOTT PEARSON.
Puritanism in England. H. HENSLEY HENSON.
Tudor Puritanism. M. M. KNAPPEN.
Rise of Puritanism. WILLIAM HALLER.
Richard Baxter. GEORGE EAYRS.
History of the Early Puritans. J. B. MARSDEN.
Elizabethan Religious History. HENRY SOAMES.
A Treatise of Reformation without Tarrying for Anie. ROBERT BROWNE.
Reconstruction of the English Church. W. USHER.
Lancelot Andrews. R. L. OTTLEY.
Church of England. H. HENSLEY HENSON.
Archbishop Laud. H. TREVOR-ROPER.
English Religion in the Seventeenth Century. H. HENSLEY HENSON.
The Reformed Pastor. Ed. by J. T. WILKINSON.
A Life of the Reverend Richard Baxter. F. J. POWICKE.
The English Revolution. I. DEANE-JONES.
Oliver Cromwell. CHARLES FIRTH.
History of His Own Times. BISHOP BURNET.
The Reverend Richard Baxter under the Cross. F. J. POWICKE.
Faith of Our Fathers. FLORENCE HIGHAM.
Summa Contra Gentiles. AQUINAS.
Bulletin of John Ryland's Library.
Life and Works of George Herbert. G. H. PALMER.
History of the English Church during the Civil War and Commonwealth. DR. SHAW.
R. Baxter. A. R. LADELL.
Making of Modern English Religion. BERNARD MANNING.
Journal of John Wesley.
Letters of John Wesley.
A Preface to Paradise Lost. C. S. LEWIS.
Martin Luther. DR. McGIFFERT.
Erastianism. E. EVANS.
Calvini Opera. JOHN CALVIN.
Calvinism. A. DAKIN.
Church and State on the European Continent. A. KELLER.
The Laws of Ecclesiastical Policy. R. HOOKER.
Diary of Archbishop Laud.
Essays in Orthodox Dissent. BERNARD MANNING.
The Case for Episcopacy. K. D. MACKENZIE.
Thoughts after Lambeth. T. S. ELIOT.
The Church and Nonconformity. ARCHDEACON GREGG.

BIBLIOGRAPHY

The Church and Nonconformity. ARCHDEACON GREGG.
The Ministry of Iniquity. T. HELWYS.
The Primitive Church. DR. STREETER.
The Christian Ministry. J. B. LIGHTFOOT.
History of the Christian Church. A. R. WHITHAM.
Commentary on the Bible. A. S. PEAKE.
Jesus and His Church. DR. R. NEWTON FLEW.
The First Congregational Church. DR. ALBERT PEEL.
The Authority of the Bible. C. H. DODD.
Press and Publications Board of the Church of England.
The Didache.
An Introduction to the Early History of Christian Doctrine. J. F. BETHUNE-BAKER.
Middle Class Culture in Elizabethan England. L. B. WRIGHT.

RICHARD BAXTER'S WRITINGS
An Index to Citations and References

Against a Revolt to a Foreign Jurisdiction, 221
Animadversions (Appendix to *Plain Scripture Proof*), 168, 169, 170
Autobiography, 13, 38, 48, 49, 50, 59, 73, 76, 81, 96, 105, 112, 125, 126, 128, 129, 130, 145, 181, 190, 246
Baxter's Answer to Dodwell, 138
A Breviate of the Life of Margaret Baxter, 74
A Call to the Unconverted, 79
Catholic Unity, 99, 100, 101
Certain Disputations of Right to Sacraments, Etc., 168, 171
Christian Concord, 45
Christian Directory, 98, 113, 144, 167, 250
Christian Ecclesiastics, 93, 95, 96, 107, 108, 146, 164, 186, 202
Church History Abbreviated, 121, 127, 128
Five Disputations of Church Government and Worship, 104, 113, 114, 119, 120, 128, 132, 133, 138, 139, 140, 141
God's Goodness Vindicated, 79
Key for Catholics, 92, 93, 94, 95, 96, 100, 103, 243
Life of Faith, 94, 97, 98, 102
The Nonconformists' Plea for Peace, 199, 218, 219
Of National Churches, 194
On Justifying Righteousness, 76, 80
The Poor Husbandman's Advocate to Rich Racking Landlords, 85
Reasons for the Christian Religion, 84
Reformed Pastor, 45, 85, 87, 88
The Right Method for a Settled Peace of Conscience, 112
Roman Tradition Examined, Etc., 175, 177, 178
The Saints' Everlasting Rest, 85, 87, 146, 153, 154, 157, 158
Second Part of the Nonconformists' Plea for Peace, 194, 199, 200, 202, 205, 208
The Substance of Mr. Cartwright's Exceptions Considered, 80
Theological Tracts, 81, 82
Treatise of Episcopacy, 92, 94, 95, 96, 97, 105, 106, 107, 108, 115, 116, 117, 118, 119, 120, 121, 122, 123, 124, 125, 126, 127, 128, 129, 134, 135, 136, 143
True Catholic, 102
Unnecessary Separating Disowned, 191, 192, 211, 212, 214
Orme, W. (Editor of the *Practical Works of Richard Baxter*), 92n., 95n., 94n., 95n., 96n., 99n., 104n., 105n., 106n., 107n., 108n., 110n., 111n., 114n., 144n., 145n., 147n., 148n., 149n., 150n., 151n., 152n., 165n., 169n., 171n., 172n., 173n., 174n., 175n., 185n., 195n., 202n., 203n.

INDEX

Abbot, George, Archbishop, 35, 37
Abraham, 169, 230
Act of uniformity (1662), 54, 62, 65, 66, 67, 129, 130, 138, 215, 216, 218, 239
Acton, 67, 68, 70
Acton, Rector of, 70
Acts xiv. 23, quoted, 106
Adultery, Puritan view of, 11
Advertisements, Archbishop Parker's, 14, 215
Alasco, John, 9
Alexandria, 124
Alfrick, Canons of, 219
Allport, J., 103n.
America, Protestantism and, 226
— South, Catholicism and, 226
Amyraldus, of Saumur, 77–8
Anabaptists, 42, 76, 168, 190
Andrewes, Lancelot, Bishop, 36, 37, 40, 210
Anglican Church, 10, 65, 66, 71, 102, 105, 133, 143, 201, 215, 225, 232, 237, 242, 252. *See also under* Church of England.
Anglicanism, 55, 65, 238, 239, 241
Anglicans, 19, 68, 69, 92, 201, 232, 237, 240
'Anglo-Catholic Party', 213
Anti-clericalism, 226
Antinomians, 76, 80
Apostles, the, 101, 103–4, 118–20, 121, 122, 123, 126, 128, 130, 131, 147, 152, 155, 157, 166, 175, 228, 230
— Creed, the, 47, 49
Apostolic Church, the, 19
— Constitutions, 121, 201
'Apostolic English Church', 37
Apostolic See, 233
— Succession, the, 103, 111, 116, 138, 142, 228–9, 231, 232
Appello ad Caesarem, 221
Aquinas. *See* Thomas Aquinas, St.
Arians, 242
Aristotle, 83, 179
Arlington, Earl of, 71
Armada, Spanish, 14, 16, 26
Arminianism, 32, 76, 77, 79, 186
Arminius, Jacobus, 37, 182, 221
Ash, Simeon, 60, 67
Ashley (Cooper), Earl of Shaftesbury, 71
Ashurst, Sir Henry, 73
Athanasius, 242
Atheism, 226
Atonement, doctrine of the, 78–9, 82
Augustine, Saint, of Hippo, 76, 93, 182, 186
Austria, Catholicism and, 226
Authority of the Bible, The, 160

Bacon, Francis, Lord Verulam, 12
Baillie, Robert, 27
Ball, Mr., 204
Bancroft, Richard, Archbishop, 19, 22, 24, 26, 27, 28–9, 30, 31, 32, 34, 35, 36, 37, 40, 138, 210, 213, 215, 237
Baptism, 92, 98, 101, 102, 135, 136, 164, 165, 166, 167–71, 183, 184, 187, 190, 206, 229
— use of Cross in, 10, 40, 199–200, 203, 216
Baptismal Regeneration, 168
Baptists, 14, 45, 58, 239
Barlow, William, 31
Barnabas, 119
Bates, Dr., 67, 73
Bavaria, 226
Baxter, Beatrice, 36
— Margaret (Charlton), 67, 68, 73, 74
Baxter, Richard:
  at Acton, 67–70
  and Anabaptists, 76, 168, 190
  Anglicanism, attitude towards, 55, 133, 135
  and Antinomians, 76, 80
  and Apostolic Succession, 102–3, 111, 116, 124, 138, 142, 229
  Arminianism, attitude towards, 76–7, 79, 186
  his doctrine of the Atonement, 79, 82
  and baptism, 98, 101, 102, 135, 136, 164, 165, 166, 167–71, 229, 241, 242–3
  — use of Cross in, 40, 199–200, 216
  birth of, 36
  and office of bishop, 119, 120, 121–8, 134–7, 140–1, 218, 219–20, 233
  bishopric offered to, 58, 70, 129
  boyhood and youth of, 37–9
  at Bridgenorth, 40, 125, 215
  and burial of the dead, 196–7
  Calvinism, relation to, 76–9, 186–9
  chaplain in New Model Army, 42, 189
  and Charles II, 57, 129
  and Church of England, 39, 46, 95, 117, 133, 134, 135, 225
  and Church government, 15, 44–5, 47–8, 55–6, 70, 80, 104–5, 114–16, 189, 216. *See also under* Baxter and hierarchical conception.
  and Church of Rome, 94, 95, 101, 104, 105, 128, 147, 151–2, 174–8, 219. *See also under* Baxter and Papists, Baxter and Roman Catholics.
  and Church's apostolicity, 102–4
  and Church unity, 44–5, 47, 57–61, 93, 98–102, 173, 205–9, 225
  civil war, attitude towards, 41–2, 181

Baxter, Richard (*cont.*):
  clericalism of, 229–30
  and confirmation, 134, 135, 165, 166, 171
  and obligations of congregation, 108–12
  and place of congregation in Church, 114–15
  his conversion, 38
  elected to Convocation, 62
  at Coventry, 41
  and Cromwell, 45, 49–51, 174, 194
  his death, 73
  at Dudley, 39, 74
  Episcopacy, attitude towards, 44, 54, 103, 121–4, 125–8, 134, 138, 144, 233
  and Erastians, 44, 129
  and excommunication, 94–5, 96, 97, 134, 135
  and Faith, 80, 153–4
  gambling, attitude to, 39
  and 'gathered Churches', 42, 244
  and hierarchical conception, 179–95, 219
  and holiness, 80–2, 97–8
  his home life, 74
  and images, 202–4
  imprisoned, 70, 73
  Independents, attitude towards, 49, 52, 190–1
  his doctrine of justification, 80–1
  at Kidderminster, 40–2, 43, 48, 66, 75, 81, 112, 115, 130, 143, 180, 210, 225, 228, 251
  and the liturgy, 59, 191, 204–5
  in London, 73
  and the Lord's Supper (Communion), 40, 45, 96, 102, 133, 134, 135, 143, 148, 149, 163–4, 165, 166, 171–4, 200–2, 208, 218
  and Luther(anism), 182–6
  and marriage, 166, 203
  his marriage, 67, 74
  and ministerial office, 132–4
  and ministry, 115–16, 117–43, 180, 189
  — growth of, 117–28. *See also under* Baxter and office of Bishop, Baxter and Ordination, *etc.*
  and miracles, 154–6
  monarchy, attitude towards, 41, 55, 194–5, 239
  and mystics, 51
  his Nonconformity, 60, 66, 71, 90, 130, 178, 196–7, 204, 210–23
  oaths, attitude to, 215–17, 218
  ordained, 39, 142–3
  and ordination, 103, 105, 114–15, 116, 132, 138–40, 141–2, 166, 207, 229
  his orthodoxy, 130–2
  and Dr. Owen, 49–50, 190–1

Papists, attitude towards, 58, 69, 76, 80, 93, 94, 97, 101, 145, 148, 151, 166, 175, 206, 207. *See also under* Baxter and Roman Catholics.
and Particular Churches, 55, 104–16, 188
his persecution, 66–7, 71–2
his philosophy, 82–4
as a physician, 89
and Popery, 197, 220–3
Popes, attitude to, 99, 103, 151–2, 153, 207
and Prelacy, 55–6, 76, 77, 84, 100, 137, 140, 184, 191, 213, 218, 219–20, 223, 229
and Presbyterianism, 44–5, 54, 128–30, 134, 193
and essentials of religion, 49
Restoration, attitude to, 57
and Roman Catholics, 92, 94, 166, 174–8, 211, 220–3, 243. *See also under* Baxter and Church of Rome, Baxter and Papists.
and his doctrine of the Sacraments, 43, 46, 55, 134, 136, 163–78, 198–202, 238. *See also under* Baxter and baptism, Baxter and the Lord's Supper.
and the Scriptures, 49, 144–62, 204–5, 212–13, 218
and Separatists, 52, 76, 77, 114, 148, 167, 189–92, 195, 204, 206, 246
and Socinians, 76
and the State, 192–5
and the surplice, 40, 198–9
and toleration, 49, 58, 69, 211, 241–3
at Totteridge, 70–1
and transubstantiation, 174–8
and the Universal Church, 90–104, 173
and Worcester House Conference, 58, 76
and Worcestershire Association, 44–8, 49, 164, 174, 181, 218, 229
Baxter, Richard, senior, 36, 38
Baxterianism, 75
Beal, Mr., 67
Beale, Robert, 18
Bedford, T. H., 168
Bellarmine, Robert, Cardinal, 142
Berry, Captain, 42
Beth Din, 125
Bethune-Baker, J. F., 243n.
Blackfriars, 66
Boccaccio, Giovanni, 157
Book of Common Prayer, 10, 25, 40, 62, 65, 105, 174, 182, 190, 192, 215, 216, 240
— *of Discipline*, 19, 28, 247
— *of Ordination*, 216
Bourbons, the, 59, 240
Bradley, parish of, 143
Breda, Declaration of, 53, 129
Bridgman, Sir Orlando, 69

Bridgenorth, 40, 125, 215
Bromsgrove, 46
Brown, F., 121
Browne, Robert, 18, 245
Brownists, 191, 245
Bruised Reed, The, 38
Bucer, M., 9
Buckingham, Duke of, 69, 71
Bunny, Edmund, 38
Bunny's Resolution, 38
Bunyan, John, 87, 249
Burghley, William Cecil, Lord, 12, 18, 22, 245
Burnet, Gilbert, Bishop, 62

CABAL, THE, 71
Calamy, Edmund, 57, 62, 67, 129
Call to Christian Unity, The, 231
Calvin, John, 91, 165, 182, 186–9, 193, 210, 249
Calvinism, 23, 37, 76–9, 80, 91, 182, 186–9, 198, 220
Cambridge Platonists, 83
— University of, 14, 15, 245, 249
Canon Law, 25–6, 33, 34, 40, 67
— codification of, 29–30
Cartwright, Thomas, 10, 15, 16, 17, 19, 21, 22, 23, 27, 36, 43, 134, 193, 196, 198, 204, 212, 218, 245, 246, 249, 250, 253
Catechism for Independency, A, 190
Cavalier Parliament, 61–3
Cavaliers, the, 54, 71
Chaderton, Laurence, 36
Channel Isles, Church in, 254
Charles I, 52, 220, 221, 223
—II, 49, 53, 54, 55, 56, 57, 58, 60, 62, 63, 64, 65, 68, 70, 71, 72, 129, 137, 138, 194, 210–11, 223
Charlton, Margaret. *See* Baxter, M. C.
Chaucer, Geoffrey, 11
Christ Church, London, 73
Church and State Two Hundred Years Ago, 63
— Anglican. *See* Anglican Church.
— Apostolic. *See* Apostolic Church.
— Early, the, 17, 108, 123, 124, 127, 128
— of England, Chapters I–V, *passim*, 75, 89, 90, 95, 117, 127, 128, 129, 130, 134, 135, 137, 138, 164, 174, Chapter IX, *passim*, 196, 204, 207, Chapter XIII, *passim*, 226, 231, 232, 244, 245, 252, 253. *See also under* Anglican Church.
— *of England and Episcopacy, The*, 231
— Greek. *See* Orthodox Church.
— *History of Britain*, 18
— Lutheran. *See* Lutheran Church.
— the Medieval, 9
— Pre-Reformation, 26, 36, 198, 202, 212, 219

— Reformed, 55, 94, 95, 103, 138, 160, 183, 207, 252, 254, 255
— of Rome, 28, 94, 95, 101, 102, 104, 105, 128, 137, 143, 147, 151–2, 174–8, 184, 212, 219, 221, 222, 223, 231, 233, 237. *See also under* Papists, Popery, and Roman Catholicism.
— Scottish, 16, 20, 26, 28, 70, 196, 239, 241, 255
'Cities of Refuge', 12
Civil War, the, 12, 22, 41–2, 43, 54, 61, 86, 181, 223, 241, 253
Clare, Sir Ralph, 55, 56, 143, 163, 202
Clarendon Code, 65, 66
— Earl of, 62, 63, 64, 65, 69
Clarke, Samuel, 253
Clericalism, 225–30
Clerkenwell Jail, 70
Clifford, Thomas, Lord, 71
Commerce, Puritan influence on, 12
Commonwealth, the, 15, 50, 52, 53, 63, 221, 245
Communion, Holy. *See* the Lord's Supper.
Communism, 78, 226, 247
Confession and Protestation of Faith, 191
Confirmation, 134, 135, 165, 171
— Roman Catholic Sacrament of, 166
Congregationalists, 14, 183
Conscience, liberty of, 11, 42, 216, 255. *See also under* Toleration.
Constantine, Emperor, the Great, 125
Conventicle Acts (1664 and 1670), 66, 67, 68, 69, 71
Corbet, Rev. and Mrs., 70
1 Corinthians i. 10, quoted, 50
Corporation Act (1661), 65
Country Parson, The, 87
Coventry, 250
Cranmer, Thomas, Archbishop, 10, 26, 138, 182, 219
Croft, Sir James, 12
Cromwell, Oliver, 15, 41, 42, 45, 49, 50–3, 174, 189, 194
— Richard, 52
Council of Trent. *See* Trent, Council of.
Cyprian, Bishop of Carthage, 124

DAKIN, A., 188n.
Dance, Rev., 58
Das Kapital, 247
Davies, R. E., 189n.
Davis, Sir Thomas, 72
Deane-Jones I., 51, 63, 64n.
Declaration of Indulgence (1662), 65; (1671), 71, 211
Dedham classes, 247, 253
Dering, Thomas, 17
Deists, 241
Didache, the, 120–1, 123, 124, 230

INDEX

Digby, Lord, 42
'Dioceses', 125
Diocletian, Emperor, 125
Directory of Church Government, A, 247
Disestablishment, Nonconformists and, 239
Dissenters, Protestant, 11, 55, 62, 64, 65, 66, 71, 72, 94, 195, 211, 236, 244
— Roman Catholic, 11, 71
Divine Right (of Kings), 34
Divorce, Puritan advocacy, 11, 203
Dod, John, 36, 204, 249
Dodd, C. H., 160–2
Donne, John, 179
Dudley, 39, 74
Duns Scotus, 39
Durandus, 39

EARLY CHURCH, THE. *See* Church, the Early.
Eayrs, G., 12n., 59n.
Ecclesiastical Affairs Declaration (1660), 58, 59, 137
Edward VI, of England, 9, 248
Edwards, Thomas, 75
Egerton, Stephen, 31
Elijah, 155
Eliot, T. S., 236
Elizabeth, Queen, 13, 24, 215, 248
— attitude to Catholics, 16–17, 28
— attitude to Church, 10, 13, 16, 25–6, 28, 30
— attitude to Presbyterianism, 32, 192
— attitude to Puritans, 14, 17–23, 28, 90
Elizabethan Settlement, 15, 28, 65, 76, 192, 231, 238
Ephesians ii. 20, 21, quoted, 103; iv. 4–7 .. 16; referred to, 92
Epiphanius, 124
Episcopacy, Bancroft supports, 27, 30, 34, 35
— Baxter and, 44, 54, 103, 121–8, 134, 138, 144, 233
— Calvinism and, 23
— Cartwright and, 15
— Church of England and, 26, 27, 35, 40
— and Church government, 213, 230–4
— Digby and, 42
— growth of, 121–8, 210
— Hooker on, 27–8, 29
— James I supports, 30–2
— Laud and, 35, 36, 37, 40, 213, 215, 251
— Long Parliament and, 43
— and ordination, 137–8
— becomes Prelacy, 35, 210
— and Toryism, 64
— triumph of, 66
— Whitgift supports, 27

Episcopalian Party (and Episcopalians), 11, 23, 24, 25 28 29, 35, 36–7, 44, 47, 49, 52, 57, 61, 62, 63, 64, 76, 129, 130, 134, 163, 174, 206, 212, 213, 244, 245
Epistles of Ignatius, 124
Erastianism, 188
Erastians, 44, 129
Et cetera Oath, 40, 70, 105, 118, 125, 134, 137, 215, 218
Eucharist, the, 235. *See also under the* Lord's Supper.
Evangelical Churches, 226
Evans, E., 184n.
Evanson, Captain, 42
Evesham, 46
Excommunication, Bull of (1570), 16–17
'Exercises', Puritan, 17, 18, 248, 252–4
Extreme Unction, 166

FAGIUS, PAUL, 9
Fairfax, Lord, 54
Faith and Order Movement, 224
Falstaff, 85
Fascism, 226
Fawsley, 36
'Feoffes', 251
Field, John, 246
Fifth Monarchy Men, 52, 195
Firth, Sir Charles, 52, 53n.
Five Mile Act (1665), 12, 65, 68, 73
Fletcher, John, of Madeley, 87
Flew, R. N., 130–1
Fox, George, 51
France, 211, 226
Francis Xavier, St., 81, 169
Free Churches, the, 232
Fuller, Nicholas, 35
— Thomas, 18

Gag for the New Gospel, A?, 221
Gag for a New Gospel, The, 220
Gallican Church, 222
Genevan Church, 188
— Reformers, 25, 182, 188
Germans, the, 131
Gibson, Dr., Bishop of London, 173n.
Goodwin, John, 77
Gouge, William, 251
Great Fire of London, 68, 69
Greenham, Richard, 245, 246, 249
Gregg, Archdeacon, 237n.
Grindal, Archbishop, 17, 253

HALE, SIR MATTHEW, 67
Haller, W., 11n., 12, 13 (quoted), 244 (quoted), 245n.. 248 (quoted), 249 (quoted), 254n.
Hammond, Dr., 44, 55, 56

INDEX

Hampden, John, 68
— Richard, 68
Hampton Court Conference, 31–2, 35, 36, 51, 59, 65, 134, 198, 251
Hatton, Sir Christopher, 12
Helwys, Thomas, 239
Henry VIII, 65
Henson, H. Hensley, 10, 35 (quoted), 40n., 43n., 48 (quoted)
Herbert, George, 87–9
— Sir Henry, 39
Heylin, Peter, 248
Hierarchical Conception, 179–95, 219–20
Higham, Florence, 75n., 88n.
High Commission, Court of, 11, 26, 28, 29, 35, 215
— Ercall, 85, 87
Hildersham, Arthur, 31, 36, 204, 249
History of His Own Times, 62n.
Hitchcock, R. D., 121
Hobbes, Thomas, 193
Holles, Denzil, 54
Hooker, Richard, 19, 26, 27–8, 29, 36, 37, 138, 192, 193, 210, 212, 213, 237, 251
Hooper, John, Bishop, 9, 252
Howard, Lord, 12
Huguenots, the, 254
Humble Petition and Advice, 52
Hunkin, Bishop, 231
Hyde, Chancellor, 56, 58, 59, 60
Hypothetical Universalism, 78

IGNATIUS, BISHOP OF ANTIOCH, 108, 124
Images, Nonconformists and, 201, 202
Independents, the, 44, 46, 47, 49, 51, 52, 53, 58, 69, 189, 190, 191, 211, 254
Institutes of the Christian Religion, 186
Intention, doctrine of, 242–3
Irenaeus, 238
'Italian' party, 222
Italy, 222, 226

JAMES VI OF SCOTLAND, 20, 24; later James I of England, 10, 23, 26, 29, 30–2, 34, 37, 51, 90, 134, 220, 221, 251
James, Duke of York, later James II, 54, 68, 69, 71, 72
Jeffreys, George, Judge, 72, 73
Jerome, St., 122, 127
Jesuits, the, 18, 110, 222
Jesus and His Church, 130
Jewel, John, Bishop, 10, 26
Jewish nation, the, 118
Jews, the, 118, 125, 230
John, St., 122
Johnson, Samuel, 59, 84, 179
Justin, 124, 238

KELLER, A., 188 (quoted)
Kidderminster, 40, 42, 43, 46, 48, 50, 56, 58, 66, 75, 81, 112, 115, 130, 143, 180, 210, 225, 228, 251
Knappen, M. M., 11n., 13n., 16n., 17n., 31n., 33n., 247n., 248n., 250n., 252, 255n.
Knightley, Richard, 36
Knightleys, the, 34
Knollys, Sir Francis, 18
Knox, John, 9, 25, 255

LADELL, A. R., 91 (quoted)
Lambeth Conference, 236
Lancashire, 43
Latitudinarianism, 90, 100, 105, 164
Laud, William, Archbishop, 35, 36, 37, 38, 40, 42, 43, 51, 64, 192, 193, 210, 213, 215, 221, 222–3, 241, 249, 251
Laudians and Laudian Party, 40, 55, 56, 94, 138, 182, 219, 220, 221
Lauderdale, Earl of, 56, 63, 70, 71, 194
Laws of Ecclesiastical Polity, 19, 192
Leicester, 9
— Earl of, 12, 19
L'Estrange, Sir Roger, 73
Levellers, the, 52
Lever, Ralph, 250
Lewis, C. S., 159, 179 (quoted), 219 (quoted)
Life and Work Movement, 224
Life of Richard Baxter, A, 142
Lightfoot, J. B., Bishop, 122 (quoted)
Liturgy, the, 59, 191, 204–5
Lollardism, 9
London, 9, 13, 43, 54, 62, 63, 68, 73
— merchants, 12
Long Parliament, the, 41, 43
Lord's Supper, the, 10, 29, 40, 45, 47, 48, 96, 102, 124, 133, 134, 135, 137, 143, 148, 149, 163–4, 165, 166, 167, 171–4, 183, 185, 187, 200–2, 208, 218, 237, 239
Low Countries, Churches in, 254
Luther, Martin, 83, 91, 148, 153, 182, 183, 184, 185, 186, 187, 189, 210
Lutheran Church, 66, 182, 198
Lutheranism, 182, 187, 188

MACAULAY, T. B., 12
McGiffert, A. C., 183
Mackenzie, K. D., 230 (quoted), 233 (quoted)
Madstard, Mr., 40
Manchester, 12
— Earl of, 54, 57, 60
Manlon, Thomas, 57
Manning, Bernard, 91, 188 (quoted), 226
— Cardinal Henry E., 221, 237

INDEX

Marprelate Tracts, 19, 250
Marriage, Puritan influence on, 11
— use of ring in, 10, 203
Marsden, J. B., 12 (quoted), 14n., 15n., 20n.
Martyr, Peter, 9, 28
Marx, Karl H., 78, 247
Mary, Queen of England, 10, 198, 244, 250, 252
— Queen of Scots, 16
Mary's Dowry, 16
Matthew xxv, 85; xxviii. 19 and 20 .. 169
Methodism, 78
Methodist Church, 105
Methodist Hymn-book, 238
Methodists, 238
Methodist Societies, 47
Micklethwaite, Dr., 66
Millenary Petition, 30
Milton, John, 11, 15, 87, 179
Ministry, growth of the, 117–28
— irregular, 232
Miracles, 154–6
Monk, George, General, 53, 54
Montagu, Sir Edward, 34
— Richard, 200
Morley, Bishop, 55, 60, 66
Mosaical Church, 118
Mosaical Law, 119, 146
Moses, 118, 155

NASEBY, 41
— Battle of, 189
Nazism, 226
Newgate, 67, 70, 71
New Model Army, 41, 42
Newton, Isaac, 84
Nonconformity(ists), 12, 17, 18, 32, 39, 40, 68, 70, 71, 91, 94, 105, 130, 144, 148, 160, 191, 192, 193, 195, 196–7, 199, 200–4, 210, 211, 229, 239, 242, 245, 249
— and Church and State, 239–40
— and Church reunion, 227, 229–30, 231
— and Episcopacy, 230–4
— Puritanism, relation to, 90, 193
— and the Sacraments, 163, 235–7, 242
Northampton, 9, 252
Northern rebellion (1569), 16
Norwich, 9, 245, 252

OATES, TITUS, 73
Oath of Supremacy, 25, 29
Oblivion, Act of, 68
Ockham, William of, 39
Ordination, 103, 105, 114–15, 116, 132, 138–40, 141–2, 166, 207, 228–9, 230
Origen, 156

Orthodox (Greek) Church, 102, 206, 212
Ottley, R. L., 30n., 37n.
Owen, Dr., 49–50, 144, 190–1
— John, 52
Oxford, 68
— Oath, 69, 70, 137, 215, 217, 218
— University, 14

PALMER, G. H., 88n.
Pan-Protestant League, 246
Papacy, the, 28, 103, 151, 152, 212, 222, 233
Papal Council, the, 151
— Infallibility, 207, 222
Papists, 58, 69, 71, 76, 80, 93, 94, 97, 101, 145, 148, 151, 166, 175, 201, 206, 207, 222
Parish Bishops, 218, 219
Parker, Matthew, Archbishop, 14, 215
Parliamentarians, 41
Parliament(s), Cavalier, 61, 62–3, 64, 71–2
— of Elizabeth, 18, 19, 247
— of James I, 30, 31, 33–4, 221
— of James II, 223
— Long, 41, 43
— Rump, 50, 52
— Short, 40
Parsons, Robert, the Jesuit, 38
Paul, St., 73, 85, 96, 118, 139, 249
Peake, A. S., 130 (quoted)
Pedlars, 38
Peel, Dr., 144n.
Penance, Roman Catholic sacrament, 166–7
Penry, John, 246
Peter, St., 230
Philip II of Spain, 17
Phillips, Colonel F., 70
Pilgrim's Progress, 87, 249
Plague, the, 68
Player, Sir Thomas, 211
Plato, 83
Platonists, Cambridge, 83
Plotinus, 83
Poland, Catholicism and, 226
Pollexfen, Sir Henry, 73
Poor Man's Family Book, The, 86
Popery, 10, 26, 196, 220–3, 248
Powicke, F. J., 51, 57n., 73, 75n., 77, 79, 85, 142, 143, 192n., 193, 194, 195, 202, 213, 222
Powis, Lord, 73
Prayer Book. *See* Book of Common Prayer.
Predestination, 78
Preface to Paradise Lost, A, 179
Prelacy, Prelatists, 35, 36–7, 44, 45, 51, 52, 55, 56, 57, 77, 100, 108, 134, 135, 137–8, 140, 184, 191, 213, 218, 219, 220, 222–3, 230

INDEX 265

Presbyterian party, 54, 56–7, 63, 129, 190, 239
Presbyterianism, 43
— Bancroft and, 27
— Baxter and, 44, 46, 128–30
— and Calvinism, 186
— under Charles II, 59, 60, 62–6, 69, 190, 211
— Church and State, attitude to, 21–2, 239
— during Civil War, 43
— during Commonwealth, 44–5, 52
— Elizabeth and, 20–1
— and Independents, 190
— James I, attitude towards Presbyterianism, 32
— and monarchy, 22
— and ordination, 138
— advocacy by Puritans, 15–16, 18, 51, 196, 210, 213, 215, 244–5, 247, 252, 254
— in Scotland, 20, 32, 35, 63, 196
Press, freedom of, 11
Principia, 84
Protectorate. *See* Commonwealth.
Protestants(ism), 13, 14, 18, 19, 184, 206–7, 222, 225, 226, 235–7, 244
Psalm cv. 28 .. 204
Puritanism, Puritans, 24, 39, 114, 255
— Abbot and, 37
— Bancroft and, 29
— and business, 11–12
— Calvinism, relation to, 77
— under Charles II, 60–1, 64
— and the Church, 15, 18–19, 20–3, 25, 26, 29, 31, 33, 51, 90, 147, 148, 163, 192–3, 210, 244–6, 255
— during Civil War, 51–3
— and divorce, 11, 203
— Elizabeth and, 14, 16, 17–22, 25, 26, 28, 30, 192, 213, 246, 247, 248
— 'Exercises' of, 17, 18, 248, 252–4
— Hooker and, 29
— James I and, 30–5
— early leaders, 36
— marriage, attitude to, 11, 203
— monarchy, attitude to, 21–2, 34, 255
— and Oath of Supremacy, 22
— origins of, 9–10
— emergence of party, 13–15
— and pleasure, 12
— political implications of, 14, 20–2, 244
— propaganda of. *See* Appendix.
— and Presbyterianism, 15–16, 18–19, 20–2, 51, 244–5, 247, 253, 255
— results of, 10–13
— rites, attitude to, 196, 198, 199, 202, 203, 212
— and the Scriptures, 144, 148
— split among, 52
— world, attitude to, 13

See also under Dissenters, Independents, Nonconformity, Presbyterianism, Separatists.
Puritanism in England, 10
Pym, John, 221

QUAKERISM, 183, 202
Quakers, 96

RAIGNOLDS, JOHN, 32, 134
Read, Conyers, 246
Rechabites, 149
Reconstruction of the English Church, 31
Reformation, the, 9, 15, 65, 143, 198
Reformed Churches. *See* Church, Reformed.
Renaissance, the, 9
Revival of Learning, the, 9
Republicans, 52
Restoration, the, 52–6, 64, 213, 221, 223
Reunion of the Churches, 224–43
Reynolds, William, 57, 129
Ridley, Nicholas, Bishop, 9
Roman Catholics(ism), 9, 11, 92, 94, 130, 145, 189, 220–3, 225, 226, 227, 234, 241, 243
— under Elizabeth, 13, 14, 15, 16, 18, 19, 25, 26, 28, 29
— Charles I and, 220–1
— Charles II and, 71–2, 211
— James I and, 24
— James II and, 72
— and the Sacraments, 166–7
— and Transubstantiation, 174–7
See also under Church of Rome, the Papacy, and Papists.
Roman Church. *See under* Church of Rome.
Romans viii. 29, quoted, 78
Rous, Sir Thomas and Lady, 42
Rowton, 36, 85
Royalists, 41
Rump Parliament, 50, 52
Rutherford, Samuel, 87

Sacramentary (of Serapion), 238
Sacraments, the, 43, 44, 46, 55, 134, 136, 137, 139, 163–78, 199–202, 225, 227, 235–9, 242
St. Benet Fink Church, 67
Saint's Cordials, 13
'Salvianus, Moriturus G.', 85
Sampson, Thomas, 28
Savoy Conference (1661), 35, 59–60, 62, 65
Scandinavia, Protestantism and, 226
Scholastic tradition, 83
Schoolmen, the, 83, 145

Scottish Church. *See* Church, Scottish.
Scott Pearson, A. F., 9 (quoted), 14n., 16n., 17n., 18n., 19n., 20n., 21n., 22 (quoted), 244n., 246n.
Scots, the, 43
Screwtape Letters, 159
Sectaries, the, 15, 50, 189
Separatists, the, 12, 14, 18, 19, 22, 25, 33, 76, 77, 114–15, 144, 148, 167, 174, 189–92, 195, 204, 206, 210, 244, 245, 249
Serapion, 238
Shakespeare, W., 36, 179
Shaw, W. A., 90
Sheffield, 12
Sheldon, Dr., 62, 64, 65, 223
Short Parliament, 40
Shrewsbury, Lord, 12
Sibbes, Richard, 13, 36, 38, 251
Silas, 119
Sion College, 129
Soames, H., 14n., 247 (quoted), 248 (quoted)
Socialist parties, 226
Socinians, 58, 76, 241
Soldier's Crown, The, 165
Solemn League and Covenant, 43, 50, 54, 65
Solipsism, 84
Southampton, Earl of, 69
South India Scheme, 224
Spain, 222, 226
Speed, John, 126
Spenser, Edmund, 11
Standen, Nicholas, 246
Star Chamber, 11, 19, 253
State and Church, 239–41
Stillingfleet, Edward, 138, 219
Strafford, Earl of, 215
Stoughton, John, 63
Streeter, Dr., 121n.
Summa Contra Gentiles, 83
Summa Theologica, 83
Sutcliffe, Matthew, 19
Swanwick, conferences at, 254
Sword of the Spirit Movement, 225
Sylvester, Matthew, 73, 80
Synod of Dort, 77

Tertullian, 124, 165
Thirty-nine Articles, the, 29
Thomas Aquinas, St., 29, 83, 145
Times, The, 232
Timothy, 119
Toleration, 11, 23, 66, 69, 241–3
— Act (1689), 65

Tombes, John, 92, 168
Tory Party, 64, 65
Tractarianism, 232
Transubstantiation, Doctrine of, 174–8
Travers, Walter, 19, 21, 36, 193, 196, 204, 246, 249, 250, 251, 253
Tremellius, J. I., 9
Trent, Council of, 207, 222
Trevelyan, G. M., 17n.
Trevor-Roper, H. R., 37n., 40n.
Trinitarianism, 243
Triple Alliance, the, 211
Tudor Puritanism, 252
Tully, Dr., 80

Uniformity, Act of. *See* Act of Uniformity.
Unitarians, 241
Unwin, Professor, 85
Upton, 46
— Canon, 67
Usher, Bishop, 57, 103, 128
— W., 13n., 29n., 31, 32, 34 (quoted), 251n.

Vestment controversy, 16, 248

Walsingham, Sir Francis, 12, 19, 246
Warwick, Earl of, 12
Weller, Tony, 224
Wesley, Charles, 234, 238
— John, 87, 89, 173
— Samuel, 87
Westminster Assembly (1644), 77, 245
Whigs, 64
Whitgift, John, Archbishop, 18, 21, 26, 27, 30, 36, 37, 40, 134, 138, 210, 213, 237
Wilkinson, J. T., 45, 87n., 88
Williams, Dr., 85
Worcester, 46, 50, 66, 142
— Bishop of, 39, 66, 142
— House Conference, 58, 76
Worcestershire Association, 44, 45–8, 49, 164, 174, 181, 218, 229
Wordsworth, William, 224 (quoted)
Worship, Freedom of, 11, 49, 50, 52, 58, 174
Wright, L. B., 250n.
Wroxeter, 85

Xavier, St. Francis, 81, 169

Yelverton, Sir Christopher, 32

www.ingramcontent.com/pod-product-compliance
Lightning Source LLC
Chambersburg PA
CBHW070313240426
43663CB00038BA/2014